THE PSYCHOLOGIST'S DAUGHTER

A MEMOIR

FLEUR C. BOAL

First published in Australia by Aurora House
www.aurorahouse.com.au

This edition published 2025
Copyright © Fleur C. Boal 2025

Cover design: Donika Mishineva (www.artofdonika.com)
Typesetting and e-book design: Amit Dey (amitdey2528@gmail.com)

The right of Fleur C. Boal to be identified as Author of the Work has been asserted in accordance with the Copyright, Designs and Patents Act 1988.

ISBN number: 978-1-923298-62-0 (paperback)

All rights reserved. No part of this publication may be reproduced, stored in a retrieval system, or transmitted, in any form or by any means without the prior written permission of the publisher, nor be otherwise circulated in any form of binding or cover other than that in which it is published and without a similar condition being imposed on the subsequent purchaser.

Scripture taken from the New King James Version®. Copyright © 1982 by Thomas Nelson. Used by permission. All rights reserved.

Scripture quotations taken from The Holy Bible, New International Version®, NIV®. Copyright © 1973, 1978, 1984, 2011 by Biblica, Inc.™ Used by permission of Zondervan. All rights reserved worldwide.

A catalogue record for this book is available from the National Library of Australia

Book Disclaimer:

This book is a work of non-fiction. While all the events are true, some minor characters' names have been changed for the protection of their identities. Almost all of the major characters' names have remained unchanged.

This book is dedicated to my little brother, Dylan. His narrative may look different from mine, but our journeys have merged in many ways. Overall, we've weathered the passage well, with thanks and praise to our Heavenly Father.

Contents

Prologue ix

PART ONE 1

1. Life Was Simple ... Before It Got Complicated 3
2. Cyclone Tracy Determines Our Future 11
3. Living with Hostility is Hard for a Kid 26
4. Blending Home with University Life 32
5. Grandparent Endearments and Turbulences 40

PART TWO 51

6. Parental Mantle of Protection 53
7. Volatile Primary Years 60
8. Mum Went Off on a Spiritual Tangent 68
9. My Curious Pentecostal Experience 76
10. High School and Other Stress 88
11. Connecting and Disconnecting 99
12. Running Away: A Quick-Fix Resolve 111

13. Marital Crash Aftermath	125
14. Dad's Newly Acquired Family	129
15. Contrary Influences and Finding Myself	140
16. The Blessing of a Step-Father	148
17. Youth Independence: Not All It's Cracked Up to Be	152

PART THREE — 169

18. Working for Dad: Traversing the Benefits and Drawbacks	171
19. A Milestone Birthday	182
20. Making a Wide Stride	187
21. Reaching a Crossroads	193
22. Life Lessons for a Sister	199
23. Graduation Day	203

PART FOUR — 207

24. The Heartbreak of Losing a Brother	209
25. Significant Celebrations and Dad's Indifference	220
26. Ephemeral Grandparent	234
27. Emotional Cutoff	243
28. Dad's Big Reveal	252
29. Mum's Death Impacts Dad	260
30. Dad's Terminal Diagnosis	265

31.	A Strategic Mistake	268
32.	A Letter for Dad, With Love	281
33.	Slippery Slope of Self-Contempt	289
34.	Our Final Father-Daughter Exchange	293
35.	A Heartfelt and Healing Funeral ... Yeah, Right!	303
36.	Embracing a New Season	314
37.	Joy and Sadness	316
38.	Restoration is Just Beyond the Veil	321
Acknowledgments		324
About the author		326

Prologue

Dad's exasperated ramblings blared from behind the old timber fly screen and its white painted panels. Through the gauze, I watched his outstretched arms and legs press the door frame, gridlocking the entranceway, his posture declaring, "*No entry!*"

I had brought Peter to Dad's Morwell home in Victoria to announce our engagement. His blatant refusal to invite us in signified that our presence threatened his home-based threshold. Did Dad expect a home invasion? Or was he confronted by an intrusion of the heart? As we remained on the front verandah, shivers coursed through my body from the cooling air, for the day's sunshine was almost gone. Searching for warmth, I moved close to Peter in a partial embrace, angling my head against his balmy, thudding chest. *Ba-dum, ba-dum.* His heartrate increased as my father pointedly addressed him.

"How dare you! I watched Fleur being born. You didn't ask for her hand in marriage. She's my daughter!"

Composure relaxed my expression, but untruthfully. I was confused. Where had this jealous and passion-driven father come from?

My legs wobbled with the rest of my body as I moved out of Dad's front yard and towards the car with Peter. I tried to convince myself that my quivering was from the evening chill not the strange and harsh reaction to our engagement news. Dad had always been hard to reach, and my Christian stance had repelled him, so his jealousy over losing me to another man made no sense.

I didn't fully realise then that my desire to achieve a thriving relationship with Dad, or to even discover a hint of togetherness, would become an achingly, long-drawn-out pursuit on my part.

PART ONE

*"Today you are you! That is truer than true!
There is no one alive who is you-er than you!"*
— Dr. Seuss, *Happy Birthday to You!*

ONE

Life Was Simple ... Before It Got Complicated

My father never truly revealed his heart to me. In my struggle to attain a close relationship with him, I wouldn't give up on what could be, resolute to claim "They lived happily ever after" for our own. I'd embraced the fanciful idiom since girlhood, and my daughter-father pursuit became the arc of my life, concluding only because Dad passed away. I persisted also in faith, which governed my choices, by reaching out with Christian love and forgiveness time and again. Oh, how Dad despised that part of me. Grievous and affirmative by turns, our story is bittersweet. While I can't deny the losses, they should never overshadow hope; I will always be Dad's little girl, and our kindred souls will come full circle. I believe it is God, the Father's, doing.

The man who gave me life shared very little of his infancy, boyhood, and young adulthood with me, so to know him better, I sought to fill this enigmatic gap in my family knowledge. My mother and paternal grandmother shared some details with me about Dad when I was growing up. By the time I was fifty, during my writing and after Dad's death, his old photos, letters, and papers became a treasure trove. I even discovered a copy of a tiny newspaper clipping with his mother's photo from 1946, published just prior to their migration to Australia. I'd hoped to understand my erratic father by starting at the beginning of his life. Here is some of what I learned.

John William Redman was born on January 30, 1939, in the County Borough of West Ham in historic Essex, England. His mother, Edna May Redman, was originally a Londoner, and her baby came as an unforeseen blessing. He defied a doctor's prediction of barrenness, and so Edna's motherly desire was gratified. Nature's verdict meant no more successful conceptions, securing her son's position as an only child.

Later in Dad's birth year, global war broke out, ending on September 2, 1945. A chunk of his childhood was immersed in an era of war, and those miseries went unexpressed; at least, they weren't shared with me. I can postulate, however, that he was a boy troubled by aerial threats, bombing devastation, and the upheaval of evacuating with his mum to Holyhead, Wales (his father's childhood town). Also, his father was absent, undertaking maritime activity, which caused unease. Would they ever reunite?

As a boy living amid war, Dad must have lived in fear. Decades later, boyhood survival through wartime hostility developed in him the voice of experience. Dad related well to ex-servicemen in his profession as a psychologist.

He provided specialist services to the Veteran Affairs community, bringing sweet release for those suffering from posttraumatic stress. This included one of Dad's veteran friends, who sang John's praises at his funeral, highlighting his empathy and support by an outstanding professional and personal effort.

Surely, austerity from World War II's effect impelled Edna to venture into the unknown with seven-year-old John in her care. They departed Southampton on October 12, 1946, for a month-long passage across the seas. Mother and son travelled aboard *Asturias* on the steamship's first immigrant voyage, and they arrived in Sydney, Australia, on November 19, 1946. They had joined masses of British passengers, quite likely through a government scheme. Edna's husband, John Thomas Redman (known as Jack), had made the trip in advance after honourably discharging from his tenure as chief petty officer in the Royal Navy. The family of three reunited to forge a new life in the great southern land, ripe with possibilities. They established themselves along the central New South Wales coastline, on the cusp of the South Pacific. There, my grandparents spent time with their son, fishing and enjoying peaceable lives by the wondrous beauty of the sea. Once grown, Dad qualified as a primary school teacher.

My parents likely met in the year 1965. It was while they were working for the Snowy Mountains Hydro-Electric

Authority in New South Wales. The company oversaw a massive engineering project at the time, known as the Snowy Scheme. Dad was employed as a clerk, while Mum worked as a communications operator. Their first-born, Owen, arrived in early October 1966, in Tumut, a charming riverside town positioned in the lower western reach of the Snowy Mountains. Mum's unplanned baby was fortunate to see the light of day. John, once aware of her pregnancy, had offered a harsh ultimatum: abortion or marriage. Her decision was to marry and keep the baby.

It was a happy day for Mum when she married Dad on May 7, 1966. The affair took place at Sydney's historic St. Philip's Church, an Anglican denomination, on Church Hill. Photographic evidence of their union is mostly gone. The majority of the pictures were blown away eight years later by Cyclone Tracy, while I suspect others were discarded by Mum at a later date.

Recently, a few remaining proofs were discovered amongst Dad's photograph collection. The pictures, I noticed, bore signs of age, though they were mostly unspoiled. One colour image portrayed a small and quaint wedding party surrounded by the old-world St. Philip's entryway. The bridal party stood on the top step, graced by a red carpet that signified the event. I took another photo, in black and white, into the natural daylight for a clearer view of the couple posing for the cake-cutting ritual. It brought a smile to my face that their frozen, wide-eyed expressions implied impatience over the shutterbug's demands. My mother's tall, slender figure was not yet showing a baby bump, though she was holding her front, giving away her gestation. The bride wore a white sheath gown made of silk shantung, overlayed with floral lace to the waistline. Atop her radiant head sat a lotus-style, diamante headpiece, clasping a bun. Soft netting layers arrayed the decorative piece, billowing over the bride's shoulders and down her back. The 1960s ensemble was stylishly uncluttered. If it had been preserved, it would now be classed as prized vintage. The bride's face, framed with tulle, revealed youthfulness through full, smiling lips and large, unwary eyes. Her fine-looking, suavely-suited groom wore a single white carnation as his boutonnière. He appeared to be distracted, not adversely but blithely unguarded. He was ready to embrace his bride, the lovely Victoria, whom he and everyone else called Ailsa. John had promised his bride a lifetime of admiration and companionship.

The couple's image evoked untainted love, though it would last just for a while, as the rest of their love story became an inadvertent lie. Alas, long before the photographs had faded, the nuptial became worn and cast-off. Concerning my parents' union, it was not all a loss. Precious lives were created with a succession of generations to come, a fact never to be undervalued.

By the year 1969, my father had a teaching appointment in Napperby, north-west of Alice Springs in central Australia, amongst an Indigenous Australian community. Alice, as the locals call it, is the focal point of the commonly known red centre. It is where I was born on March

27, 1969. Lionheartedly, John surveyed his wife's childbearing marathon, which she later described as "an exhilarating experience." For Dad, the fresh delivery produced instant love for his screaming baby girl. I abandoned the secret womb the same year as Apollo 11's lunar landing, a fun fact about insignificant me.

My father had the privilege of choosing my names: Fleur Colette, both feminine and French. The first appellation has been remarked upon by countless people ever since. "French for flower; very pretty!"

From the Alice hospital, my parents and I travelled by car to my first home in Napperby, a remote place off the endless Tanami Track. The trip covered an immense territory while I was off in baby la-la land. Owen was waiting for us in our basic outback house with our maternal grandmother, Mas'ma, as she was affectionately known, who left soon after, as she lived in another state.

Dylan joined the family two and a half years later. He arrived in the same birth month as our big brother and at the same unpretentious hospital as me. Our new fair-haired baby was robust and warmly welcomed into the family.

Papunya, a government settlement, was Dad's next placement, where he worked at the resident school. Around that time, the Papunya Tula Artists established a co-operative that produced distinctive traditional artworks. These renowned national treasures are still produced today. My early development took place in that desert landscape.

One childhood memory is of the carefree Indigenous Australian kids grouped beneath a thinly shaded gum tree near our house. Timidly, I wandered across the sun-baked earth to join them. Angling my head, I marvelled at their effortless scaling of far-reaching eucalypt limbs. Unanticipated dreams came to me many years on: memories featuring loads of red-ochre soil, sparse native scrubland, and mountainous scenes similar to MacDonnell's Ranges, which extend to the east and west of Alice.

By the time I was three, my family had moved to Darwin, the Northern Territory's capital city. The tropical environment stayed in my memory more than the coastal city. There, I attended a local kindergarten. It opened up a vibrant new world, where I made companionable friends and engrossed myself in imaginative and tactile play. Mum's farewell embrace and tender kiss brought no whimpering from her little girl, only smiles, as I was sure of Mum's return each time she left the facility. Other scant memories include frivolous sibling fun as life's simplicities presented. We scampered through the narrow halls of our modest L-shaped dwelling; a pitter-pattering could be heard across the uncarpeted flooring. Oppressive humidity and unrelenting heat called for stripping off unwanted clothing, relishing the freedom and allowing air to flow over our bodies. Under Mum's watchful eye, my brothers and I frolicked in the front garden. We dodged water shooting from the oscillating sprinkler, squealing on its return as water beaded, then soaked our skin.

Family life in the Northern Territory was simple and without threat, and as a small child, I enjoyed a carefree existence. But this would change all too soon when my seemingly innocent early years turned into hard times.

TWO

Cyclone Tracy Determines Our Future

As a tender five-year-old, I sensed sudden tension in the air of our holiday house and saw alarm in my parents' eyes. Their worry transferred onto me as they discussed the disturbing news we'd received. It was December, 1974, and my family was in Queensland's capital city on holiday and exploring a potential interstate move. While staying in Brisbane, headline news reached our ears, shocking the nation and my family, halting life's doings. Darwin had been struck down by a category 4 cyclone. Tropical Cyclone Tracy was fast and furious. Her initial brewing had gone largely unnoticed until her ferocity hit on Christmas Day. Tracy cost seventy-one lives, and much of the city's building construction was wiped out, causing rampant homelessness. Incredibly, 30,000-plus residents were evacuated. My family, like many others, never returned.

When Dad travelled back to examine the devastation, he returned with the good news that the couple who had been occupying our home in our absence were safe. They had huddled together in the laundry, which was solidly built and had proved the only structure left standing. The bad news came through the startling black-and-white photographs Dad had taken. We surveyed the pictures in disbelief. *Is that our street, our house?* It all appeared as flattened debris to be trampled over. Treasured family photographs, no longer safely stored away in our house, became historical loss, and I ached for my cherished doll, also gone with the gale. The initial days of shock wore off as a thread of hope pulled us tight as a family. Mum and Dad built on their tentative plan to establish us in Brisbane, or Brissie.

To my pleasure, our new suburb featured undulating streets with plenty of nature's greenery. It was only a few days after we moved into a rental house that I took a stroll with Mum to explore the neighbourhood. With a lively sense of wonder, I balanced on mini walls dividing terraced gardens. My arms stretched out as gliding wings, accompanied by dulcet engine hums. Flowers, in sunlit whites and assorted warm and cool colours, beautified front gardens. My fingers vivaciously snapped off as many as they could hold.

Before long, our neighbours noticed my trespassing and thieving, chiding me through their doorways and open windows. "Get off the garden. Go on! Get!"

With an innocent face, I hid the blooms behind my back, then jumped onto the nature strip beside Mum.

I wasn't deterred. *What's this shiny red thing hanging on the bush?* Mum assured me it was edible. My teeth crunched into the waxy fruit, and I waited for a taste to develop on my tongue. But there was no taste, only a slight tingling. The sensation soon became fire in my mouth. "I need water. Ahh!" We had none.

"The chilli's heat won't last," Mum laughed.

I craned my neck to view high-set Queenslanders, their timber frames painted in crisp white or muted colours, touching the sunshiny skies. Nature's aesthetics surrounded them. Spreading jacaranda trees, past their purple-blue display, provided verdant summer shade, while lofty palms and umbrella-like frangipanis brought a tropical island feel, enticing me to tuck a sweet-scented flower behind my ear. My gaze lowered, blinking and peering, making out shadowy spaces beneath these structures. Places for childish make-believe, developing plots and characters to act out. Our neighbours were now unaware of my half-crushed pickings, perfect for a white-wedding procession as a flower girl's bouquet. My fantasy soon faded. Mum cautioned me that the sticky sap coating my fingers, from plumbago, marigold, and oleander flower stems, was toxic.

Before long, my parents purchased a home in St. Lucia's well-established suburb. It was positioned on a steep slope. When facing our house, on the left was a vertical driveway made of rough, exposed aggregate. I still bare a scar from its irregular surface. Or was it the fault of the other offender, the bully Gail? I was shy and struggling to adapt in school, and my St. Lucia life was further complicated by this cruel girl. After meeting her in the schoolyard, I shortly discovered that I'd been hand-picked by a bully. Like many childhood aggressors, she sought a human guinea pig for entertainment's sake. Miserably for me, Gail would invite herself over to my place.

During one visit, she had her eye on an old tricycle. I occasionally rode it on flat ground, as it had no brakes. Delight was in her voice when she said, "Dare you to ride down. I dare you!"

My legs turned to jelly while wheeling the trike to the top of the driveway. Settling on the worn seat, I braced myself for misadventure. Gail gave a great shove from behind, propelling the trike and me forward and down the sheer slope.

"Aaaaaaaah!" The sound vibrated in my throat and flew out of my mouth. The unnerving, rutted ride ended at the bottom of the driveway, where the concrete started. Dethroned, I thudded into a metal bin near an unfriendly cactus, its spikes threatening my face. After the shock wore off, painful bloodied abrasions caused a rush of tears. I ran screaming to the only first aider I knew, Mum. She was also my safe haven. Unfortunately, she could not rescue me from all of life's cruel oppressors or that forbidding driveway!

To Gail, we were buddies who partook in schoolyard capers, sleepovers, and play dates, including forced misbehaviours, for which I copped the blame. Gail was my master, and I was her slave. Her aggressions included arm stabbing with filthy, claw-like fingernails, as she demanded, "Hold still! I don't see any blood yet. Good. Now give me your other arm." I was ordered to sit beside her on her family couch during such episodes. Recoiling was not allowed as she picked her nose for fresh snot blobs, wiping them on my bare skin and announcing, "That's a good one! Don't you dare wipe it off or I'll …" I heeded her warnings as I didn't how far she'd go. I also slowed my pace for Gail to beat me at school carnival swimming races. On went her antics, and so did my misery.

Mum came to realise some of my plight and apologised once for striking me with an electrical cord that left my calves burning with red welts. I had been punished for smashing a dozen eggs. A day later, Mum learned Gail was the real culprit. Mum may have been passively responsive, but Dad was inattentive to my needs. Was it because he was mostly away on campus, preoccupied with his studies? I was a sensitive soul but didn't want to concern my parents, though I very much wanted them to pay attention and intervene. They appeared to be caught up in their own pressures, including symptoms of a troubled marriage.

Alongside Gail's provocation, other distresses took me by surprise, none of which were subtle incidences that chipped away at the veneer of my idyllic early childhood. One involved a serious accident. On the other side of our house, a walkway was suspended above ground level. It led to the front entrance, where an ancient copper cow bell protruded from an external hook. There, we welcomed and farewelled all manner of company through our hearth and home. Family members dashed to the front door at the bell's unpitched sound. On the night of the accident, it was initially unheard as thunderous activity and torrential rain came deafeningly. The callers' persistent door pounding and bell tolling finally got Mum's attention. Two men wore sombre expressions and unmistakable law-enforcement uniforms.

Against the stormy backdrop of sheeting rain, Mum obscured the other side of the door. I inched forward for a better view, then moved back again as Owen was carried in. He was unable to walk and largely impassive due to shock. His soaking body made tiny rain puddles mingled with flowing crimson ribbons, rivulets that joined lakes on the floorboards. My brother's haemorrhaging came from his thighs. I yearned to cry at the sight of Owen's lifelessness and bloodied predicament. Instead, I nervously giggled and used out-of-place banter to awaken him while adults attended the patient. Owen's vacancy receded after what seemed like an impossibly long time. His eyes brightened, and he flashed a faint smile at me, his jesting sister. I cheered inside, but where were his glasses? My face and the fussing adults must have been a blur of activity! *Not to worry*, I thought. *They'll be found.* Owen needed medical attention more urgently. My very brave big brother didn't even cry.

Owen had been hit by a car while riding his bike, and the possibility of sustained injuries couldn't be ruled out. Cyclist helmets weren't legally required or even a consideration at the time. Earlier that evening, Owen had been finishing his paper round when Brisbane's weather had taken a low-pressure turn. His failure to return home and the weather change had alerted our mother.

Mum, Dylan, and I had driven to the newsagency to check his whereabouts where Mum had been told, "Owen left a while ago."

As the three of us headed home, we'd spotted Owen cycling in the same direction.

"Want a lift?" I'd heard Mum shout through the driver's window.

Then Owen's distant response. "No, thanks!"

Mum had allowed him some independence, despite the brewing storm. I'd felt a twinge of concern while watching Owen disappear into that rumbling, darkening night. He later received eighteen sutures to close the lacerations on his legs, and no further injuries were detected. The accident had been an ordeal for our family, but where Dad was during the unfolding drama, I can't recall.

Dylan and I stayed close to Mum, watching and wondering if our brother would be alright. Mum appeared to be in control, but her troubled eyes reflected deep concern for Owen and perhaps her own fear while navigating the trauma alone. Once my family were assured by the medics that Owen would recover just fine, we regulated back to family life as we knew it. Although, as a child, I was somewhat aware of the burdens Mum carried for us kids, and I had observed Dad's lack of presence when it came to certain parental obligations.

While I had no choice but to accept this, some other aspects of my family life didn't feel right, despite being young. The philosophy of the sexual revolution made its way into my family home through my parents. In Owen, a curious and intelligent child, Mum and Dad found an eager pupil. One clear memory of Mum sharing her liberal thoughts occurred on the timber walkway of our home. The walkway was occasionally used during the dry season as an alfresco area beneath a neighbour's massive mango tree, among other tropical plants competing for sunlight, a suburban treetop forest.

From inside the house, I passed the open door one cloudless morning. Mum called me over to join her and Owen outside. I was an unfledged girl in my tween years, unaware that I was about to embark on an in-depth sex talk. I soon discovered that it was about the birds and the bees, except that it was *way* more disgusting. Gradually, I catalogued Mum and Owen's explicit descriptions: sexual trialling and the workings of intimate body parts previously unknown. This new information appalled me, grossed me out, and incensed me all at once! I wanted to declare that I was leaving, but the words wouldn't come out. Mum's zest to pursue the matter and Owen's unbroken smirk were repulsive as they pushed me up against a wall. Mum, along with Owen's contributions, described how to self-pleasure and advocated that I trial it on my own, then share the details of my sexual discoveries with them. My face blushed with indignity.

Mum, seeing that I was affronted by the proposal, coolly stated, "You may not be old enough."

Owen pleaded for me to stay, but Mum's words had set me free, my legs hurriedly taking me away from the heavy topic. I wanted to shout at the top of my lungs, *I'm a child; leave me alone!* But the words just boomed in my head.

It was apparent that Mum and Owen had engaged in similar conversations before. I'd discerned this through Owen's familiarity and their ease with talking about the delicate subject. Owen's interest in sexual experimentation had been sparked and was growing, and there would be undeserved repercussions for me. Just a few weeks earlier, I had experienced another distress involving my older brother which I only narrowly escaped.

I welcomed in the new day, initially unaware that Owen was watching nearby, waiting to declare that we were going to visit his friend Rayleen. They were both twelve at the time, and, since she wasn't my friend, I declined. But Owen refused to take no for an answer. His pestering went on and on, so I gave in. Owen led the way, as I didn't know where we were going, my steps quickening to keep up with his hurried pace. I also didn't know why Owen was so avid in getting me to Rayleen's place. My uncertainty over his indistinct plans caused drumming in my chest. Along the way, I lost count of the blocks we'd walked. Finally, we arrived at Rayleen's beautifully restored, all-white Queenslander-style home. Owen and I traversed the outdoor stairs, and Rayleen greeted us through the verandah doors, taking us into the open living area. I took in the room's ornate structural design, occupied with vibrant tropical indoor plants, impressive artworks, antique furniture, and luxurious rugs scattered on the natural wood flooring. Caught up in the ambience, I perched on a red vintage sofa and imagined myself to be royalty, but the firm, uncomfortable surface brought me back to reality.

For some reason, my heart hadn't stopped racing since Owen and I had left our house. By this time, I also felt strong distrust. After Rayleen welcomed us in, she and Owen engaged in small talk while trying to hide their grins. *Why am I here, and what are they up to?* I asked myself.

Fifteen minutes in, Owen said goodbye, then dashed away. The flutter in my chest became stronger, and I sought to follow him, but my body failed to move. Rayleen quickly left her spot on the floor to join me on the couch. Her short, fair hair, boyish features, and a smattering of pale freckles stood out as her face was a few inches away from mine. There began an awkward moment when she asked, "Have you ever kissed a girl. Do you want to kiss me? Kiss me!"

Bewildered, I stared at her while she wound her arms and legs around mine. We were like two cosy cats, closely entwined.

Ba-dum, ba-dum! My wild heart beckoned me to release myself from the girl, who didn't stop me. I don't remember if either of us spoke, only that I was intent on planting my feet on the floor to bolt out the door, down the steps, and into the street. I pounded the footpath without stopping. Suburbia blurred past as I worried that Rayleen might run after me and if I was heading back in the right direction.

At last, relieved that I'd found my way and that Rayleen was nowhere to be seen, I arrived at home, puffing and panting intensely from the run and all that had gone on. Soon after, Owen approached me, demanding details about what had happened between Rayleen and me. At my reply, I watched his disappointed face as he tried to coax me into returning to Rayleen's place. Owen had *no* conscience. I wondered if there was a pay-off for him: sex or money, perhaps. While I was disgusted over the pair's perverted intentions, I also felt victorious that I'd escaped the ordeal unscathed. At home, I avoided contact with Owen for a while and with Rayleen when she visited. I also vowed to myself that I'd never return to her family home, regardless of my fascination with its heritage charm and lavish décor.

As a child, I dealt with my troubles one at a time, coping in my own way. I also believed that Owen would never behave menacingly again, as I wanted to see the good in him, but he made another attempt at victimising me. I was around thirteen when I noticed Owen's increased fondness. His smirking face uncomfortably close to mine as he put his arm around me. It was happening too often. It served as a warning, a reminder of how I'd felt when he'd set me up with Rayleen. One afternoon, Owen explained that he wanted to learn more about the female anatomy, and he reasoned that I was available for him to learn. His smarmy manner and inappropriate requests repulsed me as though refuse was under my nose. Although repelled, complete powerlessness was declared through a muddled voice in my head. I relented to Owen's boundary violation. When my brother approached me with a taller order in the same week, I found the courage to resist him. The misleading voice had been replaced with an empowering one. Owen was dogged, but something in me rose up, and self-dignity hailed above all else. I felt strengthened as Owen's power over me dissolved into flecks of nothing.

My older brother was also vulnerable to victimisation. Although I'll never know what most of his negative experiences involved, some I know for sure. Owen had put on what Mum called "puppy fat" during his middle to late primary school years; he wore unflattering thick-rimmed glasses and, being intelligent and articulate, he was inclined to be argumentative and sarcastic, to his own detriment. By the time Owen hit high school, he was regarded as a nerd and was so despised by his peers that a group of them formed the I Hate Owen Club. It was well past these years, in 1990, that I discovered he'd also experienced harsh rejection from Dad, which had a devastating effect. I am inclined to be sympathetic towards Owen, saddened over his suffering at the hands of enemy groups in high school and by our father. But with introspection, while writing, I realise that the effect of Owen's travails did not warrant him victimising me.

Undoubtedly, my parents' liberal attitude towards sex was not helpful for my family, as it proved to be shaky ground when practiced upon. They were strong advocates for sharing sexual partners, reflecting the height of the sexual revolution. It is likely that Mum and Dad took other partners for themselves at one time or another, but while I have my suspicions, I have no definite childhood memories to verify it. Though every so often, I caught Dad approaching the line of fidelity with other women. Then Dad flagrantly crossed over the line by the time I was fourteen, without Mum's consent, leading to a major upturn in our family.

When I noticed Dad eyeing up other women and displaying attraction through suggestive behaviour, I also saw that it upset Mum, despite her outspoken views to the contrary. I discovered it when we attended a bush dance in Brissie, after which such occurrences became obvious to me. I was nine at the time. My family anticipated a lively evening as Dad drove us to the city. He parked near Baroona Hall, a colonial-style building that originally opened in 1884. We entered through the hall's doors and were directed by staff to a staircase leading into an upper-level room. As I gripped the banister, I considered that it had served current generations and many afore. A clamour of sounds rushed at us at the top of the stairs, where I recognised customary songs as a distinctive Australian bush-style. My body was magnetically pulled towards the throng on a reverberating wooden floor, revellers thumping their heels and clapping their hands to the thrumming melody.

A bush band performed for the crowd, which paired and parted as a constant stream of rhythmic verve. Everyone was involved to the hilt. Mum and Dad quickly moved in for the dance, then my brothers and me. I beamed as my feet and hands moved to the heel-and-toe polka routine.

After a while, I realised Mum was out of sight. Then I spotted her in a dark corner. I sensed something was wrong, so I made my way over to find out what. She explained that John was far too personal with other women. Jealousy was etched in her strained expression. My eyes scanned the room for Dad's familiar form as I sought to verify Mum's complaint. Amongst the feverish crowd, Dad's head of short, dark curls came to my attention. I moved closer to see his debonair smile, swaying and close-partnering with one woman after another. Mum's intolerance continued as the song ended and another began. She winced watching her flirtatious husband on the dance floor. My brothers joined me and Mum near her alcove. Dad came over a little later. Our parents raised their voices with accusatory words at one another, though mostly from Mum, creating a public tussle. Their moment went largely unnoticed by the crowd, but it was troublesome enough that they abruptly ended our outing.

As we travelled home, I gazed at the city's expanse, the lights brightly blurring past my window. I took it as a welcome distraction from the brittle air inside the car. Dad's unbroken smirk contrasted with Mum's face, stiffened like starched laundry, while her body curved away from her untrue husband. It seemed that Mum's push towards multiple romantic partners was waning.

Mum certainly reconsidered her moral beliefs and, in fact, later changed her entire worldview when she embraced Christianity. It had happened by the time I turned ten. Although it was not until part of the way through my first year of high school that I realised her free thinking had been replaced by her support of purity in singleness and faithfulness in marriage. My parents argued endlessly over diverging views on the topic. Mum loathed Dad shoving his ideologies onto us kids well into our late teenage years. Dad remained unapologetic, as he detested the idea of setting perimeters around sex and referred to Christians as pathetic and narrow-minded. But up until Mum's conversion, during most of my primary school years, my parents had been of the same mind regarding open relationships and other aspects of sexuality, sharing these persuasions with those around them, including us kids.

THREE

Living with Hostility is Hard for a Kid

Not only was Dad forceful when airing his own opinions; he could be irritable and hot-tempered, and there were times when it manifested in physical violence. I witnessed Dad's first violent act on the top landing of the upper-level staircase in our home. As a child, I often explored the internal workings of the house, including that staircase. Countless times, my bare feet had touched its smooth wooden steps while numbering them aloud. "Nine. Ten. Eleven." With childish logic, I mused that they shouldn't finish with an odd number, as an even twelve was preferred. My petite hands skimmed the narrow stairwell walls while I skittered my way down the steeper of our home's two stairways. One afternoon, I had come out of my room when my parents' raised voices alarmed me. They stood just above the top step when Dad impetuously grabbed Mum's middle and thrust her down the stairs. From where I stood, it was impossible to see her falling, though I heard the physics, her body clumsily tumbling over hollow wooden steps and the shrill notes of female screaming. A cold sensation coursed through my body. I was stricken with fear for the victim, who soon hushed. I was also petrified of inflaming my father's temper. I remained where I was while longing to run to my darling mother's side and check if she was injured, unconscious, or even alive.

After a short while, I managed to softly walk to the handrail above the stairwell. Very hesitantly, I looked towards the landing below. Mum's face was tilted to the side, hidden by a mop of gingery-brown curls, while her collapsed body faced downward, filling the tight space. I heard her muffled, low moaning travel up from the dusty floorboards. My chest tightened and ached with sympathy pains, anguished for my closest friend. Turning instinctively towards Dad, my expression silently and futilely urged him to assist. The cold-faced wrongdoer would not. He was in suspension before leaving the room, the house, and his crumpled wife. Dad's exit only intensified my agony over Mum's trauma. At the time, I didn't wish to understand my father. He was an evil, callous creature. While I remember this horrific incident with clarity, I don't remember what happened next, except for an unsettling sense that something wasn't right. Still, I reasoned, it was impossible for me to help Mum and Dad with their relationship troubles, as I was a mere child under their care.

To the left of the short landing where Mum lay on that awful day was a dim room. It was another corner of our St. Lucia home holding childhood memories, mostly of my brothers and me constructing *Lego* creations and watching *Looney Tune* cartoons on Saturday mornings. It was a large, garishly carpeted space with a low, shrinking ceiling. Two thirds of the way into the room, flower-patterned fabric in citrus hues draped from the ceiling. It served as a partition between the rumpus room and Owen's sleeping quarters. To the right of the same landing, a few remaining steps led down to a family room. I relished the sunlit space fetched from glass panes in that generously sized area. The nerves of my feet tingled against chilled, irregular slate in earthy greys and browns. When alone in that place, I pirouetted, daydreamed, and pawed over books. Following the sunshine, out the backdoor was a patio made from the same natural slate as the family room floor. Mum, my brothers, and I scattered piles of macadamia nuts on the pergola-covered patio. We gathered the seasonal fruit from a big old tree, which dropped onto our neighbour's nature strip. With a hammer, we cracked open their outer shells, our teeth eager to crunch into the buttery, sweet morsels within.

At the patio's edge, more slate extended in uneven steps, slanting down to an extensive backyard. The outdoor setting contrasted with dense, bug-infested bush near a grass clearing that contained a swing set. I adored the yard as much as our timber home. Recently, while writing, Dylan told me that when he was only six or seven, he saw some men come through that closed backdoor, two tall figures with two others who were on the shorter side. He was afraid at the time, perceiving them as spiritual beings. As I pondered this, a heavenly assurance told me that they were angels among us, not demonic forces. They must have been guardian angels. Amid Mum's troubled relationship with my father, she needed protection, and so did my brothers and I, not that Dad ever laid a finger on us kids.

One day, when I was around seven or eight, I headed towards the family room, stopping short on the second set of stairs. I stood suspended as something peculiar was unfolding. My insides jittered at the sight of those strange parents of mine hurling items through the air and around the room. Mugs, vases, and other fragile ornaments. My shoulders flinched at every clunk, tinkle, and dull vibration as objects collided with the grate and firebricks inside the unlit, open fireplace. Dad and Mum flung strident curse words into the air while creating a virtual mountain of rubble.

What's happening in my favourite place? I wondered.

The more I watched my parents' behaviour, the more it heightened my concern. I must've given my feelings away, as they offered reassurance, telling me they were sorting out their problems without anyone getting hurt. I observed the pattern: mild disagreement became biting insults and raised voices, their hostility turning into cushion tossing and beating, then riotous yelling and swearing while destroying brittle things caught by maddened hands, ending in enervation. The opponents wordlessly left the scene, and I stepped into the deserted room, where flatness was in the air, permeating me. I saw cushions haphazardly strewn all over the place, and ceramics, glass, and earthen-ware all reduced to distressed still-life bordered by firebricks. Were my parents friends at peace or worn out enemies? Being so young, it was hard to tell. Their play-off may have been a way of venting without anyone getting hurt, but what did it really achieve? All I saw was destructive behaviour leading to utter dejection.

As a child, I knew that I couldn't do anything to fix my parents' relationship or the smashed items in the fireplace, and I couldn't get rid of that dreadful, heavy feeling in the family room. So I moved past these disenchantments and onto something more child-friendly. I'd get lost in a children's book, then copy the illustrations as best I could with a pencil and scrap of paper, or I'd head outdoors to feel a rushing breeze as I reached the clouds on my swing, hair flying free. At other times, I'd hang out with our family cats, Marmalade and Zachy.

One time, poor Zachy was flung over the walkway railing by Dad, who was in a bad mood. Dad took off, so I leapt into his vacant spot to scan the undergrowth, which seemed an impossibly long way down. Amongst monochromatic greens and brownish-black I saw no sorry cat, so I raced down the stairs, back outside, and along the unkempt neighbour boundary. There I ceased to worry with the emergence of our unscathed cat, his mouth curved into a smile. I told myself that Dad knew cats landed on their feet, hopefully.

I didn't know that my parents' hostile behaviour was impacting me. Their aggression subliminally infiltrated the unseen quarters of my mind as my middle adolescence emerged with similar aggression, re-enacted in the private confines of my bedroom. I yelled, swore, and threw things when I felt vulnerable or circumstances in life weren't going well. By these acts, I felt no relief, only feebleness of the body and mind, and I inwardly blamed Mum and Dad for their negative influence. I was angry at them and despised myself for losing control.

By the time I was a twenty-one-year-old university student, I learned that children mirror aggression, as evidenced by Albert Bandura's famed Bobo doll research. The psychologist's experimental children acted out alone, or so they believed. In actuality, hidden researchers watched nearby. And me? I was also observed invisibly. I came to realise the childhood and adolescent anguish I pantomimed in private never went unnoticed. The all-seeing God watched me from above, though he didn't wear a starchy lab coat, and nor was he confined to a laboratory. I wasn't categorised within a sample nor manipulated by variables for statistical analysis. My identity was not reduced to a flawed theory. Nevertheless, the renowned authority *did* examine me. Seeking him from the solitude of my room uncovered what had always been present. The Lord searched my heart's complexities, though he already knew me, and his conclusions were absolute. God's longitudinal study provided intervention with proven results, ongoing restoration throughout my life, including effective applications to live by. If Dad knew about my unconventional therapy, he would've mockingly laughed. By this stage, he knew that I held a Christian worldview and would have regarded the depth of my relationship with Christ as unsubstantiated absurdity!

FOUR

Blending Home with University Life

My father, a psychology student in the 1970s, undoubtedly studied Bandura's social learning theory from the 1930s. He was very much influenced by psychological theories, but he was unable to relate these evidence-based outcomes to his own life or apply them to our family. As the daughter of a psychologist, from my teenage years on, this became obvious and weighed on my mind. Similar inconsistencies in others caught my attention as well.

One account transpired when I was a tertiary student during a tutorial. I had undertaken a psychology unit as an arts requirement within my chosen welfare course. On the first day of class, I joined other youthful learners.

The teacher introduced herself, then routinely moved down the student attendance list in alphabetical order. She paused at the letter R. "You're John Redman's daughter. The psychologist's daughter. That's right, isn't it?"

I stiffened at her attentiveness, anticipating where she was heading. The teacher was greatly honoured to have me in her class because I was the daughter of the esteemed John Redman, consultant-level clinical psychologist. The impression he'd made upon her would mean hefty expectations on me. I badly wanted to leave the tutorial. Instead, I smiled away and nodded politely from my seat. Once the class ended, I looked for a way out, quickly exiting the room and seeking to withdraw from the subject. Unfortunately, the university powers that be denied me the opportunity. My greatest fears came to pass over the progressive weeks. Student inadequacy verified that I wasn't strong on statistics, among other things. Once the bubble had burst, a distinctive change came over the lecturer. I became a figment of her imagination. At most, I was treated with coolness and disregard. I observed her attentiveness and respect towards my peers by contrast. If only the teacher was having a bad day or three, but her behaviour continued throughout the term. Self-criticism followed me around the campus, repeating that I'd dissatisfied the psychology assessor and my psychologist father, convinced they were discussing my incompetence over coffee breaks at psychology symposiums. For a while, I desired to curl up in a dark corner for the rest of my student life!

Years earlier, as an undeveloped child, my antennae hadn't moved in that direction, but that big word, "psychology," had come up a lot. When we moved to Brissie, Dad left his primary school teaching role and began to pursue an entirely different path: a Master of Psychology. I soon became aware that Dad's study required his full focus. Our family visited various learning institutions, and while I understood they were for adult purposes, I also believed they were for childish exploration, heritage listed buildings and modern establishments alike. My brothers and I traipsed extensive grounds, rolled down lush hillocks, and raced through elongated passageways. We peered into classrooms branching off internal halls, built for big people to expand their vocabularies and cram their heads full of knowledge. To child-me, it was all larger than life, and I was reduced to a doll in an oversized house. Libraries were intriguing places where I became light-footed and mute, silence being the golden rule. I was a tiny figure daunted by innumerable books in various volumes, shelved across and up the walls. The elephant ladder tempted me to climb up to the ceiling to find fairy tales with pleasing illustrations, perhaps *Thumbelina*. But putting my foot past the first rung never happened. I was frightened that I'd fall. Before long, I understood that Dad's book utopia only held books which were way beyond my infantile years.

Like Dad, Mum had an examining mind, and so these places were also of interest to her. During Mum's middle adolescence, she had left school to contribute to her family's financial needs, then returned at a later date. She excelled in English, which encouraged her to pursue further learning opportunities. Once we moved to Brissie, Mum pursued a law degree as a mature-age student. She studied through the University of Queensland, where Dad also attended.

My parents took advantage of the state's free tertiary education policy, offered by the federal Whitlam government. The downside was that we had no income, so our family lived off government subsidies. Perhaps our basic lifestyle gave it away, as the mean kids at school used my family's economic situation for bullying, calling me "Fleabag." Another unflattering nickname was "Redhead Match." Being a natural redhead was unfashionable at the time, and having the Redman surname didn't help. In my defence, I didn't sport a crop of carrot-red tresses, as I was a true strawberry-blonde, my hair brightening in the sun and darkening in the shade. Also, I didn't display a face full of beige-brown freckles, only a light sprinkling here and there. Regardless, I qualified as a redhead, and I believed, like Anne of Green Gables, that being a redhead impaired one's social life.

One place guaranteeing more freckles and stressing my long strawberry waves was the Olympic-size swimming pool, located on the university grounds where my parents studied. As I entered the pool, its water stripped away natural oils, and sun exposure made its mark on my pale skin. Vainly, I charted new freckles joining with the old in the amenities mirror. A voice in my head asked who that ugly, spotted girl staring back at me was. Oh, how I wanted to erase every sun-kissed flaw! I removed myself from the image, away from the dank toilet-block and its severe chlorine smell. As my eyes adjusted to the bright outdoors, warmth spread over my cheeks, the sun's embrace melting away misery. I returned to my belongings on the pool's grassy grounds to don a pair of flippers. Waddling over to the diving blocks, I pushed myself off and into the cool water, thrashing it out in freestyle, then slowing to casual breaststroke. I later met with friends on our claimed patch of lawn, chatting and chewing our way through lifesavers, fruit tingles, and other tooth-attacking treats, giving us energy to walk the distance home.

On one occasion, my family attended a tertiary open day on the same university grounds. During the course of the day, we entered a building with an intriguing biological science exhibition. I soon became aware of Dad's interest in science. It later made sense when I was told he'd been accepted into veterinary school after graduating from Manly High School in New South Wales. Yet, after his second year, Dad had decided it wasn't for him and switched to a teaching course. While Dad was enthralled by the exhibits of this open day, I was in for a shocking surprise. My family, with a few other interested people, walked around the room at different paces. We viewed a collection of curious human and animal displays: taxidermy body parts and variously sized bottles of wet specimens, including dissections, organs, and other well-kept samplings. I squirmed inside as childish sensitivities messed with my head and gut, cautioning me to look away. Awestruck, I stared at what was once living tissue and bone turned into lifeless exhibits. I reached my limit of endurance when encountering a horse head, featured in the room's centre in a transparent display case.

The detached head was cleanly sliced in half, graphically revealing its internal parts.

My lungs forced shrill screams out of my mouth and into the science room. The words, "I need to vomit! I need to vomit!" came next as I rushed out the door. Mum followed me soon after. Dad moseyed out in his own sweet time, still absorbing information from the displays and exhaustive inscriptions he'd read. I could see it in his faraway gaze. My father loved learning and expected the same from me, but somehow, he'd overlooked my developmental age.

Dad's single-mindedness for study meant his conspicuous absence from our daily lives. Our family home was his quasi-base as he spent a lot of time at the university campus. Mum was left to balance her law studies with parental obligations. Her collapse eventuated from overarching pressures, and she dropped her course.

Dad failed to support his wife and even degraded her. "You're not the brightest kid in the cabbage patch," came repeatedly from his smart-aleck mouth.

Ailsa had chosen a full-time parenting role, requiring less brainpower, according to her husband. Mum was by no means stupid. She returned to study at a different college in the early 1980s and qualified as a high school teacher. Her further education and work accomplishments went on from there. I observed her balanced approach to work, study, and family over the years, along with the ability to rise above a husband's discrimination. Mum's fortitude and enduring hope included Jesus Christ as her companion, who strengthened her to no end. She viewed herself a sojourner, someone just passing through this earthly life before entering an eternal place where life really begins. This Christ-centred ideology gave Mum the capacity to deal with hardships in the interim.

My father also proved his competence, as his high work ethic demanded. Unfortunately, it came at the cost of family, as Dad lacked work-life balance, and his study focus often meant he was unable to find value in places beyond the academic realm. Nonetheless, as a kid, I cradled deep admiration for Dad when he graduated in the late 1970s. On his graduation night, our family arrived at the event in plenty of time, and then Dad disappeared from sight. Just as I was asking Mum where Dad had gone, he re-emerged in time-honoured master's regalia. He was resplendent! My father's formal appearance and glowing countenance captivated me for the entire evening. While I couldn't fully comprehend Dad's hard academic slog, I knew he had earnt an important piece of paper and a position name worthy of acknowledgement. The hooding ceremony wasn't mere adult pomp and ceremony. It was a family celebration. Dad wanted us all involved.

While I tend to remember Dad as a student, I came across his staff identity card during my writing, and it reminded me of his work in 1979 and most likely in 1980. The card stated Dad's psychology lecturer position at Kelvin Grove College of Advanced Education. Amongst Dad's memorabilia collection, I also found two related photographs. One was of the faculty staff, where he featured in the middle, wearing a light pink open-collared shirt. With a relaxed expression, Dad's arms were around male colleagues on each side of him. The other photo was of the heritage-listed building where they worked. I instantly recognised the towering pillars and two sets of stairs at the building's entrance, which took me back to that place where I joyfully raced up and down the steps. Dad's joy, at the time, would certainly have come from his educationalist role.

FIVE

Grandparent Endearments and Turbulences

Family holidays often meant travelling north along the Sunshine Coast to Bribie Island, Maroochydore, and Noosa Heads. At Christmas time, we also alternated between staying with Mum's relatives in Adelaide, South Australia, where we had access to metropolitan beaches, and Dad's parents' place in Terrigal Beach, New South Wales.

Visiting Dad's parents meant a mixture of banter and quarrelsome times were had. Food was emphasised, oodles guaranteed, mostly English-style. Nana and Grandad's overabundance must've been recompense for lived extremities — the Great Depression and World War II's effect. Hospitality was also Nana's way of showing love.

We stayed in Nana and Grandad's double redbrick flat, constructed by Grandad's large, dexterous hands. At night, I lay on the bed in their spare room, where my fingers poked at cold potholed bricks, bumping over unevenness, tedium lulling me to sleep. Grandad had shaken hands with a business partner shortly after arriving in Australia. They'd established homes dotting Terrigal Beach's scenic seaside town, Nana and Grandad's home base. While my grandfather had never acquired papers approving his building business, he was a shrewd businessman as he built flats on prime land, including his own, where we stayed. They brought in tenants for a steady income, sustaining him and his wife throughout the years and into their golden ones.

My grandfather was a towering man, unlike his son, with a decent shoulder breadth connected to powerful arms, but he had developed a paunch over time. The greatest comfort for Grandad was his wooden pipe. With childlike fascination, I watched its red embers glowing and fading from the carved bulbous end and puffed smoke-curls escaping Grandad's contented mouth. His habit may have been one of the last few pleasures from a former hard-knock life. Aromatic smells came alive and drifted from the antique pipe, mingling with the stale kitchen air long after Nana's roast. There, they met with her sickly-sweet perfume, ammonia fumes from cleaning fluid, and the choking scent of mothballs. Fresh air brought relief as it entered through a newly opened window. The breeze rattled and clunked the aluminium venetian blinds and disturbed dust motes, illuminated by sunlight from open slats, some flying up my nose. The odour subtly remained, though strangely, it was neither pleasant nor unkind, as it represented family occupying the home.

Looking back, I regret my lack of appreciation for two generations above me. As a granddaughter, why didn't I fully value my grandparents' company and lived experience as contributions from history's page, now long-lost? I'd switch off from Grandad's war blathering and Nana's bossiness, her genuine efforts at communicating. Even so, these were slight niggles compared to perturbing family disputes that stemmed from Dad failing his father's expectations in days gone by. He was embittered by rejection. Between the two, a constant flow of argumentativeness, mockery, and blame manifested. I was on edge each time they had a flare up.

I witnessed son provoking father, at least as a pitiful attempt. "Have a go, Dad. Go on. Hit me!"

I'd stepped out onto the balcony at my grandparents' Terrigal flat when I heard Dad's repetitive demand. I saw his fists, clenched and at the ready. Dad's features were strained as he glared at his father, who stood a few feet away. Dad danced around like a palooka in a boxing ring while I cringed at the ringside, relieved that no one else was around. I felt embarrassment mingle with fear as the puny man goaded his hulking opponent. I expected Grandad to knock Dad to the ground, but he didn't throw a single punch. With a pained glance, which I took as pity for his son, he shook his head and left.

They were both hurting but struggled to amicably work through their issues. It seemed that Dad's resolution was to battle it out, while Grandad coped through unresponsiveness. My Welsh grandfather lived with his own heartaches from the past. His father had been a wife beater, and from boyhood, he was profoundly affected. His teenage reaction had been running away to join the navy. He'd avowed permanent separation from his dad while faithfully sending money to his beloved mother. Bitterness remained towards his father until the end. A mournful anthem sung from Grandad's childhood — violence, rejection, and running away, leading to generational cutoff. My family line testifies this pattern has filtered down for at least four generations.

One of the most brutal displays occurred during an incident one Christmas. Grandad was no pacifist this time around as he lashed out as a true goliath, but not at his son.

Megan, a cousin from Mum's side who, like me, was in her middle primary school years, had come along on our holiday to visit Nana and Grandad. For some reason, her parents weren't forewarned of the edgy environment in my grandparents' home. Perhaps Mum and Dad didn't think to mention it, as it was our norm.

The summer holiday was going swimmingly. That is, until a slight disagreement festered between mother-in-law and daughter-in-law. We were all in my grandparents' flat, most of us in the family room. But no one initially responded; discord between them was nothing new. Then the heat turned up, and a massive row ensued. Mum displayed astounding vigour as her playful cushion tossing became storming the place. The madwoman sang sassily for all to hear, though I can't recall the song. For those of us who were lounging on Grandad's handmade settees, the reality of the situation didn't immediately sink in. In our disbelieving pause, we watched objects raining down, from soft furnishings to Nana's pot plants. Terracotta pots thudded and smashed into sharp chunks as plants and gritty soil dislodged, exposing spidery roots to hate-filled air.

Nana fumed in her chair. Her eyes peeled at the chaotic mess soiling her prized carpet. She screeched at Mum, commanding her, "Stop, woman! Stop!"

Mum would not stop.

As the frenzy continued, Nana disappeared down the hall and into her bedroom, returning with Grandad. She had awakened a sleeping giant. He emerged lofty and larger than life, his face hardened and eyes tight. Grandad's pace increased with each long-legged step, enraged over the pandemonium in his castle. Whoever upset his wife *would* regret it!

I was immobilised, as I was seriously afraid. My limbs seemed to lose all sensation, and my rear was fixed to the couch. I waited numbly with bated breath, waiting for the monster to tear my mother limb from limb. *He's going to kill her in front of us all!*

Suddenly, Dad was part of the scene as a flustering mother hen gathering up its chicks, activating my brothers, Megan, and me to get out of that place, *pronto!* I willed my body into action, and we took flight down the stairs and over the road like greased lightning.

Dad's parental assertion was for our protection, I understood. Even so, I agonised over his husbandly cowardice. John had left his wife and the mother of his children in certain peril. While I wrestled with this thought, both Dad and I knew Grandad could have crushed him with one hand if he'd intervened. At first glance, the five of us appeared to be on a treasure hunt. We arrived together, then dispersed around the reserve, our heads down as we paced with tense anticipation. The bird-colonised area, situated beside an estuary, was no more than a safe place for us. I kept my cousin close, feeling responsible for her wellbeing. For her sake, I tried to keep calm and composed. Inside, I was a fretful child, utterly torn over my mother's uncertain fate. I continually glanced in Dad's direction, anxious about his next move, whatever that would be.

Dad was a bundle of nerves, his head and shoulders stooped low, legs frantically moving him around and around in rough circles. He had withdrawn into his own headspace, so my stare went unnoticed. Was Dad fearful over what may be happening to his wife? I desperately hoped she was enduring injury over death.

After what seemed like an endless time lag, Dad decided to check up on the situation at his parents' flat. We kids were instructed not to follow, only to wait for his word. Dad finally appeared on his parents' driveway, frantically waving to get our attention, then beckoning us to cross the road, after which we were told to hurriedly pack our bags for the homeward run. My memory becomes foggy from that moment, as I don't recall re-entering the flat, only packing my bag. I also don't remember if I made contact with my grandparents, just a sense that I should keep away. The point where my memory becomes clear is when I saw Mum, the rest of my immediate family, and Megan as we piled into the Chrysler. Seeing Mum get in the car stirred feelings of relief that she'd survived her ordeal. I also felt deep distress, as she had been severely beaten.

Dad drove with a wooden expression and gave his wife neither words of comfort nor the offer of a hospital call for observation and treatment. I stared at the victim, limply furled in the front passenger seat. With one hand, she attempted to conceal swelling with shades of purple, black, and blue around her eye, the other hand nursing her middle. I could tell Mum was carrying a great deal of pain in her body and in her soul. We all sat mutely in low spirits. The solemn journey was impossibly long, as we lived a whole state away, my cousin two states.

Nana and Grandad truly brought a mixture of likeable and turbulent times to my childhood. On reflection, I remember Mum telling me about Grandad's exposure to family violence as a boy. I believed Mum's words because, when he wasn't playful, he became a formidable man in charge, his face hard like flint, cautioning me to stay way. The impact was also evident when he lashed out at her on that troublesome day. At the time, I didn't blame Grandad because Mum knew of his fearsomeness and took a great risk when she began stirring up trouble. Rather, in my thoughts, I blamed Dad most of all. He should have defended his wife, even though he had reason to fear his father. I've no doubt that Dad's upbringing involved Grandad's brutality or at least a detrimental authoritarian parenting style. As a young adult, I made the connection between Dad's volatile relationship with his father, his aggression towards his wife, and his disconnect with me and my brothers, confirmed through our shared sense of rejection from him.

As for Mum's terrifying ordeal with her father-in-law, it was around ten years later when she told me she'd barricaded herself in the spare room, weighting her body against a mattress to secure the door. The enraged man had ripped the door from its hinges, leaving Mum with no defence, only a frightful predicament. She volunteered nothing more beyond that point, averse to re-entering her nightmare.

Mum also gave me some insight into her bizarre hysteria. The backstory began in our Northern Territorial days, when Mum and Dad had loaned an undisclosed sum of money to Nana and Grandad, and it was squandered away. Nana's prized carpet had been bought with some of the money, along with other unaccounted-for purchases. My parents found themselves in deep financial trouble some time later, struggling to feed and clothe a young family. Quite understandably, they asked for the loan to be repaid. Dad's parents refused to pay their debt, despite financial success from the flats that brought in a steady income. Over the years, they acted as though there was no debt. Mum resented this and harboured bitterness, which came to a head during that school holiday visit. Mum's anger targeted Nana's carpet as a settling of scores.

At least the abysmal Christmas would not be repeated, as Mum never returned to her parents-in-law's home. The rest of us, apart from Megan, made visits to see Nana and Grandad later on. For me, that intense episode, and many other Christmases with my grandparents, had a residual effect. One Christmas, it all came gushing out as unforeseen grief. I'd turned twenty-one, and it was the first time I'd connected with Mum's relatives since my teens. I was keen to see Megan and her affable family. Their house was nestled in Adelaide's foothills amongst a rustic bush setting, a delicate habitat for native flora and fauna. The home's internal vibe mirrored its outdoor tranquillity.

Christmas morning came with festive greetings, gladdening our hearts and gracing the home. A decorative pine stood self-importantly, spangled from its pointed top down to its ornate skirts, with handsomely wrapped gifts scattered at the base. I sat nearby, cross-legged on the carpet, enjoying time with my aunty, uncle, and two cousins beyond the glittery Christmas mood. Within minutes, my happiness disappeared when I was struck by a bothersome thought that I was unreasonably encroaching on another family's custom. I shared my concern, which was dismissed as nothing. I was unconditionally accepted, just as I'd always been. My strange reaction must've baffled Megan's family. It certainly took me by surprise.

Gifts were given one by one. Bronwyn, my youngest cousin, reached one out to me, her smile sparkling with the festively lit tree. I took her tissue-wrapped gift, and as I opened it, a silk scarf came free. My hands stroked the delicate cream fabric that glided like butter over my palm. While I savoured the gift, it had a disconcerting effect. Repressed grief bubbled up and out in a whoosh of tears, like the surge of shaken soft drink. Fitfully, I tried to explain my trouble reconciling this experience with past Christmases. "All … all those C-Christmases with Nana and Grandad … Your … your love has overwhelmed me." My sharing and blubbering felt uncomfortable, especially as four pairs of eyes stared blankly into mine.

Bronwyn glanced at the silk scarf and then asked, "Don't you like it?" She offered to exchange it for another one.

"I … I l-love it. I r-really do," came my stammering reply.

The lull of silence that followed only held the sound of my quiet sniffing. I lowered my head and shielded my eyes, struggling to hold back tears. I dishonestly told myself that I was the only one who had noticed them.

After mentioning Christmas with my grandparents, I was very conscious of Megan. Knowing she'd been present during the awful episode involving her aunty and my grandfather, I wondered if it weighed on the mind of her parents, who would've also known. But it wasn't mentioned, so I let it be.

We had a few quiet moments together, which brought me to a realisation; my need to grieve had gone. Like soft drink when it loses its fizz, my blubbing had fizzled out. But I wasn't flat. *Cheer up,* I thought. *It's Christmas!* I had collected myself just in time for the arrival of more relatives. We revelled in good spirits for the remainder of the day, as loving families ought to.

PART TWO

*"Life is like riding a bicycle.
To keep your balance, you must keep moving."*
— Albert Einstein

SIX

Parental Mantle of Protection

As a child, I wished to safeguard Mum against all her trials, and I shared her burdens, though she didn't want that. I was also aware of my inability to provide the help she needed. As for my protection, Mum and Dad assumed a parental gatekeeping role, hedging me in from childhood wiles when they could. I never considered that their relaxed parenting, like promoting sexual freedoms, would compromise their protectiveness towards me.

This was proven once when my family and I visited an outsider in his home. The call was for important adult business, I presumed, while I was looking forward to meeting someone new. I'd never met a person with dwarfism before. Youthful curiosity captured my attention, but my interest faded once I realised he was another person just like me. The man, whose name I forget, encouraged me to look around, so I did. I soon found a doorway off the main hall, leading to a small clinical space containing an adjustable massage table and a chair. After stepping into the room, I sensed someone's presence behind me and took it as a cue to leave. I turned to find the man my parents had come to see, his kindly face beckoning me to stay as I moved towards the doorway. Having noticed my curiosity about the bed, he urged me to test it while closing the door. I relented.

"How's that feel?" The man's voice was pacifying. "Are you comfortable? Would you like your feet tickled?"

We removed my shoes and socks, and I lay back comfortably on the firm padding, stretching out lazily. My feet tingled with a pleasant sensation as his warm hands caressed them. A few minutes in, I heard my parents' distant voices. They repeatedly called my name, which came in crisper each time.

The man's voice became stern as he told me to relax and say nothing.

The next thing I knew, Dad and Mum practically fell through the door, causing me to sit bolt upright. Their wide-eyed, ashen faces reflected deep concern before they urgently whisked me out of the room, out of the house, and into our Chrysler across the street.

Once my family were all in the car, Dad drove us home.

Mum, still pale, spoke rapidly, asking, "What happened? Did he touch you? Are you hurt? Are you okay?"

I assured my parents that all was well. My feet had simply enjoyed a rub-down from the nice man. I didn't understand their parental reflex, as opposed to reflexology from a stranger to an innocent child. But their disturbed expressions imprinted in my mind and resurfaced as a warning the next time.

It was a couple of years later when I recognised the same uneasy look in my parents' eyes. Our family had been invited to a friend's beach house for a weekend stay. We arrived with other guests, and good vibes were amongst our gathering. That is, until I sensed something was amiss when a couple I didn't know turned up. During introductions, the male partner's unflinching eyes enlarged over my physical appearance, disproportionately flattering me. I felt decidedly queasy. A hush came over the other adults, who were statue-like, wearing the same disconcerted looks as Mum and Dad.

Throughout the day, I stayed close to the other kids, believing there was safety in numbers. I also took solace in Mum and Dad's vigilance that day. Once the shady character left with his wife that evening, it brought ease to my mind. I expect it was the same for my parents and the remaining adults. A sense of freedom meant we could make the most of weekend capers.

A greater danger came in my early teens. I'd forged a special friendship, only for it to be spoilt by a menacing father. Not mine, as Dad rightly stepped in. Cherry was an only child and the apple of her father's eye. She was my high school friend, and we had regular sleepovers at her place, never mine. Her dad hung out with us girls. We often cosied up on the front bench seat in his ute's cab, where we shut out winter's rasp, our rosy pink cheeks seared by the heater's hot air blasts. Cherry's dad, as I'll refer to him, would adjust the shift column with one hand while the other clutched a beer; it was a familiar sight.

One night, Cherry's dad offered us his queen-sized bed. *Is this okay? Am I overstepping a boundary?* I asked myself.

Cherry, aware of my unease, reassured me that he'd be out of our way, sleeping in her bedroom down the hall. Ready for slumber, my body sank into the bed's softness then stiffened as the man of the house entered the room and hovered at my side. Now *he* was crossing over a boundary! Even in the lamp's soft light, I saw a leathered face, aged beyond his forty-plus years. His boozy breath and reeking pores were equally repulsive to my senses; I yearned to cough out what had been breathed in, to run and hide, but I didn't.

The man's slurring words came sickeningly. "Hoooow … How 'bout a good night's kiss, luv. Coooome on. Donbe shy. Give uza kiss, luv."

Under the quilt, my body was deceptively relaxed. Inside my head, I was freaking out. *Where's Cherry? Where's Cherry?* Like a nightmarish dream, my lifeless legs were incapable of taking me to safety. Just as the rank mouth inched towards mine, my head impulsively wrenched away.

"Go away, Dad. Goodnight!" Cherry's words came abruptly with her appearance, taking me out of my wide-awake nightmare. The timing of her arrival was impeccable. Although greatly relieved, I was still unsettled and felt drumming in my chest. *How could I sleep?* Worst-case scenarios taunted me — child kidnap and rape, being left for dead while my friend floated blissfully unaware in a glorious dream.

Although I knew this parent was dangerous, Cherry's place became my second home. At one sleepover, I woke from a dreamless sleep to find my gatekeeper gone. I was a defenceless lamb abandoned to a wolf's care. Argus-eyed, I dressed speedily and gathered up my gear. I needed to get out. Inexplicably, I did nothing to escape. Instead, my nose followed appetizing smells wafting from the kitchen.

A domestic man greeted me with a lilting voice. "Goood mooorrrning! I made breakfast for you. Bacon and eggs. Cuppa tea? I've dropped Cherry off. She'll be back late."

Sirens whirled in my head as I took in his words.

The unsavoury man urged me to sit at the table, playfully serving up breakfast with a devilish grin. His performance troubled me all the more.

Help! I cried internally and desperately hoped God would intervene. I also hankered for my parents' consoling voices, imagining myself screaming into their ears. *I'm in danger. Get me out of here!* I didn't know what to do. Like a senseless lamb, I followed my beguiler, climbing into the car beside him as he continued to deploy his playful manner. I was told we were off on a mystery trip somewhere out of town. I pretended to be intrigued. Inside, I was scared stiff over what may happen. *Oh, God, protect me,* went my SOS call, on a wing and a prayer.

Once we reached our destination, we moved from the car's interior to a lightly gravelled track. As we walked beside a river, its muddied brown bed and rippling silvery surface attracted my attention. I breathed in eucalyptus scents from the dusty blue-green leaves of gum trees, which framed the sky while warbling magpies rested on their limbs. I took in the sublime surroundings for as long as possible. It was a distraction from the droning of my unwanted companion's dull oration.

Inside, I screamed, *Shut up!* Outwardly, I politely listened.

According to the hoary man's wisdom, "Women sit on a gold mine, though they don't know it." He slowly offered further explanation, convinced that I was his budding student. "There are riches to be gained from prostitution …" With an air of benevolence, he offered to get me into the profession.

I was *dumbstruck.* At the age of fourteen, I was a fledgling who hadn't yet experienced a first period.

The predator then asked me for sex in a honeyed tone. His mouth twisted into a sinister smile as he explained that he'd been looking for an ideal spot, and it had finally appeared. His finger pointed towards a bush area nearby, intended as our seedy bed.

Terror and repulsion joined hands with mine, compelling me to speak out. *No!*

Attempting a more persuasive voice, Cherry's appalling father asked me twice more, but I would not relent. His mood instantly soured, and I was taken back to his Morwell home in silence. As we travelled, I lengthened the distance between us by clinging to the car's cold, rigid door panel, graciously ignored. I felt sweet relief over my escape, relief that I had not been raped. A sense of gratitude welled up inside of me. It reached to the heavens, headed for the Great Shepherd, who had been my secret gatekeeper.

I didn't tell a soul about the close call. But just a day later, Dad became aware of the offender in our midst when an independent source warned him about the devious rogue. Dad was righteously angry that a sexual deviant had been near his daughter, and I was forbidden to stay with Cherry. Being made to stay away meant our friend connection ended, but to Dad, my safety was paramount. Despite our struggling relationship, he was looking out for me. If it weren't for him, I'd have returned to Cherry's home and placed myself at further risk. I didn't understand my folly until much later, as an adult. The insight came while I was working in the child protection field. A child's ability to leave a grooming paedophile is nearly impossible. Children at risk need intervention. In my case, the intervener was my father, and I am ever so thankful.

SEVEN

Volatile Primary Years

I learned that not all of my childhood struggles would compel Dad's intervention, nor Mum's. As a child, I never doubted their love for me, but Dad's lacking devotion and Mum's somewhat wavering ability to reach out meant, for the most part, I navigated school pressures and lurking bullies alone, too afraid to seek help or stand up for myself. My readiness for school was uncertain, as I was a year younger than my peers and insecure at that. Mum and Dad decided to send me anyway, only for my teacher to later recommend that I repeat Grade 1. My education began at Ironside State School in St. Lucia, Brisbane.

My teacher, Miss White, pulled off an iconic 1970s style. She, and almost every other female teacher, wore lanyard-length necklaces over turtlenecks or summery tops and mini-skirts skimping upper thighs with knee-high leather boots. Crotch-hugging bell-bottom pants worn with clunky shoes was also a favourite.

Unfortunately, Miss White's impeccable appearance did not compensate for her waning warmth. She unsettled me from the start.

On the first day of school, I raised a hand to request a trip to the loo. The teacher quickly sent me and another student off to the toilet block. On return, we were met with Miss White's terse explanation that toilets were only available during designated breaks and that we should *never* ask to use them during class. The next day, heavy arms pulled down to my sides, though I desperately wanted to raise one, as I was busting. It was too late! The chair's plywood layering slurped up some of the warm liquid beneath me, and the rest over-flowed, leaving a light yellow puddle splashing at my feet. My ammonia-soaked dress turned to glue, as I couldn't leave the seat. I also couldn't speak, petrified of the outcome. In my sorry predicament, I saw a small girl walk forward to whisper something into Miss White's ear. The teacher's head turned in my direction, and her dirty look said it all. I was in *big* trouble. Alas, it was a precursor to many more schooling tribulations.

My timidity meant lagging behind my peers, which at times led to trouble. On one occasion, I was loosely present but uninvolved in a relatively serious incident in the schoolyard. The particulars later vanished from my memory, apart from someone getting hurt. I do, however, remember the consequence for my vague association with the misbehaving students.

The ominous announcement piqued my attention, along with fear. "Fleur Redman, come to the office. Fleur Redman …"

Hearing my name repeated over the school's loudspeakers was double the humiliation! Nerves had me running to the redoubtable headmaster's office. The man in charge remains nameless and faceless in my memory. But what I do recall is a man who towered over me and wore walk-shorts paired with knee high walk-socks, much like my grandfather. The headmaster's black leather shoes gleamed with notable spit and polish, qualifying him for the defence force. Another standout feature was his knobbly knees, ugly, hairy joints jutting out.

The man's deep-toned voice delivered a stern lecture, harping on with a moral lesson. I knew it wasn't applicable. Still, I complied by lowering my head, too afraid to look into the disciplinarian's eyes. My posture was likely misread as that of a shame-faced troublemaker. I flinched at each whipping as the cuts caused instant smarting against my knuckles. When the ordeal was over, I cupped shaking hands together to self-sooth reddened and swollen fingers, stinging with each movement. Hot tears flowed for reasons the headmaster didn't know. I had no voice to protest the unwarranted corporal punishment. That afternoon, I found Mum's comforting arms, but she didn't speak out in my defence. Even worse, Dad was silent on the matter. His deficiency in supporting me as a student was a pattern he exhibited throughout my schooling. He only cared about good marks, which I didn't attain, and acceptable handwriting.

I recall a moment of fatherly advice in my early high school years, after my family moved from Queensland to Victoria. Dad noted that my cursive Queensland penmanship had become Victorian printed letters. We stood in the entranceway of our Churchill home, where we completed a form for school administration purposes.

He skimmed my writing twice. "What's this? Printed block letters? Printing is an immature writing style! You should be using cursive letters. Do it again!"

I had been influenced by my school peers. "Everyone else prints," I explained, but Dad still disapproved of the simplistic writing style. It was genuine coaching, but his tone implied that I'd committed a sin. Dad didn't know my lacking confidence affected my writing quality, in both ways. His criticism did not improve my lettering or self-assurance. Today, I alternate between each script, and at times, my penmanship deteriorates if I'm feeling under confident.

Back at Ironside State School, I was greatly relieved when Miss White released herself from worrisome and frail me. I moved up in year levels and gained a teacher upgrade. Mrs McKay was a student's dream, as she was even-natured and nurturing. We established an instant rapport. Her kindly eyes and exceptional patience told me I was accepted, no matter what! Mrs McKay was gifted in bringing children's literature to life. Her perfect intonation and character animation transported me into a fictional realm, tonic for an unsettled child. Sadly, my happy place ended all too soon when I moved up a grade and away from my classroom champion. I braced myself for another unsympathetic teacher.

Mum witnessed my melancholic moods yet again, later telling me I was unhappy. "You came home from school crying every day."

Was I really that much of a blubbering mess? If so, why didn't she do something, like rescue me from Gail, that mean-spirited oppressor? In truth, I was incapable of asking for help. The driveway incident was just one example of when I should've solicited Mum's help beyond a hug and a Band-Aid. I needed guidance on how to protect myself against sneaky adversaries.

Looking back on the day that two school peers intercepted the bully in my life, I'm certain that their valiant effort came from divine intervention. God knew I needed them. That morning, I stood alone in the school quadrangle, facing away from the summer sun. My uniform dress clung to my back with dampness from heat and rising humidity. The bell had rung, and students dispersed from the area. Why was I waiting, melting?

Turning towards the direction of my classroom, I spotted two figures striding my way. The girls walked with certitude, one being slightly taller, leaner, and blonder than the other. Once their features came into view, I saw their open faces, but who were they? Neither of them were in my class. Perhaps they attended classes a year above mine. Besides, why were they approaching me? Their opening line demanded verification of my identity. "Are you Fleur Redman?" Then they confessed to spying, "We've been watching you."

Initially, I suspected new bullies had come into my life, except that they were set on helping me.

"We've seen how Gail treats you. She won't bother you anymore. We've come to your rescue. We're your friends now."

Their words came as a surreal delight, but surely, I would wake up from the beautiful dream. I would return to real life's disenchantment. No. I *was* awake.

The girls, who introduced themselves as Natalie and Emma, soon bid me farewell, armed with their watertight plan to ward off Gail. I honestly can't remember what their tactic was or even if they told me, apart from saying, "We'll see her today."

That wasn't my concern anyway. As tardy students, we went off to our classes, and with good reason. I didn't witness Gail's disarmament but revelled in the effect. She was literally nowhere to be seen from that day on. Natalie and Emma kept their promise, and new relationships were created. These beautiful souls joined with mine through the bond of youthful friendship.

Our allied triad changed my life for the better, and as it turned out, our houses were within walking distance. A neighbourly couple permitted me to cut through their extensive backyard to visit my friends. Lingering at the fence line, I would snap off sugarcane stalks for chomping and sucking. Their unadulterated sweetness came euphorically to my mouth. Once satisfied, I'd clamber over the wire fence, detangling my legs before adopting a comical running style, feet kicking up like a performing clown. I was dead serious as my bare feet avoided red-bellied black snakes, or some other type, sheltering in the long grass. I ran the distance to Natalie's house, sugarcane juice fuelling me, as it was on the steeper side of our hilly neighbourhood.

Her South African family resided in a neat and orderly home that displayed antique furnishings. At Natalie's place, I sampled edible luxuries my parents could never afford. It was a bracing change from homemade Anzac biscuits, bread and butter pudding, and four-ingredient pancakes. Natalie offered an assortment of cream-filled biscuits and the wonder of vanilla ice-cream. We piled our bowls high with frozen rippled curls that numbed our tongues and cooled our insides, a delightful treat on hot summer days. Emma's home was unlike that of our shared friend but a shambolic place in the best sense. Everyone was welcome in her cosy family abode, regardless of feathers, fur, or skin. Emma and her mother's open-handedness drew us all in, along with their adorable ducks.

While my renewed life was travelling well, I loathed senseless shenanigans but understood that they had factored it into our friendship treaty. It was a better alternative to being bullied. Emma, Natalie, and I poured custard over parked car doors to give unsuspecting motorists a sticky surprise. My conniving friends taught me how to master the art of shoplifting. We pinched bubble-gum, lifesavers, and other items small enough to hide from shop assistants. Sweets in my hand became unpleasant tidbits on my tongue, retelling that I had acted against my conscience. I was free from worry once the phase had passed. I was never caught out, to my relief, unlike Owen for his troublemaking. My older brother and his friend once stole a stockpile of calculators worth thousands of dollars, bringing officious police to our front door. I suspected that it wasn't his only misdemeanour. Still, I had no proof, and having been a thief myself, I couldn't point the finger. Dad rose to his parent role on this matter, attempting to sort out Owen's delinquency. From a distance, I scrutinised our father's sudden attendance. I gathered that something unscrupulous had to come to his attention to activate his parenting. He and Mum strictly kept me out of the commotion, which meant I wasn't present at the police station. Consequently, I couldn't tell exactly how it panned out.

EIGHT

Mum Went Off on a Spiritual Tangent

With my new relationships established, Mum and Emma's mum also formed a friendship. It served as the catalyst for change in Mum, and she was eager to share her revelation with me. One lazy afternoon, I was enjoying the sun-warmed back patio in solitary bliss when Mum showed up. She had just returned from Emma's place, and although I didn't immediately know it, the energy Mum had brought with her came from a spiritual awakening that would create a ripple effect through our family. Mum sat on the slate beside me. Her sombre tone and incisive eyes commanded my attention as she shared her soul-searching confessions and newfound answers.

Her voice, laced with churchy and other foreign words, toppled out with fanaticism. "… experimentation with mysticism through transcendental meditation … sin and horrifying blackness within. I found the answer: salvation through Jesus Christ!"

To me, it all sounded like nonsensical prattle. While Mum maintained her gusto, I preferred to be elsewhere, content to remain as an unwitting child.

Emma's mum, as I knew her, had led my mum to salvation, whatever that word ending in "shun" meant. Mum's perplexing talk continued, so I determined to find a reasonable conclusion for her weirdness. Soon enough, I accepted that Mum had been handed something, or someone, as a source of strength and purpose. It was a helpful proposal when considering her recent meltdown. I had certainly seen Mum suffer through a volatile marriage and bend under life's mounting pressures, including financial strain and little support from Dad in raising us three kids. Her source of hope seemed to come that day, but would Christ himself be the basis for her fulfilment? Perhaps it was another phase, like the community Mum found through the women's liberation movement and her immersion in Eastern meditative practices. I told myself that only time would tell if the personage of Jesus Christ would endure, like the constancy of seasonal change, especially in light of Mum's existing season's ravages. Meanwhile, Mum shared her strange and wonderful spiritual experiences, and I politely listened and mirrored her smiles, hiding my personal disinterest.

Apparently, I'd been educated in the ways of God. Mum must've agreed to religious instruction, a non-compulsory subject in addition to the school curriculum. But I only retained the Christmas narrative. Walking home from school one afternoon, I began questioning what

I'd been taught. How could a conception take place in a virgin, a so-called immaculate conception? And why was our world told it was fact? The more I contemplated the idea, the more ridiculous it sounded. I cradled resistance towards God over the idea that he'd sent his son as a babe, destined to save the world. I gladly cast off the original Christmas theme as nothing more than a feel-good fairy tale. My conclusion came satisfyingly, so I chose to leave the matter where it was, only to be faced with Mum's opposing view. Annoyingly, my soliloquy occurred around the time of Mum's conversion to Christianity. Her conversion was impactful enough that she took my brothers and me on an unexpected spiritual journey as she embraced the experiential through classical Pentecostalism.

While still in my non-believing mindset, a children's program was commencing at the local Anglican Church. It became the talk of the playground at my school, while a blasé attitude washed over me. Why would I want to attend a church event? It would be religious, boring, and irrelevant! On the first day, I gave in. Peer pressure had me following along, just as a sheep instinctively keeps to its mob. As we entered the church building, we were handed glossless books in miniature size by willing parishioners with toothy smiles. Father himself also welcomed us. His good humour and expansiveness reminded me of Santa Claus.

I tuned into the sounds of childish chatter, giggles, and our clumsy plonking onto hard timber pews, echoing through the internal chapel space. The priest began his introduction. His rich, modulated voice created a lull amongst us, down to the last shuffling shoe. The scene was set for the storytelling performance. While the storyline escapes me, I recall monsters were afoot and larger than life characters featured in an enthralling plot, gradually revealing the fable's underlying message. Dazed kids gained a reward for keeping quiet and sitting still. Each week's protagonist featured a separate monster face as a lick-and-stick stamp for our booklets. It was all very entertaining, though the effectiveness of the moral teachings was uncertain. I had no fresh convictions and no God encounters during the program, though that probably wasn't the purpose. Still, I quietly wondered if God was in that holy place. It *was* his house. Was I reconsidering God? If so, did that mean the Christmas account held some weight after all? My softening heart came from witnessing Mum's remarkable transformation. Her despondency was turning into hopefulness, even in the face of a troublesome marriage.

One afternoon, Mum announced that our family, bar Dad, was going to a worship service in Brissie somewhere. I assumed it would involve music and song to honour God's name. Attending a worship service would be a different experience for us, so I was in purely out of curiosity. When the day came, we arrived late. The four of us gathered at the front of an undistinguished building with no indication of a church denomination. Dylan has since reminded me, as I write, that we attended a Christian Outreach Centre, or COC. The brand was founded by Pastor

Clark Taylor, who was known for his evangelistic ministry, strongly emphasising healing miracles at the time. During the few minutes that we lingered, I glanced at Mum and my brothers. Her eyes were bright with expectation. Owen and Dylan were wide-eyed with apprehension. They reflected my own uncertainty over what to expect. Then again, I wondered if anyone was actually inside the building, as I detected no sound, movement, or any other goings-on.

An intuitive thought interjected. *There is a lot going on, and I will be impacted!* Fresh eagerness came skittishly, preventing my hand from grasping the door's handle. Mum reached past and opened the door, like a lid unhurriedly drawn back from a mysterious box. Escaping light prevented me from deciphering what lay inside. As the threshold came into view, I stepped up and into the building, where weightlessness overcame my body, drifting me halfway up the aisle with Mum and my brothers. I was mesmerised by a presence of aliveness, and its novelty wooed me. I took in the peculiar scene; people jubilantly leapt and swayed, sang and chanted praise to the lively music, their arms and hands reaching towards the ceiling as an act of adoration. Some of the gathering conveyed distress as they extended stiff arms or frantically moved them about while crying out through anguished tear-marked faces, seeking a cathartic experience. *So this is what Mum meant by a worship service!* We were amongst a community of people, and while they expressed themselves individually, they were collectively seeking something bigger than themselves. For me, the lightness in my spirit carried both delight and contentment. I oddly felt at home for the first time. In the months ahead, I understood that God himself had filled that place with his presence, and it was impossible to be unaffected. I knew this because the sublime touch of God, which came upon me then, was the start of many to come.

Mum took us back to the COC for healing services. It was yet another eye-opener. Dad offered no comment, as he hadn't been informed of the events Mum had taken us to. Once aware, a heated argument broke out between my parents, mostly from Dad as his foul temper got the better of him. He banned his wife from exposing us kids to the vices of Pentecostalism, claiming it was all fundamentalist sensationalism as a dangerous form of brainwashing. By contrast, he was quite okay with the local Anglican establishment. It was the same place I'd attended with my peers for after-school activities. Apparently, the church and its rituals were non-threatening to our well-being. I couldn't understand Dad's stance. My Pentecostal experience only whetted my appetite to explore more uncharted spiritual territory. Precisely his concern!

The next service we attended, again without Dad, was the safer Anglican alternative: Christ Church, St. Lucia. Heading towards the front entrance, I strained my neck to view the silver cross atop the landmark bell tower. The structure went way up high into the endless sky, reminding me of Rapunzel's fairy-tale tower. To relieve my neck, I shifted my head towards the vast brick building and its glass window walls. As we approached the entrance, I had questions on my mind about what the church offered beyond hearty greetings and monster stories with value-laden lessons and how it would contribute to my mother's divine pilgrimage.

Once inside, we found a pew, where I melded into Mum's warm, pliable side, as I was feeling hesitant about the unaccustomed service. The pipe organ's resonances came with amplified sound, instantly correcting my posture. Along with the choir, it sounded churchy to my ears, lofty and out of reach. *Does God like it?* I wondered.

As I fumbled, Mum navigated me through pages of hardcover books for congregational prayer and song. "Can you see, up there, a hymnal board with numbers on it?" Mum pointed as she spoke.

To pass the time, I gazed at sun brightened stained-glass windows, deciphered as old religion. I also observed beautifully honed items around the building. Later, I discovered they were liturgical objects with consecrated purposes: glowing candles, pristine cloths, carved wood, gleaming metals, and the central sacramental cross, which required a nod from parishioners. I half expected a light to appear above their reverential heads.

"Should I bow?" I asked Mum.

"It's up to you," came her unhelpful retort.

I wanted to know if bowing made a person more acceptable to God. I was perturbed by one particular artefact, a life-sized resurrection statue. The coppery, emaciated figure suspended out from the wall above our seating.

I wished we didn't sit so close to the suffering man. Or was he already dead? Whenever I caught a glimpse, I shuddered with infantile fear. Was the real Christ that haunting? I also detested Sunday school, running away each time Mum forced me to go. I didn't know why she said it was good for me, and when she asked why I didn't want to go, I had no answer. So she let it be my choice.

Owen's involvement in the church boys' choir was also mystifying, as I was unable to make out how he felt about the experience. Overall, I found little inspiration in that religious place. The consecrated objects and archaic traditions were all extraneous to child-me. I wanted to know if God was personally accessible. Veritably, I knew he was, having felt God's presence amongst those odd Pentecostals, despite Dad's warnings about that precarious lot. At the time, I was confused about why reaching God had to be so complicated, questioning if it was people who complicated how we reached God.

Later, from my early teens, I would experience God as a loving father who reached out to me with notable simplicity. It would happen through more manifestations of his presence and hearing his voice in various ways. Mum was also a recipient of God's love, continually over the years. Once established, her eternal focus never waned, and it rubbed off on me.

NINE

My Curious Pentecostal Experience

The summer of 1981 presented cause for lament. My family travelled well over 1,500 kilometres by car to Churchill, Victoria. I was forced to abandon my precious trio friendship and our familiar family home with its tropical haven and my backyard swing. I was also unhappy to be far away from the vast Sunshine State with its glorious coastline. We were no longer proud Queenslanders but foreigners in a southern state. The way I saw it, we may as well have moved to the moon when we relocated to Churchill. The town had been named after the British Prime Minister, Sir Winston Churchill, officially in 1966. The township is based in the Latrobe Valley in the middle of the Gippsland region, east of the state. We moved because Dad landed a job as a community psychologist at the Churchill Community Health Centre. It seemed to me that Churchill was a dreary place, and I discovered that my newfound peers felt the same way. They referred to Churchill as "The Hole" because of boredom and lack of inspiration from limited opportunities due to slow economic growth. If Sir Winston Churchill were alive, I wonder what he would've said about that. Although, I'm certain that he'd approve of my return to the town further down the track, as I had a renewed sense of purpose.

On the upside of things, Dad's salary significantly improved our lives. Mum also contributed soon after. I relished walking into clothing shops as my eyes expanded over racks of hanging textiles, begging to be explored. Mum would generously say, "Get whatever you like, Fleur." I never took advantage of her generosity as my younger days of dowdy, second-hand clothes had fostered gratitude. Since our move meant starting high school amongst an unknown crowd, I was determined to attain a reasonable level of popularity. From the first term, I dressed en vogue, knowing the school had a non-compulsory uniform policy. My 1980s fashion picks included denim staples and knitted legwarmers with flecks of sparkle to be removed only under sufferance, not to mention Cindi Lauper's fun fashion style. Admittedly, I was unadventurous by comparison. Cindi's sassy personality was something I lacked, believing that I wasn't made to stand out.

Our rendered brick house had been renovated since it had been constructed in the late 1950s or early 1960s, during the building boom. We all appreciated novelties like gliding kitchen drawers and effortlessly functioning taps. Also, newly purchased must-haves. Our first food processor was a remarkable culinary help, as was a microwave oven, which was a convenience marvel. Our family room was richly carpeted in unfussy cream with an oversized modular couch in lively cobalt blue. They were both good enough to nap on. The internal upgrades were a welcome change from our characterful place in Brissie, which was highly appealing to the hippies who bought it. Each of these houses were split-level designs, likely to have been built in the same era.

It wasn't long before our new home lost its charm, as material improvements couldn't compensate for Mum and Dad's declining marriage. Terse arguments escalated into domestic abuse again, Dad directing his aggressive behaviour at Mum before Owen, Dylan, and me. Hushed sibling talks came from our anguished minds as turbulence filtered through the house. During one of these times, Owen and I met by coincidence in the hall as vulnerable teens. Our edgy eyes fused in an unspoken agreement that our childhood had ended. Sibling solidarity came as a clear-cut decision, at least between Owen and me. We stopped our childish banter to join alliances. In reality, we had virtually no resources to pool. Our vague efforts at camaraderie were merely passing moments of empathy. Our struggles were mostly kept to ourselves, becoming adult complications later on. Something we wouldn't have considered at the time.

Mum wore a perpetually tear-stained face. Beneath it were layers of pain I couldn't fully understand. But even so, the heartache she carried deeply troubled me. Aching for my mother meant resentment towards her rival, the detached figure I called Dad. Perhaps I was the detached one, slipping into survival mode amidst the marital storm. I constantly slammed my bedroom door, then shut myself away. Poster images lined the walls with recognised bands: AC/DC, Suzie Q, and KISS. They screamed profanities from rebellious mouths. My mind and lips followed their cause as a false belief that I was in control. Staggeringly, God visited me in that miserable dungeon. Somehow, he reached in and tempered my troubled mind, his soul joining with mine in sweet amity, mostly filling my room with his comforting presence but also through visions containing spiritual truths, providing answers to my unasked questions. In his presence, I also received fresh revelations. God wasn't restricted by church buildings or manmade traditions, and he truly was the God who sees, devoting himself to insignificant me. I still find his dedication astounding, as over the years, his personable approach has remained unchanged. Yet all the while, I was caught in a spiritual battle, a quandary. *God or rebellion?* Both enticed me as a hurting adolescent.

Soon after our move to Victoria, Mum put out feelers to find a thriving Pentecostal church. Her chosen place of fellowship, The Revival Centres of Australia, was indeed buzzing with in-house activities and evangelistic outreach beyond its walls. Dad must've lifted the ban on Pentecostal worship by that point. Mum, my brothers, and I gained biblical teachings and doctrine according to the church's version of Christendom. It was a major influence in my youth, spanning three and half years from the age of eleven. Within that place, Mum constructed impermeable theologies, which she personalised and vehemently clung to for her remaining days. Her dogma was just as zealous as the church community, a force to be reckoned with. Some oddities became a part of my world. Revering the pastor above all others, as he held a privileged position, was one. Another was that the church's doctrine was absolute, overriding that of all other Christian denominations as heresies, despite similar foundational beliefs and practices.

One Sunday service, Mum pressed me to step forward and join an animated crowd gathering for prayer ministry. Obediently, I made my way towards the sanctuary, where a small circle of men hemmed me in. They bellowed at God to free my tongue as though he was deaf and confused. The church's main player, Pastor Aidan, took over. He was a gregarious man with a large faith capacity. Overshadowing my small frame, the pastor was intent on commanding tongues into being. His bulky hand spanned my forehead, transferring clammy heat while forcing me backwards. I resisted just enough to avoid a fall. All the while, I felt like a timid church mouse, eager to scurry away from the hullabaloo. Free at last, Mum and I were homeward bound, though my tongue had not been loosened.

As Mum drove, her words, "Never mind, maybe next time," came with a sympathetic look.

I responded with a weak smile, secretly hoping that the experience would not be repeated.

One evening a week later, we joined others in an overcrowded room at the church for charismatic prayer.

Standing beside Mum, I slid down the wall and into a squatting position. Praying in a whisper, I closed my eyes, as they were heavy for sleep. In that moment, an anomaly occurred. All the people vanished, along with their noise, and across the room was the man I recognisably knew to be Jesus Christ. He appeared to be neither young nor old and was dressed in a loose-fitting tunic of pure white, falling below the knee. The man I beheld was, in some ways, like Akiane Kramarik's renowned portrait of the *Prince of Peace*. The Jesus I saw also had brown wavy hair and a beard, though longer and far less styled, while his smooth, olive-toned skin matched the painting. As I didn't study the shape of Jesus's nose or the curvatures of his cheeks, I cannot compare these features. Kind and tender eyes exemplified his character, not gemlike with a mysterious glint like those depicted in the painting but as an authentic human being. I sensed that Jesus knew me well as he transferred peace and calm onto me. His outstretched arms and open hands offered an invisible gift. My heart was supple as the gift instinctively became mine; phonetic sounds came repetitiously from my mouth as an unfamiliar language taught by the Holy Spirit.

The instant I opened my eyes, Jesus's appearance vanished, and all the people returned to the room with a rush of noise. The new language I received was still forming on my tongue, spoken in a soft rhythm. As I stood with the boisterous crowd, they became distant. Their voices reduced to nothing more than a murmur, for I was enveloped in awe and repose. By Christ's own hand, I had been given something remarkable, a treasure unlike any other.

I wanted to guard my secret, but it was impossible. It was expected that I reveal my gift to the church crowd, so I shared while Mum drove us home. I kept the vision part from her, lest it become headline news. Mum rang Pastor Aidan shortly after arriving at our house, despite the late hour. My body flinched at his celebratory shout through the receiver.

According to church doctrine, tongues secured my place in Heaven, so the next Sunday, Pastor Aidan declared, "Fleur has come into salvation, with the evidence of speaking in tongues."

Within that place of worship, there was jubilation amongst the congregation as numerous heads turned towards mine with hallelujahs and rapturous applause. It was more attention than I needed at the tender age of thirteen. At the time of this soul-stirring experience, what mattered to me was that only Jesus and I knew my unabridged story, which was very personal, and the effect has remained ever since.

If my church involvements were regarded as larger than life, then Dad's response was grand offence! Broaching anything mildly related to the subject was like igniting an explosive. Yet, for a time, he entirely changed his tune. I watched Dad's behaviour as he trundled off to Sunday morning services with the rest of our family. I understood Dad's decision was an attempt to salvage his tattered marriage by supporting his wife. I believed it was a noble gesture, despite many misgivings about my father as a teenager.

Dad had little nerve, yet he boldly placed himself amongst raucous ecclesiastical activity. He resigned himself, at least outwardly, to an insistent shoving towards God by those attending the church. Dad was plainly out of place, as he was unable to traverse the foreign territory. His demure nature swung to the extreme as he avoided interactions by keeping a low profile. I suspect Dad spent more time outside than inside the building, acquainting himself with the car park. Granted, both Dad and the church were well-meaning, and the reception he received was warm and welcoming. All the same, Dad's restlessness would not settle as everything cramped his style. Though, I did wonder whether he was looking for evidence of God's existence in the deep recesses of his mind. My only suggestion for this thought was that I'd never heard Dad deny the existence of God, only that God had little relevance. My speculative position didn't last for long, as my baptism raised ill will in him.

The idea of baptism wasn't initiated by me; it came through church influence and my pushy mother. The Revival Centre's fear tactics served as doomsday warnings, homing in on apocalyptic events. It was a tendency amongst many denominations. Church attendees, including me, were exposed to this thinking through fire and brimstone preaching and film enactments; the rapture of God's chosen ones and the disturbing aftermath for those left behind, all inspired by Revelation's prophetic book.

My internal question repeated itself. *Why did God draw people to himself through trepidation?*

One afternoon, Mum was ironing clothes in the laundry, which was located near my bedroom. I was innocently passing by when she stopped her chore and launched into preachy mode. Her judgement day lecture was tailored just for me, strongly emphasising God's dissatisfaction that I hadn't been baptised. As I listened, fear crept into my mind and inundated me. I retreated to my room and sat on the edge of my bed, hoping for some respite. None came as I shook uncontrollably and imagined a wrathful, punitive God mapping out my destiny, forever scorned. His punishment was justified by my insubordination.

In my terrified state, I fell into another consciousness, being neither awake nor asleep. A vision came as a movielike viewing with vibrant colour and surround sound. My physical eyes were closed, but I could see spiritually, like the vision in the church. On this occasion, I was compelled to look skyward instead of across the room. Similar to Jacob's dream, I saw angels on steps to the left and right of the scene, coming down from heaven. The hosts were dressed in timeless robes, and the whole picture was brightened with gold and white colour. I heard Heaven's pure sound. Cathedral crescendos emanated from the unaccompanied angelic choir, their voices initially mistaken for music. The worship was intended for the one they heralded, the principal figure in the vision: Jesus Christ. The hosts lightly faded as my eyes fixed on their ruler, steadily descending between them. Christ's glory was not from kingly apparel, as he dressed in a plain white robe, yet he was profoundly and inexplicably wrapped in majesty. The Son of God's personal effect transferred peace as he bore the message that his coming was for me. I was wholly accepted. I was *not* scorned as I'd supposed. My eyes snapped open to the reality of my room. I had been altered with lightness in my spirit with a distinct absence of fear. I'd also gained a new take on God's character. He saw me with grace through the eyes of his son.

My decision to be baptised was no longer fear-based. So I joined my angelic friends by donning a robe for the emersion, as was customary in the church. I crossed my arms over my chest.

Pastor Aidan held me in his firm grip as he declared, "I now baptise you in the name of the Father, and of the Son, and of the Holy Spirit."

I relented to full-body dousing, then sprang forward as quickly as I went down, resurrecting from my watery grave, which sprayed the already half-soaked pastor. I felt cleansed beyond the water's refreshing, light in my spirit and unnaturally jubilant.

Pastor Aidan assisted me as I wobbled my way out of the baptismal tank. I dried off and got changed in a closet-sized room, my body comically refusing to cooperate. It became apparent that I was spiritually drunk!

I floated back to the congregation and my reserved seat with wet hair dripping down my back. An atmospheric charge could be felt amongst the people, as baptism was a celebrated occasion, though unlikely for Dad. He'd attended the service, but I hadn't considered him at the time of the ceremony, and I don't remember seeing him until afterwards. People congratulated me after the service, adding to my joy. Then I spotted Dad advancing towards me. He had a look of tenacity as his fiery eyes flashed at mine. I had seen that aspect of Dad before but never in the church, where he was usually reserved. Something had offended him, and he set out to disempower it. It was soon discovered that I was the offence.

Dad was without pretence when he confronted me, to the extent that people took a wide berth as they passed us. We stood near the foyer entrance when he blurted out, "You are a stupid, stupid girl! That was the worst decision you have ever made. You'll regret it! You'll regret it!" Dad continued to emphasise how stupid I was, with as much abrasiveness as he could muster.

I watched Dad's lips move with each discouragement. On an ordinary day, I would've completely fallen apart, but it was *no* ordinary day. My unassailable spiritual high meant I was entirely unshaken. I knew, beyond doubt, that I'd made one of the best decisions of my life. I would *not* regret it!

Exasperated, Dad finally backed down, as he could see his dissuasions held no effect. He huffily muttered to himself while walking away. My extreme sanguine mood continued, shrugging him a goodbye with a smile. I couldn't help it. Sadly, I discovered later on that Dad pursued someone else with his temper. His target was Owen, who had also been through the baptismal tank that morning. I'd wondered if Owen's decision to be baptised was made through coercion from the powers that be or by his own free will. As uncertain as he might have been, I shuddered to consider Dad's heightened aggression after it had failed with me.

That was the last time I remember Dad attending our church. My brothers agreed that Dad's church-attending efforts had reached their limit. We could see that his attempts at salvaging his marriage proved null and void!

TEN

High School and Other Stress

Just before moving to Victoria that summer, fellow Queenslanders pre-warned us about the bitterly cold winters in the Gippsland region. So we expected mild temperatures, only to be faced with a relentless heatwave. Naturally, the chilly weather caught up with us once wintertime rolled around. I remember too many unpleasant mornings while waiting for the school bus, guaranteeing chattering teeth and numb extremities as I shivered from damp fog creeping into the internal parts of my uniform.

It was my first day of high school, which I wasn't ready for. Feeling alone in the school quadrangle, I was plagued with anxiety. Parts of my body were numb, while my throat pulsated intensely. But the isolation I sensed was all in my head, as I was surrounded by scores of other students, their restless bodies and tense faces reflecting my apprehensiveness. *They can't be as insecure as me*, I thought. I was the same scared little kid I'd been on my second day of primary school, but at least I had control of my bladder. Since my hearing went dull when the school authorities gave student directions, I tagged along with the rest of the clueless horde during orientation.

Soon after the daunting high school years began, I became aware of a new socio-cultural scene. Unlike my previous school experience, there was a rough element. I quickly fell into line with the school's culture but was never fully resigned. Neither my school existence nor home life provided much stability.

Dad launched himself into his new role, his first opportunity as a registered clinical practitioner in the real world. This meant his extreme work ethic was reassigned from study days to his occupation. What didn't change was that he still missed daughter details. As I convoluted my way through pre-teen to teen existence, it was Mum who noticed me. She remarked on my hair-dye experiment in the school toilets and detected freshly pierced ears. She and Dad had forbidden these actions. I explained that the ear-piecing antic was done by a high school friend with a needle. "But she used ice, so it didn't hurt too much," I told Mum.

Mum examined my lobes and determined that they were infected.

I yelped when they were touched.

"All right, let's go to the chemist. How many holes would you like?"

Mum's question thrilled me. My extra piercings, a fashionable short hairstyle, and newly discovered make-up helped me maintain a bold and trashy 1980s look. The revamp and my curves coming in meant it wasn't long before the opposite sex noticed me.

Peer culture dictated an unwritten rule that those without love interests were a lost cause. Naturally, I had to oblige, and my shallow network coaxed me into meeting a guy. "Matty likes you. He's been watching, waiting to meet you. There he is!" The giggling girls virtually pushed me onto my pursuer. They believed that intimate connections should never be subtle. Then they dispersed, spying from somewhere nearby.

Matty and I stood together in a high-foot-traffic area, under the cover of a monochrome locker-bay. It was morning recess, so students came and went with the sound of relentless chattering, yelling, and swearing. They stridently clanked locker doors and dumped their bags like they didn't care.

Weirdly, the flurry and clatter around me faded into the background. I was with the boy in an insular bubble, our bashful faces up close in an unspoiled stranger-to-stranger encounter. Matty was tender-eyed, radiating sweetness as tousles of sun-kissed hair brushed with his pretty-boy face, suiting him to a tee. I *was* facing a boy, for he had no manly characteristics, at least none that I could see. Matty's physique was small and wiry and covered with hairless bronzed skin. We considered each other to be extremely cute, and a relationship of sorts developed. My new boyfriend was smitten with puppy love, wanting to dive into an unexplored pool of love. I, on the other hand, offered a half-hearted girlfriend commitment on account of his fawning and the sway of my friends. Upon meeting his two older brothers, I was taken aback by their blatancy about their active sex lives. Matty indicated that we would head in the same direction, even though we were only twelve and thirteen. As I considered Matty's young adult brothers' professed sexual behaviour and their crassness, I also considered how sex was rife amongst my school peers. I was under the impression that students who didn't succumb to these social pressures were subjected to ridicule. *Do I really want that?* I asked myself.

"Okay!" I flippantly replied when Matty, using lewd speech, suggested that we lose our virginity together. The conversation occurred over the telephone, and at the start of the call, I suspected that Mum was eavesdropping. But I dismissed the thought after hearing nothing further. That is, until a treble scream theatrically came from another line, confirming that she'd heard everything. I swiftly ended the call, bracing myself for the awkward Mum talk. Admittedly, I'd felt a twinge of conviction, but teenage indignation overruled it. My agitation came in anticipation of Mum's reaction, explicitly declaring God's disapproval of my choices.

Quite surprisingly, she didn't go there and Q&A time was less uncomfortable than I'd expected, though still unwanted. "You wouldn't, would you?" Mum queried in her serious lower pitch.

"Of course not, Mum!" I lied. Or at least I was half-hearted about the idea. It seemed that Mum was satisfied with my reply, as she didn't revisit my questionable intentions with Matty. Perhaps she trusted me, believing that I'd moved on from hers and Dad's push towards sexual partners from my primary school years, though Dad still advocated it. Since the pendulum had swung the other way for her, she likely accepted that biblically based chastity until marriage would become my conviction too. What she'd missed was that her journey wasn't mine. My inclinations towards Mum vacillated between "religious nut," as Dad sometimes called her, and my significant other. Then again, I considered him to be a hypocritical "head shrink," as psychologists were commonly known. I was also constantly uptight over Dad's antagonisms towards Mum and her dogmas, despite my own struggle with her fanaticism. Essentially, my parents sat on opposite sides of the spectrum, and I found these extremes confounding. I needed someone to navigate me through such intense crescendos, especially throughout my early to middle teenage years.

While sex was a hot topic, so was cigarette smoking. The Quit Smoking Campaign came about to raise risk awareness. Dad acquired a role in the anti-smoking movement as a community educator. Late one chilly Friday afternoon, he returned home from work, staggering up the railway sleeper steps with armfuls of equipment, pink faced and out of breath. It piqued my curiosity. When I asked what was happening, he announced between wheezes that we were having a family get-together that night. It was getting dark by the time Dad rested. A smile spread across his face as he admired the lounge room alterations;

kitchen chairs faced a large white screen on a tripod, with the movie projector ready to go. The cinematic experience was about to begin, except that the audience was scattered and disinterested, much to Dad's astonishment. Still, efforts were made to round us up like resistant sheep looking further afield. We were finally seated with Dad out the front in eager educator mode. He gave an overview of the teaching about to commence, as endorsed by the Quit Smoking Campaign, keenly adding our privilege as first viewers. I yawned away, as my attention was elsewhere. By the end of the viewing, the teacher was deflated by the lack of enthusiasm from his family, though his wife feigned support. I truly hoped that our psychologist father got a clear message from us kids. A forced psychoeducational approach would never work for our family! Why couldn't he organise a family camping trip like other dads? He had promised to take Owen, Dylan and me camping but avoided discussing it over a number of weeks. Dad eventually told us he had to forgo the trip due to work responsibilities. It was a typical excuse.

Admittedly, I flouted Dad's smoking warnings on the school front, along with the school's risk prevention program. My first smoking experience occurred in the toilet block at thirteen years old. My shaking fingers put a half-smoked cigarette to my lips, and I inhaled deeply. Searing pain instantly attacked my throat's velum. Spasms of choking and coughing had me in a low bow while I exhaled thin plumes of smoke. I didn't expect to survive, but I did.

With a laugh, the girl who'd given me the cigarette asked, "You haven't done this before, have you? Do you like it?"

Reluctant to admit it was nasty, I responded with a croaky "yes" to liking it. Once recovered, I tried the experience again and then again, finding it strangely exhilarating. Was it the thrill of unruliness, the tobacco leaf flavour, or the novelty of playing with an ignited thing? Perhaps it was desirable for all three reasons. I had to finish it, down to the bitter-tasting butt. I wasn't quite there when the sports teacher stormed into the bathroom, the smell of smoke putting her in a bad mood. Her presence meant rushing the last few drags, and I did so in open view.

The rest of my company scrambled to flush their smokes and hid themselves in locked toilet cubicles. Since I remained unmoved, the teacher flew into a rage. "What are you doing? Put it out, or you'll be disciplined. I said now! Are you listening?"

I was unapologetic. Sassing the teacher only added more buzz to the excited feeling I had from underage smoking. While Dad would have been furious, I don't recall him being notified of my unruly moment … or any others, for that matter. As for Mum, I vaguely remember her somewhat indignant look when she mentioned a concerning phone call from the school, and nothing more.

Maryvale High School, or "Mary-jail" to disgruntled students like me, had some peculiar disciplinary measures. Smokers caught in the act collected and disposed of butts around the school perimeter with unprotected hands. We offenders grumbled and swore our way around the yard, picking up used cigarette butts by the handful, overseen by teachers. I doubted the reprimand's effectiveness, since most of us went back to our smoking behaviours. We students also complained about the disciplinary measures for those caught chewing gum. This involved wearing our pre-chewed bubble gum on the ends of our noses while sitting outside the staff room. The idea was to provoke mockery from passers-by. What teachers didn't know was that blowing bubbles provided mild relief from school tedium. Also, in my defence, I didn't stick gum blobs under school desks for unsuspecting fingers to find, unlike some students. *Ugh!*

My smoking experience emboldened me to push the boundaries even further. I revelled in graffiti scrawling on school property, wagging class, swearing at authorities when I felt brave enough, binge drinking, and making out with schoolboys, just for fun. This behaviour was endorsed by all the high school kids I knew. It was also a warranted diversion from my miserable life, even if it added further messiness to my youth.

Comparatively, I wasn't as rebellious as some students, and the school pecking order terrified me. I'd shudder whenever school fights broke out, often ending with blood noses and *"I'll get you after school!"* intimidations, yelled at casualties as teachers ushered the perpetrators away. Cat fights amongst the roughest schoolgirls were often the worst. Mercilessly slapping, punching, scratching, grabbing hair, and screaming insults into enemy faces. *"You *ugly bitch!"* was a standard choice of words. My survival strategy was to stand back from the crowd, but I didn't entirely separate myself, avoiding attention as a conspicuous hanger-on.

Dad knew virtually nothing of my school life, except through progress reports that screamed underachiever, both in marks and remarks. He also commented that I had few interests. Dad was worried about me. Guiding would assist with my journey, he decided. It was the solution to all my teenage problems. One ordinary afternoon, Mum tricked me into taking a car ride. I had no idea where we were heading until Mum pulled off the road and into the local guide hall car park. Her casual "Dad thought guides would be good for you" raised contempt in me.

I got out of the car anyway, my legs involuntarily following Mum's into the building. My heels made sharp, attention-grabbing click-clack sounds against the timber floorboards, ending once we stopped in the middle of the hall. In a trice, I was aware of an all-girl troop gawking at us and my blushing reaction. The girls stood composed in their pressed uniforms, complete with neatly sewn insignias, earned through diligence and enterprise. I felt out of place, inferior, and disorderly before my female compatriots. I wanted to leave but remained in the same intimidated pose, oblivious to Mum's quick getaway. Once realised, I flouted Dad's futile plan in a temper and hurried towards the open door. By then, I was unbothered by my click-clacking kitten heels echoing through the hall. I bolted in the direction of our moving car, across the car park and onto the bitumen road. My mirrored reflection pricked Mum's conscience, and I was soon seated beside her in our Ford, parked beside the road with the engine still running.

When Mum turned to face me, I was naturally drawn to her features; layers of loose curls touched her cheeks, and pale lashes and brows softly framed hazel eyes, conveying kindness. "Okay. I won't make you go." Mum's words and sensibilities took the flush of heat from my face.

While Mum had considered me, Dad proved to be disappointing. He'd decided what was best for his daughter, then roped his wife into actioning his decision. We could've talked about why I was unyielding, but he never broached the matter.

Despite my lacking girl guide ambition, Dad kept me within his sights. But his good intentions didn't work out well when he cottoned on to a ridiculous career notion of mine. The audacious 1980s drew attention to modelling as a highly alluring career choice. Unfortunately, I had nothing to offer the industry, lacking height and being short-waisted. Let's just say I'm not modelling material. Even so, Dad made efforts to move me towards my unrealistic dream, soon organising an appointment with a modelling agency. When the day arrived, Dad drove us to our Melbourne destination. We stretched our legs after finding a car park, then made our way towards a high-rise building. The address was a vast warehouse space, branching off into smaller quarters. I'd equipped myself with a little confidence, which vanished when a tall European-looking woman greeted us. We followed her prissy walk to a confined, windowless room. I felt a chill when she shut the door behind us but kept my closed-in feeling to myself. Dad verified our reason for meeting as I sat in the chair beside him, leaning slightly forward and bracing myself.

The polished woman sitting opposite us studied my appearance, eyeing me twice over. Laughter exploded from her mouth, then abruptly ended. Her face turned unfriendly. "No vacancies!" She frostily asserted.

A quick departure for Dad and me was my only thought. Rising from my seat, I was sternly told to sit back down by the agent who wouldn't allow me to leave without a complimentary lesson on poise and grace, starting with my deplorable posture. The woman's pretentious manner implied she believed she was doing a tremendous service for the pitiable girl in front of her. All I wanted was to see cracks beneath my feet so I could will them wide enough to swallow me whole. I didn't care that we were a few stories above the ground floor!

Still in humiliation's clasp, I travelled with Dad out of the city and towards our home in Churchill. I pondered the take-home message that day. I was *not* one of the glamorous people of the world, nor was there any flicker of potential. Dad's absence of words and stoic face came as no recompense. It confirmed all the more that I'd embarrassed us both.

ELEVEN

Connecting and Disconnecting

Memories of my extracurricular sporting endeavours during my schooling are neither good nor bad, though Mum's encouragement and attendance feature most prevalently. There was, however, one activity that always involved Dad, and that was golf. His passion for the club-and-ball sport meant he constantly worked on his swing and practiced putting on the green. Dad had spells of playing the game proficiently, starting with a good drive with the aim of lowering his handicap. At other times, he was not performing well, cussing at the windy grounds and sometimes at his unremarkable caddy. That caddy was me. In my modest role, I followed Dad around the golf course, carting his prized clubs for the ready and providing tees and balls. My brothers often came along, bringing some variation from Dad's austere attention on keeping to par. They also assisted Dad on the golf course and were never dissuaded by murky water hazards as they searched for his vanishing golf balls. Successful finds meant good news for our dad. Any bonuses brought in extra pocket money for Owen and Dylan, especially the big brands, from other golfers.

My motivation was also monetary, as well as the refreshments at the end. Hours of caddying always guaranteed a parched mouth and a big appetite. We found a table at the clubhouse restaurant, where we sat down, and I stretched my tired legs, accidently kicking my brothers' shins. Inevitably, I copped one or two back, adding to my bruise collection. My belly made angry groans as I looked across the table. Owen and Dylan were quieter than usual, showing they were also hungry and thirsty, while Dad nattered on about the game. Our drinks arrived, and I eagerly took mine. Fizz tickled my nose as I sniffed in aromatic, sarsaparilla tones before satisfying my thirst. A waiter delivered springy, crust-less squares, layered with fancy fillings of creamy whites and flecks of pink and green, harpooned with bright cellophane cocktail sticks. Club sandwiches were my absolute favourite. These caddying rewards must've been worthwhile, especially since my lacking golfing proclivity got me into trouble time and again. My golfer breathed out frustrations over details I continually missed.

"Dad, which wedge do you use for the sand bunker again?"

He persevered with me in his gruff way. Still, I suspect Dad was harder on himself. The contorted faces I watched him pull while undertaking the game's challenges indicated it.

If golf was a trial for me and my father, then squash was *way* off beam. The fast-moving sport proved no simpatico relationship existed between us. Dad became a daunting coach, determined to get me onto the squash court. I found the very idea of performing for him induced negative self-talk. My confidence also lessened as spectators appeared at the see-through back wall. I was given Dad lessons, observing his drive, drop, and other techniques. Nothing stuck, as I was terrified of missing the mark. Dad demonstrated how to play, his instructions more assured than his performance.

He and another squash player I didn't know moved around the court in a mad flurry, determined to home in on the ball, determined to outdo each other. After some final guttural grunts, Dad shook hands with his partner, who fled the court. I then watched him double over. His laboured breathing and high-pitched wheezing disconcerted us both. Dad straightened up, revealing sweat patches darkening his shirt, while his face was beet red and dripping wet. I was repulsed by the vigorous noises and sweat. Plus, the sight of Dad torturing his body came as a complete turn-off.

Since I was not athletic, bowing out politely was my plan. Vexingly, Coach Dad would have none of that. Despite my protesting, he badgered me into having a go. I was constrained to chase the black orb with the racquet he'd placed in my hand. As I blundered around the court, that sneaky ball got away each time, and with my energy sapped, I made no apparent headway.

Thankfully, the spectators had all fled, as they were bored. All except Dad and his disbelieving features. I had failed miserably, making a mockery of his training efforts. But *why* did he make me do it? Couldn't he see my ungainly athleticism and dubious spatial awareness were unintentional? I couldn't improve on what wasn't there. Dad hardly spoke, shaking his head incomprehensibly at his unteachable daughter. I was physically weak and emotionally wrecked as I berated myself in my head. *I'm not enough. I'm not enough. I'll never be enough for Dad!* I wanted to get away from that steamy sports stadium and even further away from that mean coach! Instead, I shamefacedly followed him out the door and towards our car, apologising profusely. I was truly sorry for my sporting weakness, sorry for being me. My father remained silently bemused.

Our squash activities may have been associated with torment, but mercifully only on a few occasions, while my caddying experiences occurred repeatedly. Dad and I did make one positive sporting connection, nonetheless. It included my brothers at a mega-event: the 1982 Victorian Football League Grand Final.

Experiencing footy fever at the Melbourne Cricket Ground brought its own heightened atmosphere. Countless fans injected life into the game, their team colours emblazoned from the sidelines. Augmented uproars filled the air as adored players sprinted onto the ground, cheers or jeers shouted out at goal sounds and spine-tingling crowd chants, all adding to the thrill of the game. We merged with the grandstand masses in the chilly September air, scoffing hot footy food and other junk like everyone else. My jeans copped a staining mess from meat pie filling and tomato sauce. Groaning, I wiped the solids away then shrugged it off as evidence of a great day at the footy. Beyond the game's hype, the event meant togetherness for me, Dad, and my brothers. I was especially stoked that Dad took us to the game as he'd promised.

Dad and I shared another occasion, also related to entertainment but without the sports theme. It was my fourteenth birthday, and Dad offered to take me to a movie. I was naturally delighted about the idea. We drove to the Traralgon village drive-in, where the unconventional movie *Flying High (Airplane)* was screening. In the front seats of our trusty Ford, we cozied up with blankets and movie snacks. It was a real birthday treat, just the two of us … until distaste took over. I was confronted by what I saw and heard on the big screen. Some of the humour was above my head, as I didn't know it was a parody of an earlier film, or what a parody film was, for that matter. Dad laughed wildly at all the comedic scenes and was into the catastrophe theme. Meanwhile, I struggled to get into the crazy plots, as American humour was unfamiliar. We rarely watched movies, and television viewing was generally from the British Broadcasting Company or the Australian equivalent. That said, the satire and slapstick comedy styles weren't too different. They just didn't appeal to me. I wondered if the movie targeted people in Dad's time of life or if I wasn't worldly enough. Whatever the reasons, he and I couldn't relate or even speak civilly. So we chose reticence while driving home. There was no doubt that Dad's sulky silence was over my prudery. At the drive-in, I'd expressed disgust when Dad laughed at nudity on the screen. Then I'd exited the car to find the playground swing. He followed me to where I swung back and forth, paying no attention to him. On the way home, my sulk came through an unhappy birthday girl pout.

I'm sure my prudery always irritated Dad. A few years later, it was fully deployed when Owen was turning twenty. My brother booked tickets, which Dad paid for, for the three of us to attend a live theatre event in Carlton, a popular Melbourne suburb. But I started to hold some reservations around the evening. As we walked from the parking bay to the venue, it dawned on me that I hadn't taken into consideration Dad's and Owen's senses of humour, which were *not* on a par with mine. When La Mama Theatre finally came into focus, a festively lit courtyard graced us with a friendly tree, its leafage garlanded above us with a cheerful bunting. Still, I resisted the desire to unwind.

Within the building's walls, we found our seating, with the downstage directly before us. The lights dimmed, and the drama commenced. Almost immediately, I realised the play was a sex comedy, and it upset my moral gut. At first, I thought I saw nudity, but a second glance made it clear that the male actor had only exposed his torso. Nudity or not, I was in for quite a ride, as erotic subject matter was in my face.

The artist's eyes met mine, dark and alluring, his expressive, masculine brows perfectly framing them. He was unfairly good-looking, and it wasn't just the make-up. The young performer's winsomeness and powerful dramatisation claimed my unwavering attention. His close proximity and blatant amatory language brought a flush of heat to my face, which refused to fade. The man had a message just for me, the youngest member of the audience. "Ha! You will succumb, whether you like it or not!"

I told myself he was only acting, and besides, the performer had a bright spotlight in his eyes. To him, I was merely reduced to a dark figure amongst the crowd. But it was no use, as the performance held its potent sway. Heady feelings messed with my sensibilities: sensuality, embarrassment, and rising anger. My wrenching conscience and galloping heart urged me to escape the seductiveness ensnaring me. Instead, I turned my head to the left of the seating to observe Dad and Owen. Along with the audience, they were in raptures of laughter: knee slapping, open-mouthed, teeth-bearing hysterics. I was the odd one out. Should I grimace or hold a passive expression? I couldn't decide, fluctuating between the two while stiffly occupying my seat. Dourly, I waited for intermission to come around. It would be my chance to break away, though it would come at the cost of Dad's fury. He would tear strips off me for being a disagreeable prude of a daughter.

Finally, my body lifted from the seat as every soul, prop, and vacant space abruptly lit up. I made my way with the crowd out of the building to join Owen and Dad in the courtyard. They clapped each other's shoulders with jollity while discussing the performance. Contrastingly, my body was taut as I was about to extinguish their frivolous mood. It happened when Owen asked me what I thought of the play. I bravely stated my offence to Owen, with Dad listening in. As I spoke, their faces reflected a perplexed air, inquisitive eyes staring into mine, wordlessly asking, *But why?*

I explained that the performance diminished the sacredness of sex through debased humour, and since I detested it, I would not return to the production. After stating my piece, an inward sigh released, fretfully waiting for the repercussion.

Dad's fury came alive just seconds after. His puce face screwed up like crumpled paper, and his arms and legs became restive. Dad's pithy words came through gritted teeth, keeping his voice low for the sake of the crowd. Dad called me narrow-minded, a favoured phrase of his. He made it clear that it was on account of my limited moral conclusions, believing I had not critically thought about different perspectives to form an intelligent outlook. I should have ignored Dad's overused words, but they struck a nerve in me. I was already insecure, doubting his confidence in my capabilities. Feeling pathetic and weak, I absorbed Dad's opinion of who I was. Yet a part of me promoted strength, resolutely following my moral compass.

Dad's outburst continued, focusing on my faith as nothing more than a pitiful crutch for religious people. This time, I wasn't threatened by Dad's familiar tact, nor was I apologetic for what I believed. Since it didn't have the desired effect, my father moved onto his next line of attack. Apparently, I had made an unfair judgement on him.

"How dare you! How dare you judge me!"

My response was that I was *not* condemning him but solely following my personal convictions. I then suggested that he and Owen return to the play. Secretly, I wished they would so Dad could show me up for the narrow-minded person he thought I was. Surely, that would settle our feud. For some reason, he didn't have the guts.

What *were* my father's true convictions anyway. Did exposing his adolescent daughter to sexually explicit content prick his conscience? At the time, it certainly wasn't my intention to challenge his sense of right and wrong, and I repeatedly told him so. But Dad, in his foul predicament, misconstrued my words, harping on about my judgement against him. His angst transferred onto me as I unintentionally mirrored him, my face twisted in a hot cheeked flush as I agitatedly moved about. Our voices rose in a senseless quarrel while Owen wisely chose a spectator's position. Conscious that our fight was escalating, we left the courtyard. By then, the gathering had re-entered the building. My quarrel with Dad carried into the city streets, our voices echoing as we walked.

After a while, Dad and I somehow became civil enough to enter a restaurant. We were hungry, and Owen had chosen Italian cuisine for after the event. Genteel staff ushered us to a formal dining arrangement, and as we followed, Dad and I bit our tongues. From our table, a trickle of hushed, exasperated words could be heard as slow instrumental music clashed with the hostile mood. While contending, we gulped down mouthfuls of pasta with rich sauce and pale-yellow parmesan shavings. Every so often, Owen interjected with a sensible voice. To the attending staff, our intense discussions were all part of the dining experience. Or they pretended all was well as a complimentary part of the service. It is a good reason to revisit a fine dining ristorante.

When the day was done, I reflected on my evening with Dad and Owen. My father had discredited me for upholding a standard, and although we were at loggerheads, his reaction only solidified what I believed. Did he know that? All in all, I recognised that I was astute enough to form and follow my own opinion, contrary to his words.

In my recent writing, I found a forgotten letter I wrote to Dad. It was dated October 16, 1986, sent shortly after our heated episode. It includes an apology for my behaviour that night, adding, "… if we go somewhere, let's choose an interest of mine as well as yours …" I also stated that I didn't want anything to "get in the way of a good father-daughter relationship."

Dad must have valued my honesty and good intentions to have kept it.

Back in my early to middle teens, Dad made efforts to bond with me. We travelled to psychology seminars in pursuit of ongoing professional development for Dad. Our car travels covered various places around Victoria and some in New South Wales.

Dad would approach me with a sprightly invitation. "I'm going to a convention. Would you like to come?" He implied it would be loads of fun.

I took up his offer each time, falsely believing we'd find some commonality. Sadly, our initial togetherness turned into separateness of mind.

As for my brothers, I don't remember Dad inviting them to join him, or me, on such trips. Dylan recently confirmed that was true for him. I can only assume that Dad handpicked me out of concern for our waning relationship. If so, it didn't work out as well as he'd hoped, as we were intolerant of each other's standpoints.

Our heated discussions centred on theoretical points of difference, specifically on the topic of God. Dad supported agnosticism through a humanistic philosophical lens, his angle being that humanity is progressive through achievement, promoting freedoms individually, and through community, ruling out the relevance of an overarching higher being. I came from a biblical worldview, authenticating a triune God, giver of life, the Alpha and the Omega. Evidenced human weakness called for a redemptive solution through Jesus Christ, reconciling individuals with their Creator. I also favoured the need for community but with the major variation of eternal understanding and functioning.

Despite being young and inarticulate, I contended with Dad's position with passion, albeit parroting church teaching at the time. We were uninspired by each other's perspectives, and our mutual isolation of heart and mind did nothing to build up our parent-child relationship.

Looking back, our vied discussions were never worthwhile. If only we'd respected the other's worldviews simply because we're all entitled to think differently. That way, at least we could acknowledge one another's value as fellow humans.

Our connection was complicated by my father's intellectual inclinations. One day, he was keen to tell me about a friend of his that I hadn't met. "His children have done really well. They've been accepted into a high-ranking university in France. In France!"

Dad was extremely impressed. Whether this came from his intellectual pursuits or the allure of status, I'm not sure. Either way, I was disheartened by his comment, convinced that I would never reach his ivory tower of academia. I didn't have the smarts or the confidence to make it into a local university, let alone a prestigious one! I am pleased to say that this negative self-talk was negated at a later date when I was accepted into a course through Monash University. But at the time, my insecurities over what Dad thought of me were persistent, often arising in his company and amongst his social group. I recall instances when I mingled with his cultured circle as we viewed exhibition artworks. Along with my self-consciousness, I found it bothering that Dad thrived on snobbery amongst his friends. I sensed a lack of genuineness, as the air was thick with pomp and artiness. Since I didn't know how to read art, I avoided stumbling over my words by saying very little, nodding away and putting on my practised highbrow face. I wasn't a fake, only justifiably inconspicuous.

TWELVE

Running Away: A Quick-Fix Resolve

My father's true passion was his vocation, and he single-mindedly prioritised his time accordingly. Needless to say, Dad's family rapport was waning. The assaults against Mum had also increased. Messy times attended my adolescence.

At the age of fourteen, I made a runaway attempt to test my parents' devotion. My destination was a thinly wooded scout property, about fifty metres away from our Churchill home. It was early evening when I snuck out with an overnight bag slung over my shoulder. I stuffed it with survival items, just in case I moved further afield. While I had no courage or skills for living rough, life on Melbourne's streets held appeal. I crawled into the densest patch of bush available and transformed into a chameleon, waiting for the low-slung sun to disappear. For about half an hour, I relished the brief interlude away from family troubles. After that, my squatting legs longed to stretch, and my body shivered from lack of warmth. Boredom added discomfort to my stiff and cold predicament. *When will Mum and Dad realise I'm gone?*

In the dark, I listened to crickets chirping. Then, finally, I heard stifled voices from a search party. Their shoes crunched over the ground, then travelled in all directions. I froze, holding my breath for as long as I could, like a child in a game of hide-and-seek, exhaling gradually and noiselessly.

The seekers were advantaged with torches, and one suddenly blinded me. "There she is, in the bushes!"

My absconding was met with little fuss, except that a police officer was present, but I could've been mistaken since it was dark. Mum and Dad thanked the helpers, who quickly dispersed. I was left with my parents' examining eyes in the torch light. With a troubled look, Mum questioned my intentions, then gave a short address. Her genuine concern was enough to satisfy me. Dad, on the other hand, displayed a bewildered face as he searched mine for clues. Neither of us could adequately communicate.

My pathetic disappearing act was never to be repeated. That was my empty self-promise. Distress pushed me to run away yet again, starting on the school grounds when a teacher triggered me. Unkind students had dubbed her "Spidereyes" because of a cosmetic blunder. Her black, clumpy lashes curled out stiffly, like creepy spider legs. I reacted to her abrasiveness over a misbehaviour I was probably guilty of. Feeling threatened, I took off to escape the severe woman, my peers, and everything else in that harsh school environment. While the teacher remained on the curb near the school property, I lingered on the nature strip across the road.

"Come back! Come back! We can talk about this. Everything will be okay," she bellowed, continuing her plea for what felt like a long time.

I wanted to stay away but had nowhere to go. So I relented. Just before returning, I checked that no students were around to avoid schoolyard gossip. Back on school property, I broke down in tears as the teacher did her best to reassure me.

The next day, I became the subject of gossip. But it was not in the schoolyard. It occurred in the staffroom, no thanks to the taleteller Spidereyes. As a credulous student, I stood by the staffroom door, hoping to see one of my class teachers for a study-related reason.

A nearby teacher attended me with warmth and an invitation. "Come in, Fleur. You'll find her down the back." Her words and kindly manner didn't ring true. My high school experience advised that entering the staffroom was strictly taboo for students, except for teachers' pets, which I wasn't. Again, I was invited in, so I gingerly entered the building, nervously making my way through the teachers' hub. I felt numerous eyes boring into me and then audibly gasped with a realisation that yesterday's foolish runaway attempt had become common knowledge to the *entire* teaching faculty. My nervous tension turned into mortification as I made an about-face for a quick exit.

She's about to do another runner, came the implication from teachers' pitiful looks, especially from those hastening out of their seats while imploring me to stay. I was not running away from the school facility, but I *was* running from the staffroom with its judgemental teachers. The mortifying experience reinstated my distrust towards teachers and put me off future attempts at solo runaways.

Mum, not Dad, as far as I knew, had been informed of my school absconding the day before. She arrived early to take me home, and as always, she provided maternal care through affection and a listening ear. Not that I gave anything away. I didn't want her to problem-solve on my behalf. My struggling parent had a problematic marriage with no solutions in sight, so how could she stretch herself to help me? Besides, the ramifications of Mum and Dad's declining relationship only fuelled my desire to run in the first place.

My family was stuck on a carousel ride that none of us enjoyed. We wanted to get off! Eventually, Mum found the courage to take the first step and jump off, leaving Dad behind in his own dizzy world. A heinous act from him was the catalyst for Mum's decision to take control.

Late one morning, my family got into our most recent car, a Ford Falcon sedan with copper bronze duco and a dual-tone white roof. I don't recall where we were heading or why, as Mum and Dad flouted our plans when they came into conflict. Their argument quickly converted to a one-sided rant from Dad. As it did so, Mum mouthed supplications to God, feeding her husband's temper. I wanted to express my loud thoughts. *Stop, Mum! Stop praying!* But I couldn't.

Her lips kept moving with minimal sound while our red-faced driver struggled to maintain control of the thin-rimmed wheel, distracted by his hot-headed insults and accusatory pointing. Dad's short emotional fuse was ready to blow. I had seen it many times and urged myself to stay calm. But the word left my vocabulary as Dad reached across Mum's body, fumbling with frustration to open her door. He intended to shove his wife from the moving car and onto the Princes Highway. Fortunately, Dad couldn't unlock the door. He then turned towards Dylan, seated behind Mum, commanding him to release the lock. My unbearable ache of injustice for Mum momentarily stretched towards my brother. Dad's cruel intentions were unchanged, so Dylan rightly disobeyed. Dad was all the more infuriated by Dylan's inaction and stridently declared, "I'll do it myself then!" I stiffly braced myself the whole time.

Dad turned the car sharply into an approaching car park at the Trafalgar railway station. As we slowed, I heard soothing tyre sounds crunching over pale-coloured stones. It was a distraction I wanted to prolong. What would Dad do next? I didn't want to know, though the answer would come soon enough.

The irate driver stopped the car, released his seatbelt, and moved towards the front passenger, intending to cause harm. He lashed out at his wife in any way he could, grabbing, shaking, punching, and slapping her arms, torso, and crestfallen face. Dad breathed out profanities and emphasised her worthlessness, shouting, "Get out! Get out, you stupid bitch!"

Mum was unresponsive. She was strangely disconnected from her shocking reality, resembling an inanimate doll being manipulated without a care. Her lips no longer moved in prayer.

After stretching further to unlock Mum's door, Dad swiftly left the driver's seat. I watched him brush with the car's bonnet and grille as he was eager to get to her external door. While pulling the handle, he repeatedly shouted, "Get out of the bloody car!"

The victim remained impassive and unyielding.

Dad furiously grabbed handfuls of Mum's hair and her clothed flesh, groaning with the strain of heaving a dead weight out of the vehicle. He finally dragged Mum onto the ground. Her body slumped to one side with no movement or sound, as though her living soul had departed. Dad knew she was alive, attacking her with his hands and repeatedly kicking her side. One final kick came with a slur. "You bitch!" Dad hastily returned to the driver's seat, started the engine, and put the car into gear.

My emotions suddenly climaxed in profound fear. *He's going to kill her! He's going to kill her!* The voice screamed inside my head. I held my breath, waiting for the rising sensation of the car tyres bumping up and over Mum's body, but I felt nothing. I only heard the crunching sound of wheels driving over loose gravel. The vehicle did not rise and fall as I'd anticipated. Dad, thank

God, had enough humanity to allow clearance between our Ford and Mum. In that horror-stricken moment, I hadn't thought he would. I exhaled long and slow once realising my mother hadn't been crushed to death by the weight of our family car.

The offender gunned the engine, dust and stones fanning in Mum's direction as he made a quick getaway from the crime scene. Through the rear window, I watched Mum's motionless body become smaller and smaller, wishing she wouldn't disappear from view. Since she did, I shifted my head towards the windscreen. I wanted to lie in the gravel beside Mum, to wrap my arms around her and cry uncountable tears over her battered body. But there was no way, so I sat dry-eyed with my brothers on the rigid rear seat. Silent and solitary, our worlds were suspended for a moment in time. After a while, I managed to find some words, asking Dad how Mum would get home.

"She'll find a way," he deadpanned. He was simmering down during the thirty-odd kilometres home.

Mum's image featured in my mind as we drove. Her wilted body on the stones beside our car. Then her image shrank as we moved away, never fully disappearing as it replayed.

I wasn't told the rest of Mum's story. What injuries she had suffered, if she found help from a Good Samaritan, or how she got home. All I know was that my poor mother appeared at our Churchill home just after sunset. I came out of my bedroom as I heard the front door gently close. Stepping into the hallway, my eyes barely adjusted to the dusky house, but I didn't think to switch on a light. I turned right, then walked towards a shadowy figure near the front entrance, recognising it as Mum's curvy shape. We were separated by the landing where I stood, with three steps raising her above me. The house was completely silent, even calm. But I was *not* calm. I felt unsettled, like a persistent, steep ocean swell. My heart pleaded for my legs to run to Mum, to throw my arms around her and hold her tight, to sob away all the pain I felt. But I fought against it, trying desperately to supress the disquiet within. Surely, my embrace would increase Mum's physical and emotional soreness. I wouldn't deepen the pain already leaving a tender scar for her remaining days. Instead, I reached out from a distance with questions. "Are you alright, Mum? Are you hurt?"

Without the slightest quiver, she gave a vague yet satisfactory answer, "I'm okay, Fleur. I'm okay."

Perhaps I should've shown my true feelings, messy and raw. It may have been the very thing my darling mother needed. But how could I be sure?

It was around three weeks after Mum's ordeal that she communicated with us kids that we were running away. It was another runaway attempt for me at the age of fourteen, but at least it wasn't my idea, and I wasn't alone. A lot of drama was happening for my family that year.

"Pack an overnight bag. We're leaving your father. I'm waiting for the ideal moment," Mum said softly, though Dad wasn't home to hear. The plan was vaguely feasible, so I was in, not that I had a choice in the matter.

Keeping our secret over the next couple of weeks proved a tantalising challenge. As it happened, Dad became mildly ill with a virus or some such passing ailment, convalescing in bed. According to Mum, it was the ideal moment.

One school day, I heard Owen's name blaring from the classroom's loudspeaker. As expected, my name came next. The teacher's nod of approval to leave came sweetly. Without delay, a ball of energy had me gathering my school belongings and heading towards the administration building.

Mum's solemn face told me she'd been edgily waiting for me. Her voice was deeper than usual, reserved for serious moments. "We need to go now. Owen and Dylan are already in the car." Mum must've given the staff some details of her plight, as a few of them lingered to say goodbye, and the principal's eyes misted over. I pondered this for about three seconds, quickly moving on, as I was eager to leave the school and our life with Dad.

All it took was Mum's decision to get us away from our misery; escaping life's troubles should always be that easy, I mused. In my fickle-mindedness, it didn't occur to me that Mum's decision would've been quite an ordeal for her. With our bodies and gear occupying the car, Mum revealed our destination was Adelaide, South Australia. It was the state where her relatives lived. Mum's mission meant travelling for about nine hours without stopping overnight. The thrill of escape remained with me for a large part of the journey. Eventually, I was overcome with travel exhaustion. Mum woke me up when we arrived in the backyard of a house at an undisclosed location. Bleary-eyed and disoriented, I clambered out of the car with my brothers. I fumbled with my bag and pillow through the overgrown yard in the pitch black.

A woman emerged, one we heard more than saw, telling us to "Shush!" We hadn't made much noise. She ushered us into the house, then a room where we claimed our bunk-style beds. I was soon fast asleep, as it had reached the wee hours of the morning.

The next day, I was better able to orient myself with our accommodation. Insipid surroundings gave me a cold feeling, while edgy women, some with clingy children, diverted their eyes from us. I didn't judge them, for who knows what they'd endured. I told myself that we were in a temporary situation, a woman's shelter for Mum's safety. We weren't there for cosiness. Our time away, two weeks or perhaps closer to three, was a blur of tedium. My brothers and I had no schoolwork to do, though we didn't complain. While writing, Aunty Joy (Mum's sister) told me we stayed a day or two with her family in Adelaide's south-east. She also said we first arrived at their place, quite unexpectedly, before we went to the shelter. This explains the late hour, though I have no memory of this or any other time spent with them, except for a conversation in their home at some point. The chat with Mum was about Dad's aunty and uncle, who lived thirty kilometres from Adelaide. The couple had called by Aunty Joy's home, looking for Mum, my brothers, and me. Thankfully, Mum's relatives gave nothing away. The impromptu visit implied that Dad had made a phone call, asking his aunty and uncle to seek us out. They never found us, as we were at the safe house.

Our family kept a low profile while waiting. I didn't know how long we had to wait or what we were waiting for. Mum provided no clues about our future plans. That is, until she picked up the telephone's handset on the shelter wall.

"Who are you calling?" I nosily asked.

"Your father," Mum said, using her typical reference for Dad.

"Oh. Um … Is that good?" My words came with a feeling of disappointment.

Once Mum finished her conversation with Dad, she told us kids to pack our things. We made tracks soon after, away from South Australia and across Victoria's western border. Mum was positive about the return. I wasn't. Strong doubts came to me regarding Dad's redeeming qualities. Owen and Dylan's subdued responses supported my scepticism. Although Mum was treated with kindness and respect by her husband back at home, I clung to my opinion. It was only a matter of time before his despicable character would re-emerge.

Soon, the school holidays rolled around, and my brothers and I travelled to see our paternal grandparents in New South Wales. Hours-long coach trips included vomit stops, just for me. I rushed past ogling passengers and the driver, then down the stairwell to relieve my roiling stomach beside the road. Embarrassed, I stepped back into the coach as the driver smiled sympathetically. Otherwise, our vacation went well with Nana and Grandad, as it was entirely drama free.

Back in Victoria, I made my way out of the coach, my shoes touching the ground with a realisation that the vibrating and swaying had come to an end. I'd soon recover from motion sickness.

Mum greeted me with exceptional joy, as though we'd been separated for many months.

After sharing in a hug, I asked, "Where's Dad?"

"He's over there, collecting the bags," Mum answered while waving her hand with a flourish.

I walked towards the coach's luggage compartment, where Dad turned to face me with a cheerful greeting.

"Oh. Oh. Hello, Dad," I spluttered, surprised by his newly grown gingery-brown moustache. My pleasant expression was insincere as I asked why he'd chosen the whiskery look.

"Thought I should try something different. Do you like it?" Dad beamed, thinly stretching his upper lip with the patch of hair. It depicted a live caterpillar as a horrid, prickly thing. In my adolescent opinion, moustaches were reserved for people like Freddie Mercury and Tom Selleck's signature looks, helping them make their mark on the world. For Dad, the look was simply too try-hard! I eyed him with suspicion, as his new look came with another change. Dad's uplifted tone and gush towards Mum was excessive. She enjoyed the attention — his tender eyes, flirty smiles, and constant fondling. I found it repelling, even nauseating, as it gave me the same terrible feeling I'd just recovered from.

That afternoon, we were in the kitchen area at our Churchill home when Mum spoke on her husband's behalf. "Your father has something to tell you."

Our eyes followed Mum's gaze towards Dad, who was speechless and rooted to the spot.

My brothers and I gave each other quizzical looks.

Mum broke the silence, blurting out, "Your father is born again. He's accepted Jesus as his Lord and Saviour."

The awkwardness in the room amplified as we kids gawked at Dad.

Our eyes and mouths were wide open as he blushingly confided, "Yes, it's true." His shy smile turned downwards, pained by our astonished expressions. It was then that Dad played the family man and attended The Revival Centre's services for about a month, a grand attempt at salvaging his marriage. He even extended himself to attend a church tent ministry at a beach location in Geelong. We stayed for a week, as far as I remember. On the surface, we looked like a happy, churched family. But I knew that Dad had used his cunning to appear committed to the event. He disappeared from the time of our arrival until we left, apart from opportune appearances. It was a tactic to appease his wife. She was caught up in the tent ministry hype, so his absence didn't register. After the camp, Dad continued with his Christian guise over a short while. That is, up until my baptism, when he moved on from the whole pretence. The moustache also went, as neither worked well for him. By then, Mum realised that John was no longer sold out for God or their marriage, or even vaguely committed. His initial respect for both had slipped back into disregard.

Dad's antics became something of an embarrassment. He was using me as a sounding board or perhaps his sex therapist. "Your mother won't have sex with me anymore," he revealed.

This happened a few times, and I was flabbergasted. My father *shouldn't* talk to me like that. I'm his daughter!

While I was still processing Dad's exposé, Mum told me of a change in bedroom arrangements. "You are to stay with me, as your father wants your bedroom."

"What? Why?" I was stunned yet again. I didn't know what was more affronting: relinquishing my sacrosanct teenage space or being caught up in my parents' unhealthy relationship.

THIRTEEN

Marital Crash Aftermath

Our family mess was about to become messier. Dad was having an affair. When the rumour reached the ears of Mum, my brothers, and me, we held inklings that it was true. We sat around the breakfast bar the same afternoon we heard the rumour. Sombrely, we discussed the situation in hushed tones as Dad's absence dominated the space. The next day, Dad confessed his marital unfaithfulness to Mum. Perhaps she had boldly confronted him. Her husband also told her that she and I should pack our bags. We females were being exiled to another place, somewhere not yet determined. Dad planned to make room in our home for his lover, Sandra, and her eleven-year-old daughter, Lilah, while Owen and Dylan stayed.

After I received the news through Mum, I could hardly breathe. The blow had winded me. The shock was over Dad's sheer willingness to let me go, *just like that!* I was also miffed that he chose Owen and Dylan over me and that he was replacing me with a girl he didn't even know. It was the first time I experienced blatant rejection from my father. I tried to make sense of his evasive approach, passing the message to me through Mum as though passing on footy results. Dad's unwillingness to join me in working through our losses was not just bruising but astounding. As I considered his chosen profession, I wondered why he didn't think to broach the matter with sensitivity. Dad could have admitted that it had been hard for us all and explained that his decision was for practical reasons. He could have added that I was, and would always be, his cherished daughter. If only my inept father had confirmed this to be true or offered some other rationality. Alas, this was not the case, so my young mind concluded that I was *not* worthy of my father's love.

Soon after, Dad aborted his original plan for Mum and me to move away and make room for his lover and her daughter. Instead, our entire family was about to flee our Churchill home. Dad and Owen would be going one way, while Dylan and I would follow Mum in another direction. My first response was immense relief for my mother, who was finally unfastened from her fragmented marriage and all that it implied. Little did I know that the full impact of the separation would catch up with me, and painfully so.

On the cusp of our parents' separation, my brothers and I were offered supportive help through Dad. While his intentions appeared to be genuine, the approach was truly lacking. It was on a Saturday afternoon when Owen, Dylan, and I were casually invited to join Dad for a drive.

The destination was revealed once we reached a walking trail in Trafalgar south, West Gippsland. I was dubious about Dad's intentions, as he was the only one who knew why we were there.

Before long, a mystery man arrived. Dad met him with a firm handshake and a smile of relief, implying indebtedness at his coming. Whatever they'd planned Dad's jittery movements told me he wanted the deed done, and quickly. We were introduced to his solicitor friend, whose name I forgot right after. Butterflies in my stomach bothered me. They came with the man's intimidating height and formal way of relating.

As we all gathered in the bush surroundings, Dad offered a loose explanation for the meeting. My brothers and I were to each have a little chat to Dad's friend, as he was looking out for our best interests. Since the three of us had nothing to say, he ended with, "I'll see you soon."

The man I thought I knew resembled a little boy wanting to cry before turning his face away, his shoulders hunched forward as he dashed along the leaf-scattered path. What would Dad be thinking while trekking along the beaten track? Surely this father didn't suppose his children would return to him fully intact!

Distrust was my guide when it was my turn to talk with the stranger. I was certain he would relay my every word and gesture back to Dad. My butterfly feeling increased as his head angled down towards mine, a giant approaching a fragile flower. As it turned out, Dad's solicitor friend did almost all the talking. He also implied that he knew my inner thoughts. "Now, Fleur, I know you don't want your parents to be apart. I know you don't want them to get divorced. I know."

My internal monologue sang. *Yes, sir. No, sir. And three bags full, sir!* As the mentoring circuit was ending, we approached Dad on the path where we'd begun. His posture had corrected, and a look of satisfaction glowed in his eyes. Were these signs that Dad had ticked off a difficult task on his pre-divorce checklist, a task he'd handballed to some else? If Dad thought his strategy was helpful to me, then he was *wrong!* I suspected that my brothers were just as dispirited as I was, considering their subdued behaviour and forlorn faces.

By then, the butterflies in my stomach had all fluttered away, replaced with a great weight of cynicism towards Dad.

FOURTEEN

Dad's Newly Acquired Family

When my family dispersed from our Churchill home, Dad and Owen moved into Sandra and Lilah's house in Trafalgar. I was under the impression that Dad didn't want his eldest child, but he had no choice since his wife refused to take him. She was only willing to take Dylan and me. I didn't know why Owen wasn't wanted by either of our parents, and their harshness upset me. Dad provided Owen with a roof, food, and a bed but not much more, barely meeting Maslow's lowest hierarchy of needs. Owen also endured Dad's jealous partner, Sandra, who conveyed the message that John firstly belonged to her and Lilah. My big brother was in a less-than-ideal place.

I was well catered for by contrast. Mum, Dylan, and I had each other's company, softening our transition into new circumstances, as our lives had altered considerably. My divided family was occupying two homes in two different towns. One commonality was that we all lived in the same West Gippsland region surrounded by the

Strzelecki Ranges, dressed in a shawl of avocado and olive green amidst winding undulation.

My younger brother and I, at the ages of twelve and fourteen, had our first Christmas with Dad since the separation. Arriving at his new living situation, I was surprised to see his downgraded commission-style home. I chose to focus less on the colourless house and more on Owen, as I badly missed him. We'd been apart for weeks while settling into our different contexts.

"Where's Owen?" I asked as we entered the house through the back door.

Dad said he didn't know. He then wandered around for a while, Dylan and I shadowing him. Our parent left us in a dark corner with a wilted figure on the floor. Owen's dusky appearance was sighted below our eyeline, explaining why he was so hard to find. Initially, our presence didn't register, despite calling Owen's name multiple times. Dylan and I glanced at each other, and our eyes filled with alarm. I could only presume that our brother's detachment came from a lonely existence in an unloving household. Once he returned to the present, the three of us chatted.

I urged him to live with Dylan, Mum, and me. "We can find space."

Owen grinned at my proposal, amused by my desire to help. He declined the offer, as he and Mum could never meet in the middle. Their relationship was fraught with animosity. Mum's avid push towards Christianity provoked him to argue against her convictions just as avidly. Owen chose one unhappy circumstance over the other.

With clarity, I remember waking up the next day. It was Christmas morning, and I met Dad, Owen, and Dylan in the kitchen to wish them a merry Christmas. Then, like any ordinary day, we kids quietened our noisy stomachs with a rushed bowl of cereal. Sandra and Lilah had been with us in the house the night before, so their absence that morning mystified me. I considered asking Dad where they were but decided to save my question for later. It certainly seemed like Dad's new family wasn't supportive of him or his children. I found this troubling, along with the fact that he didn't mention them. My concern led to another internal question. *What's Dad seeking in his new relationship?* I wanted to ask him but did not dare to. It would've angered him.

We gathered in the dingy, boxlike lounge room by a synthetic Christmas tree strewn haphazardly with tacky trimmings. As we exchanged unremarkable gifts, a lacklustre atmosphere robbed us of the smallest suggestion of festiveness. The unfriendly house applauded the dismal Christmas mood. Oh, how the Grinch would've been in his element!

Soon after we opened our gifts, Dad headed for the front door. He paused to inadvertently answer the question I'd been saving, "Okay. I'm off to join Sandra and her family down the road. Meat pies are in the freezer. Help yourself. Don't know when I'll be back. Merry Christmas!" Dad spoke cheerfully. Then? *Poof!* The illusionist disappeared in a devastating puff of smoke. His words and subsequent disappearance hit me like a slap in the face. It caused a nasty shock, stinging me like crazy.

My brothers and I tried to process what was happening. *Did our father just abandon us on Christmas Day?* Our miserable reality meant moral support was a coping necessity, though it brought little consolation. I wanted to cry, but tears wouldn't come, only a feeling of utter deflation. *Dad hates us!*

I'd expected Dylan and me to spend Christmas Day around Dad's table, joining Owen and his new family, who we'd get to know. I'd looked forward to feasting and fellowshipping like families do, clinking glasses filled with something sparkling, followed by cheers. Pulling bon bons, donning silly paper hats, and reading corny jokes, making us sigh or laugh aloud. Dad would set aside the turkey's wishbone to dry, then snap it apart that night with one of us kids. We would wash up together and laze around while complaining about the summer heat, maybe play a board game or two and enjoy the Christmas chorus. Then we'd begin feasting all over again on Boxing Day. There was none of that. I just knew it was going to be a long, drawn-out, wretched Christmas Day!

I couldn't ignore it any longer. Weakness slowed my legs, and lightness fuzzed my head. I needed to eat. So I opened the freezer door. My fingertips moved their way around the icy space, as I was too short to fully see inside. Dad's freezer contained meat pies and a pack or two of dim-sims, and that was all. Perhaps there was something Christmassy in the fridge. Or maybe not, only unidentifiable dregs covered in plastic wrap. The fridge was virtually bare, and the pantry had nothing for a teenager to grab for a treat, only packets of rice, flour, pasta, and the like. Besides, I'd been raised to believe that it was rude to rummage through someone else's kitchen cupboards. I'd never been fussy with food preferences, but this was another matter. Dad's disregard for us was plain unloving, and what was Sandra thinking? They were killing our Christmas!

With my stomach hassling me, I settled for a microwaved meat pie, which tasted of bitter rejection. A tightening in my throat made it hard to swallow lumps of meat and pastry. Each unpleasant mouthful came with Dad's words revolving in my head. *"Help yourself."* He'd sounded so ... so ... *benevolent!* The only help was that my brothers and I were together, and even then, I carried an added burden for Owen. He was submerged in a quagmire the whole time. Owen's body wilted as his muscles refused to work. His eyes were darkly obscure, and speech evaded him. I pushed past my own gloominess with bursts of playfulness, hoping to bring him back to the present. But Owen had fled to that ethereal place. A trampoline offered Dylan and me some relief from boredom. It was shoved against the house in a derelict yard, mirroring the dingy, unloved residence. Much like my brothers and me, it was devalued and neglected. Our father was the inattentive landlord.

The sun dipped low on the horizon as it was done with the day. I had also had enough of the vexatious day. The front door swung open, grabbing the attention of Owen, Dylan, and me. Dad stepped in and greeted the three of us at once. He was in a good mood. We were asked to join him with Sandra and her family at her brother's house. Dad implied big-heartedness with the same sentiment as when he'd left us hours ago. I didn't believe he had a generous bone in his body. My brothers and I hardly leapt for joy over the invitation, but my growling stomach hoped there may be food, even something appetizing and festive.

We walked along the bitumen road with little to say. Then Dad pointed out the house we were about to enter. Inside, I mused that it was just as basic and gloomy as his and Sandra's place. A flurry of people, whose names I was never told, drifted into the kitchen, then out to the backyard. I don't remember seeing Sandra or Lilah, and Owen and Dylan had vanished. Perhaps they were with the crowd outside, while I was in the house. I got the sense that no one seemed to care about who I was or that I was even there. Their appalling manners came as another unpleasant surprise that day. When I asked about dinner, I was told to source my own leftovers. I felt like a hunter-gatherer in a harsh terrain as I discovered food was scarce.

"Sorry. It's mostly all gone," said a woman I didn't know. She was about the only one who acknowledged me as a human being, genuinely smiling as she introduced herself.

I managed to find a lukewarm sausage, a piece of bread, and maybe the luxury of tomato sauce. I honestly can't remember. Either way, I was still hungry afterwards.

I decided to entertain myself, since I'd had enough boredom. Plus, some amusement would distract me from the uncharitable people in the house. Seated by the breakfast bar, I swivelled around to observe Dad in his new place of belonging or lack thereof. He moved about disconcertingly, as he was sorely out of place. Despite Dad's broad Australian accent, he was unable to communicate in an Aussie bogan style, unlike the company around him. It was hard to decide if the stark contrast was comical or just sad. I wondered what Dad's take was on the situation, since there was no laughter in his eyes. It appeared that his only source of comfort came from a glass of something alcoholic, and I'm sure many more saw him through the day. What on earth had Dad gotten himself into? From what I'd seen, there was no foundation between Dad and Sandra. I seriously doubted that their relationship could endure life's inevitable storms. Dad would never have asked for his young daughter's thoughts on the relationship, of course, and I would never have offered them.

Blind sightedness had its way as the couple secured a wedding date. I was seventeen by then. The wedding day arrived with fine weather, but I was *not* fine from the outset. Grief filled me, as I was overwhelmed with heaviness of heart, though I didn't know why. A funeral theme rose inside of me as I entered the church doors, clashing with the matrimonial theme filling the space. I was sickened by the floral garnishes embellishing the sanctuary, along with the unduly loud romantic music and the bride and groom's lovey-dovey performance. As guests choked up with romanticised emotion, I choked up with misery. Yes,

I believed the wedding was nothing more than a romantic travesty! But was that my reason for being so disconsolate?

I breathed in Trafalgar's fresh country air, feeling slightly calmed as the service had finally ended but still carrying heaviness of heart. The newly married couple stood at the front of the church to have their photos taken, while elated guests arrayed around them. I lay low at a safe distance, quietly bereft, while watching the photo shoot. Until I was spotted and rudely singled out.

A mature woman bellowed at me while extending her arm in my direction, ordering me over. "There's Fleur! Come on! It's your dad's wedding! You have to be in the picture. Come on!" Ignoring the inclination to run, I allowed the cameraman to capture my image with the bride and groom. Standing next to Dad, I glimpsed his pained expression. It exposed his hidden feelings towards me. He didn't want his daughter around, as he was ashamed; I felt it intuitively. Although in my insecurity, I might've misread him. Dad gave me a photo after the event. The couple's faces express delight, while my forlorn eyes are longing to cry. Even as I write, the picture takes me back to those raw emotions.

Finally set free from the groom, his new wife and the ebullient crowd, my feet found traction. Stopping at the back of the little church, I was certain Dad would not come after me, as it would've been embarrassing for him. I bent forward for great sobs to come from my depths. My tears plopped like fat raindrops, discolouring a patch of dry earth. Soon after, a woman startled me with her presence. As much as I tried, I could not rein in my emotions, so my unsuccessful rescuer left. While writing, I now reckon that she was the woman who beckoned me to join Dad and Sandra for a photo and the one who spoke to me that disagreeable Christmas when no one else bothered to. It's just that I was far too distressed in the moment to recognise her as the same person.

The wedding crowd relocated from the churchyard to Sandra's brother's place, whoever he was (I don't recall ever meeting him). The garden was festooned with twinkling lights and draping wedding whites, as expected of an outdoor reception. A celebratory atmosphere came with ample tasty fare and wedding dancing songs for guests to show off their moves. Small children were adorably outfitted in miniature three-piece suits and A-line frocks in summery pastels and white. Holding hands, they danced around and around, barefoot on the grass, adding youthful wonder. Alas, the appealing scene did not bring delight to me and my brothers. We were our own forlorn gathering. Closely seated at our white-dressed table, I watched Owen move away from the present. His low mood was far more ominous than the gloomy cloud threatening Dylan and me. I tried to break his stupor with my pointless chatter, but he had already departed.

To make things worse, Dad was nowhere to be seen, apart from one brief interlude. A few twittering women coaxed him to see his children and then uneasily moved away from our crestfallen table. I'm sure that my grandparents were present and speeches were had, but I have no memory of them. The likely reason was the funeral theme overshadowing me the entire day.

The Christmas and wedding occasions may have been hard for my siblings and me to cope with, but still, there were some positive times with Dad and Sandra. Though, I'm not sure about Owen. For me, being given the opportunity to ride Lilah's horse was one of them. While the horse's name is long forgotten, I'm certain he was a gelding with a brown or bay coat. At the horse paddock, I stroked his warm neck while breathing in his rich, sweet scent. Just as I was becoming familiar with the animal's temperament, Lilah had to meet her father elsewhere. I didn't want her to leave, as I was beginning to relish her company in a sisterly kind of way. So I remained with my new four-legged friend, snorting and shaking his head, along with Dad and Sandra.

Dad stood back while Sandra showed me the basics of how to handle a horse. Once I was mounted, we began a gentle walk. Everything was going smoothly until he started napping as I tried to move him forward. Our beginner's ride ended by the time we reached the other end of the paddock. The horse balked and dropped beneath a tree, rolling pleasurably in the dirt. I immediately dismounted the saddle to avoid being crushed by the creature's great weight. Afterwards, we all laughed over the comical situation. We connected really well that day.

Likewise, Dylan remembers a good time during a stay with the couple. Sandra had organised a drum set for him to play as a first-time experience. As it turns out, Dylan is now a proficient drummer and runs a successful cymbal business, using his own brand name.

At one point, Dad admitted to having relationship problems. As a quiet getaway, he purchased a hobby farm, nestled amongst Trafalgar's sublime hilly landscape. Dylan and I visited him without Owen, as by then, he'd moved to Melbourne. Dad was satisfied with his new investment, and I was genuinely pleased for him but also a little concerned. Grandad came to mind, as he had expressed qualms over his son's practical abilities from the past. It was a major cause of contention between them. I didn't want to bring discouragement, so I showed interest in Dad's new property. Though, admittedly, I laughed at farmer John's primitive crofting one day. He ran amusingly, arms propelling him, while chasing the neighbour's agisted cows back to his paddock for grazing. Those stocky beasts regularly escaped his property, much to his chagrin. As the windy weather carried my laughter away, it struck me that Dad should stick to psychology. It suited him far better than farming. Grandad, most likely, would've agreed.

Unsurprisingly, Dad's marriage dissolved eighteen months after the wedding affair, heading down the divorce route.

FIFTEEN

Contrary Influences and Finding Myself

Back when my parents first separated, Mum, Dylan, and I moved to the rural town of Warragul, where we lived for a year. This was also when Owen stayed with Dad. We took up residence in a rental cottage near the town's social centre. Warragul is about a hundred kilometres east of Melbourne. Our location gave us closer access to the city, either by train or car, than Churchill. The well-established township also came with historic charm and lush surroundings to enjoy.

Unfortunately, my new teen reality on the school front cast a shadow over these improvements. I braced myself for schoolgirl brutishness, which became unavoidable. I'd hardly adjusted to Year 10 student life at Warragul High School when a peer lied to the school heavyweight, Michelle. She was told that I was liable for offensive graffiti aimed at her in the school toilets. Her entourage tracked me down, declaring a fist fight.

"Michelle will see you on the oval, twelve o'clock, Friday. Be there!"

My sympathetic mother allowed me a sickie, but Monday inconsiderately came around. The first part of my school day was a haze of incoherence. Then the lunch bell rang as a rude awakening. Sitting with my two friends on the grassy banks of the sports oval, I wolfed down my lunch, as food and school fights don't mix. They chatted without a care, while I anxiously waited for my mystery nemesis to show up.

At least half an hour later, Michelle's entourage came with a message. The fight was still on, only at a different location. My friends and I made our way to the girls' toilet block, where I lost sight of them. As I took in the school's entire female student population, I sensed their eagerness for the fight to begin. I looked around at the obscene graffiti covering the walls and doors, Michelle's name printed in bold writing. This turned my anxiety into palpable fear, and my body shook violently.

Michelle suddenly appeared, separating herself from the crowd. I felt numerous hands pushing me forward.

The girl commanding attention asked no one in particular, "Where's Fleur? Where is she?" My adversary treated me like I was her property, though we hadn't met before. Grabbing my uniform collar, she slammed me against a partition between toilet cubicles. My tormentor's close proximity drew attention to her eyes, heavily lined with black make up, glaring daggers at mine. Michelle breathed out scorn as her warm, moist breath misted my face. She swore to avenge me for the slur she believed I was guilty of, pointing to the evidence all around us.

"Wake up. Wake up. Get up!"

I opened my eyes, suddenly aware that someone was shaking my shoulders. It was Michelle. She wanted me off the concrete floor, the cold, hard place where I'd been lying unconscious. The bell had rung, and almost all of the students had vacated the area. Michelle was concerned about getting into trouble, so she shoved me into a toilet cubical. She commanded me to shut the door and stand on the lid in case prying teachers saw my feet. I came to my senses while holding the walls to steady myself. My fingers poked a fat, bloodied lip then rubbed a sharp pain at the back of my head. Still shaking, I reassured myself that the ordeal was finally over. Later, Mum offered some understanding but mostly treated my misfortune as something I should work through myself. As for Dad, he knew nothing of my high school banes. Would he have known if we still lived under the same roof? Would he have cared?

In late July, Mum and I exchanged Gippsland's dreary weather for warm sunshine via an international excursion. We travelled to the United States, which included free entry to events at the 1984 Olympic Games in Los Angeles, California. Owen, then seventeen, had won the trip for two through a commercial promotion.

His excitement was short lived. "No!" Mum told him. "You will not be taking a girl along."

This aggravated their already strained relationship, and Owen's usual argumentativeness became withdrawal.

His second response pained me more than the first, as his previous feistiness showed some verve. Mum offered to accompany her son on the trip, as though it was her prerogative. His aggrieved response was one of refusal, pessimistically handing over the prize.

I can only guess that Mum made the decision for Owen because Dad appeared to be preoccupied with his own complex world, regardless that they lived in the same house. I remember Dad attending the shop in Morwell, where Owen won the prize. He stood at a distance away from the rest of our family and remained uninvolved. Owen, who came with him, was also a sorry sight, as he'd been caught in the rain. His wet hair flattened against his head, and sodden clothes trickled onto the floor beneath him. He must've stood in the downpour as not-so-subtle defiance against the adults around him. It had the desired effect when the shop manager, well turned out in business attire, remarked on Owen's sodden and dishevelled appearance. It was also obvious that he was far from being a happy prize winner, so the man advised that he return at a later date in appropriate dress for a publicity photo. Owen refused to return on another day to have his photo taken. The manager moved about aimlessly, as he was confounded by my family and didn't know how to handle the situation.

Concerning the trip, I was sad for my older brother but also thrilled that I was next in line, though I minimised my excitement around him. Dylan didn't get a look in. Perhaps Mum thought he was too young. Owen said he no longer cared about the trip, but his dejected face and dragging body told me otherwise.

Mum and I enjoyed a fortnight of fleeting fun during our United States summer visit. As a sprightly teen, I tried everything on offer. We indulged in five-star accommodation, beginning in Los Angeles as spectators at the Olympic Games track cycling events. We also sampled speciality hot dogs and bottomless coffee, depriving me of sleep. Most importantly, we learned about sales tax and avoiding hostility from cabbies through generous tipping. More than Mum, I delighted in Disneyland Park's magnetisms in Anaheim, California. Las Vegas dazzled its twenty-four-hour neon lights and alarmed us with the presence of armed guards. San Francisco's street life and contrasting natural beauty also shocked, entertained, and fascinated us.

Hawaii was the last port of call. Shortly after arriving, we took a walk outside our hotel, where a skater approached Mum. He casually asked, "Wanna buy some drugs?"

She declined, and we watched him skateboard effortlessly towards more pedestrians.

Mum decided we should splurge one night on Japanese cuisine at the hotel where we stayed. But once the meal arrived, I couldn't eat a thing, as my stomach churned when a waiter flirted with me. Away from Mum's line of sight, he began winking, grinning, and gesturing, then slipped me a note at our table.

I read it to Mum in the elevator. "Meet me in the lobby at 10pm tonight."

She burst into laughter, and I burst into tears. It was all a bit disconcerting to fifteen-year-old me. Needless to say, I didn't meet with the stranger. I wondered how many teenage girls he had approached and what he'd gotten away with. Sleaze!

The highlight of our stay in the Aloha State was on the last day. We went snorkelling for hours in the pristine waters of an ancient volcanic crater amongst colourful marine life. Then my paradise experience turned into suffering as sunstroke struck me down. I discovered the symptoms back at the hotel room. Nausea sent me running to the loo, and my head throbbed like it was about to explode. I tried to lie down but couldn't settle. On top of the other symptoms, I was burning up, and my limbs ached unbearably.

Mum packed my things, as we were due to catch a plane back to Australia. By the time we reached the airport, Mum and a man from our tour group dragged me and my luggage along, as I was feeling faint. As we waited for the plane, I draped myself over some spare seats, sure I was dying. I felt even more vulnerable when Mum demanded that I should stand up and pray loudly in tongues. I was uncertain I could stand without collapsing. Mum refused to accept my decline, so I forced myself up and into a standing position. Fortunately, we were away from the main crowd, though I was hardly concerned about embarrassment since I desperately wanted to be well. While I obediently prayed, the throbbing headache and light-headedness soon left, along with the heat, aching, and nausea in my body. I remained standing, staring at the ceiling as my tongue rested, utterly amazed that I was back to my usual self. I was completely well for the long flight home.

After the two-week trip, a pang of guilt bothered me. I believed Owen should have enjoyed the United States trip. Still, I had other things to think about, and before long, my guilt released.

Around that time, I struggled with feelings of hostility towards Dad that ebbed and flowed. Undoubtedly, I had been influenced by Mum's condemnations of her ex-husband. A symptom of their marriage split-up. Still, he was my father, and our geographical separation wasn't vast. While Dylan and I made efforts to visit him, I quickly became aware of parental manipulation coming at us from both sides. Dad targeted Dylan and me when we stayed with him, pushing his ideals as a tactic against our mum. At home, Mum forced her beliefs just as tenaciously. They were each bent on overriding each other's influence over us. I suspected the same was happening for Owen. We kids were caught up in the crossfire of our parents' battle. It was still a volatile time for us all.

Dad and Mum's dogmatisms were voices shouting in my head, telling me what to believe and how to live. I had to form my own worldview. I began from a spiritual premise, aside from Mum's assertions. While my visions of Jesus bore evidence of his existence and character, I needed something more. I needed to know who I was and how I fit into this crazy world and beyond. My burning two-fold question looked for a definitive answer about my origin. From my primary school days, the subject of ancient human beings had been taught, and I believed that seven primate species had progressed to the homo-sapiens we are today. That is, until the Genesis account cancelled out evolution, according to the church. Both concepts were convincing, but I had to come to an absolute decision about what I believed. I called out to God from the confines of my tiny bedroom. "Was I created, or did I evolve? I need to know where my origin lies. Are you my Heavenly Father?"

After I prayed, I sensed a great presence had entered my room, recognised as God's spirit. It overpowered the space, filling every crack and crevice and infiltrating every fibre of my being.

Breathless and speechless, I stood terrified against the wall. Although I felt afraid as my body trembled, there was no confusion about what was happening. In an instant, the awesome presence left. I leant forward, hyperventilating as a repercussion of the disturbing visitation. While I didn't see or hear anything, my spiritual encounter *was* undeniable. The awesome presence left me with an indelible revelation: God, my Father, is the author of life!

SIXTEEN

The Blessing of a Step-Father

The year 1984 also brought significant changes in my family circumstances. One change that directly affected me was dropping out of high school that October. Well-meaning adults told me I would regret leaving school so early, that I'd made a serious mistake.

You have no idea of the trials I've been through, I thought. I didn't care to share them. My decision to leave meant walking away from destructive peer influences: truanting, smoking, binge drinking, dope smoking, and fooling around with boys. At least I hoped so, as they were behaviours I didn't want to maintain for the long-term. My point of decision came after a Year 10 work experience stint. It didn't go well, and I just couldn't bring myself to return to school. A great weight lifted off my shoulders once Mum signed the student exit papers. *Phew!* I was no longer a dispirited high schooler.

Mum took me to a local adult learning centre, where I hardly felt like an adult at the age of fifteen. Even so, I was accepted into a short course on drawing techniques. The other students were all middle-aged women who were very talented at drawing. A lesson or two in, the teacher asked us to sketch a tree stump outside the classroom window. She took my smudgy sketch and showed it to the class as an example of how to use light and shadow in a drawing. The woman who taught me provided more encouragement over those few short weeks than all my high school teachers. The only exception was an art teacher at Maryvale High School.

Our period in Warragul included a twelve-month waiting time. It was a separation requirement for my parents' divorce to be finalised. It was when Mum fell hopelessly in love. I watched her saddened face turn into beams of happiness. A renewed outlook entered her life, and she attractively slimmed down, contentedly forgetting her need for food. Mum was free from care overall. I could tell she had met someone special. I connected, for the first time, with her soon-to-be husband on a minibus. Making my way up the steps, I expected a fun-filled day with people I knew from church.

The short isle took me to Mum, who was already seated. Her smiling eyes held a glint that grabbed my attention. "You haven't met Barry, have you, Fleur?"

As the day trip unfolded, many conversations occurred between Barry and me. By sunset, I had no doubts about his bona fides. Barry was a keeper.

On November 27, 1984, Mum and Barry tied the knot. The couple, in their late thirties, were ready to begin a new journey together. Their wedding was a simple affair and took place in their newly purchased home in the countryside. A brief service was conducted by a civil celebrant, witnessed by a small gathering of family and friends. The bride wore a flowy hot-pink dress and gushed with gaiety for the entire occasion. I felt a quiet assurance for the couple, certain that flourishing days were in store. I embraced our new family dynamic. Barry brought evenness and calm into our daily lives, treating us like we mattered. His realness came with warm hugs, and his presence activated joy for Mum.

We lived in Buln Buln's small rural town, which was less than ten kilometres from Warragul, towards the north. The 1950s two-bedroom home had limited space, so extensions were needed. Barry, being a skilled handyman, added a bungalow, a double garage, and other improvements to the place. While my love for Barry and his love for me was certain, I'd realised he wasn't exclusively mine. Apart from Mum and my brothers, Barry shared his bloodline with four kids from a previous marriage. It was clear that he also loved them dearly. They became a part of our lives over alternate weekends and school holiday periods, when they stayed at our house, the bungalow addition making it possible. As far as I remember, we all got along fine. When issues came up, Barry and Mum addressed them with minimal fuss. Once I approached independence, my step-sibling ties broke away but for no ill reasons; our connections only lasted a short while.

After Mum and Barry had moved in together, with Dylan and me in tow, Mum gave me her original engagement and wedding rings from Dad, which she no longer wore. Many months before then, my greedy eyes had coveted the cool, smooth gold and shimmering, light-refracting stone, so I was satisfied when they became mine. I wore my first pieces of fine gold like a proper woman. Then my conscience began to trouble me. What audacity, to grasp at another's love symbol so flippantly! I knew too well of my parents' fragmented love, so I shamefully returned the rings to Mum. We stood together on the linoleum floor in the kitchen, where she turned them into landfill. My eyes followed the once esteemed metals and solitaire, gleaming as they fell from my mother's hand, lost amongst refuse in the bin. In my head, I sought to redeem them. But my conscience declared a final ruling: *no!* Mum was entitled to keep or throw away as she pleased. To her, monetary value was inconsequential. Besides, why revisit my guilt?

Over time, my predictions were proven to be true. Mum and Barry's marriage thrived until the end. They enjoyed twenty-seven years together, separated only by my mother's accidental death. Barry's outpouring of grief, though agonising to watch, attested further to their bond. Through the years, Barry and I have remained in touch and have a loving relationship. I am grateful that he supported Dylan and me in adolescence, and especially that he esteemed our mother. I'm reminded of this each time I wear the ring Barry put on her finger as her beloved groom.

SEVENTEEN

Youth Independence: Not All It's Cracked Up to Be

While Mum was still with us and newly married, Owen had moved away from Dad's place, having finished his final year of school. How he managed Year 12 under the circumstances, I'll never know. Owen was studying a Bachelor of Arts at Latrobe University in Melbourne. The wider cosmopolitan environs proved to be a bracing change from the small-town thinking that previously encroached on Owen's style. He was intensely philosophical, like our father, and so university life suited him perfectly. He was free to theorise with likeminded students. I was overjoyed when I heard Owen had been accepted into a university course, especially as it meant he was far away from Dad's unsupportive household. I also hoped he'd moved on from his depressive bouts. Naturally, I wanted my older brother to thrive and achieve all that he desired.

I was also free to leave home, having matured into a stately seventeen-year-old. Independence was beginning to take shape, as I was employed full-time at a local supermarket. But I felt anchored with Barry around, and leaving home wasn't much of a consideration. Then, one day, he and Mum dropped a bomb, announcing that they were relocating to Mount Beauty in north-eastern Victoria, around 430 kilometres away. Barry had been offered a job in Falls Creek, thirty kilometres from Mount Beauty, while Mum had a teaching position at the local high school. After some discussion, I made the daunting decision to leave home. Collecting my things, I said goodbye to my chief support system and my little brother.

I lived with Robby and Trish, a sociable young couple. The first-time homeowners lived in Drouin, which fell under the same Baw Baw Shire as Buln Buln. My connection with the couple came through my boyfriend, Alyn, Trish's brother. Their parents supported our relationship, and I was warmly received by the family. I was well set up with the essentials of a room and board, paid for by my regular income. Other staples in my world were spiritual and social as I circulated the local Christian loop.

I often travelled in the car with my provisional family to Sunday church services. Typically, I held hands with my steady date in the back seat. Our eyes would tenderly meet, affirming fondness. One weakness was that our relationship lacked passion and depth. I felt it acutely but never mentioned it to Alyn. We spilled out of the car in our Sunday best. Cheap court shoes bit at my feet as we navigated our way through the gravel car park, then entered Warragul's established community church. Alyn and I found our peers and exchanged quick greetings, settling in our seats, as socialising was saved for after the service. The church offered essential worship, sound doctrine, and warming fellowship. We were spoilt for choice with varying activities, all holding magnetic family appeal. Church conventions were also adhered to. It brought comfort to the people. Nothing wrong with that, I convinced myself. I never shirked what was expected of me in God's house, partaking in Holy Communion, tithing, and other practices, which I wholly supported. At another level, there was something the church didn't offer: the experiential. I longed to get into deeper spiritual waters but kept this desire to myself. I didn't want to concern others, who appeared to be satisfied with their revolving Christian circle.

When a youth pastor couple came on the scene, I saw it as an opportunity and hoped they might fill the gap. The charismatic husband and wife, likely in their early thirties, exuded drive and good looks, and they were stylishly dressed. I pretended to be brightly assured around them. The man, whose name I can't recall, gained the youth group's interest from the first time he spoke; my attention was drawn to his clipped circle beard as it animated with his mouth. We young people sat around a large room in a curve, facing the pastor as he coached us, referencing psychology theories he'd learnt. We were told that he'd provide youth guidance as long as he filled his role, supporting and equipping us well for the real world. The pastor educated us through a whiteboard affect, words written in black, red, and blue.

I squirmed inside, forcing myself to sit calmly and focus on the leader, along with the collective. While observing him, I saw and heard my psychologist father. But why did my peers look so relaxed? Did their minds wander elsewhere, or was the teaching style and content genuinely to their liking? I doubted it, as no one asked questions or engaged in discussion. The gathering quickly took flight at the session's end, apart from me. The room's empty, open space felt excessively big as the pastor and I tentatively glanced at one another. My irritated voice broke the silence. I spoke my mind about Dad's discrepancies between the roles of father and psychologist. Then I sassily compared him with the pastor, focusing specifically on their patronising clinical approach. I complained to the pastor about his distinct lack of spiritual teaching, emphasising my disappointment.

As I spoke, the man's placid face turned into a scowl. It signified that he hadn't read between the lines of my outburst. He'd missed that my unflinching message came from unresolved hurt and that I desperately needed to talk to someone about my dad-baggage. Unfortunately, I was too fired up to explain or apologise.

The pastor was on the defensive by the time I finished speaking. He resembled my father all the more as his suave facade and learned ways left him. The man's comeback was more pithy than loud. "I'm not your father. Don't you compare me. You need to work on your issues!"

Yes, I had issues. I was not in a good frame of mind, and I was unreasonably accusatory and hostile. I had no excuse, though I *was* struggling. Clearly, I'd presented the youth pastor with a startlingly difficult challenge, and he was a newbie at that. But then again, wasn't that why the church had employed him? Wasn't he there to work with an array of young people, even troubled ones like me?

My disclosure to a stranger was attached to trust, not to a particular person. Someone equipped to serve in a pastoral role. I expected the hands and feet of Jesus to offer a brotherly hand out of life's muck, a friend to those in dark places. I expected abundant grace, acceptance, and an offer of prayer, wisdom, and viable answers, denoting a presence of hope. Was this too much of a tall order? It must have been, as the pastor offered no validation, no support or strategies of any kind, only a rebuke with a fuming face. Yet he championed himself as well able to equip the entire youth group with the skills to deal with life's tempests. I couldn't help but compare him to my unremarkable father.

In a pause, we stood stand-offishly, having nothing more to say. The pastor's face was filled with distain, his eyes glowering at me beneath furrowed brows. Even his beard didn't soften his features. It was my cue to leave. I first took another look at the whiteboard. The black, red, and blue writing was nothing more than a useless theory, devoid of Christian love and care. *Hello, Dad, and goodbye!* The words came harshly to my mind over the bitter irony of the situation.

The moment I left the building, I beat myself down. Why I had to upset the man, I didn't know. Why couldn't I just pick myself up, shut up, and go through the motions again? That night, I cozied up in my bed's cocoon. My thoughts discriminated between God and people. God is perfect, while all humankind is stained with imperfection, I realised. I took this simple truth as Heaven's wisdom, which brought me to a decision to trust in the All Sufficient One and never elevate others based on their position. With that certainty, I resorted to a weepy prayer. "Holy Spirit, it's up to you to fill me. I am done!"

The great Counsellor came into my lodger's bedroom, where I was tenderly restored.

My circumstances changed some months after moving away from home. I'd finished one job to start another, only for it to fall through after a few short weeks. Life's unexpected deviation was disorienting. I needed to recourse to plan B, quickly, only there was nothing beyond plan A. That is, apart from Alyn and I having called it quits. Our relationship hadn't moved beyond a shallow connection, indicating a directional change.

I made a phone call I didn't want to make. "Mum, I lost my job. Could I live with you and Barry?"

The couple took me in without reservation. Their kindness and understanding brought peace of mind.

As the name Mount Beauty suggests, I found nature's beauty all around. I savoured the high-country experience while meandering through the serene countryside on my bike, especially when summer's greenery circled into autumn's colourful display. Dylan was also in his element during the snow season, skiing in the alpine heights of Falls Creek.

But I didn't make it through all four seasons, as I found my happy valley place clouding. I was a young adult back under parental care and without a wage, a licence, or a car, among other independent privileges. I was stuck. Purposelessness and boredom messed with my ability to communicate well, particularly with Mum, bringing stress into the home. It was time I moved on.

Wodonga was my chosen destination, about an hour's drive north of Mount Beauty. It is a bordering municipality referred to as Albury-Wodonga. I resided on the Victorian side, serving a smaller population than Albury's thriving New South Wales city. In Wodonga, my bike became a handy workmate, transporting me to and from appointments. I travelled across the adjoining causeway above the Murray River banks, lined with native river red gums. I rode flat strap across the border bridge, taking a cardiovascular workout, then cruising if the traffic flow allowed it. The routine ride took me to an Albury institute. There, I attended a nondescript government program, as my attendance was a requisite for gaining financial assistance. It was the state government's answer for unemployed youth like me. I'd realised that my employment opportunities were limited, having left school early. My Wodonga life required focus and determination in churning out job applications, attending subsequent interviews, and receiving knockbacks that crushed my self-esteem. Straddling the saddle, I rolled and swayed with my bike's wheels and steel frame. I was on a ride of disillusionment, on the road to nowhere.

Lodging, at times, was also a thorn in my side, or should I say a thorn in my bike tyre, leading to deflation? My boarding and house sharing experiences came as a mixed bag, as credulous relationships were often the theme. My first port of call was with a young couple. All went well until the husband noticed me, leading to jealousy from his wife. Next, I took up bed and board with a nice enough family, but couple feuding brought stress into my life. I tried again with a friend in a one-bedroom flat as a temporary setup. The lack of space proved to be a problem when her sister moved in. Tensions swirled between them, creating a storm in a teacup. I was caught up unintentionally, guilty of hand towel ruffling, a felony they accused each other of.

I trialled another short-term stay with a young woman I hardly knew. Dragging my stuff into the entrance of an affluent Albury home, I was greeted by my new friend, who was house sitting. When I was told we'd be sharing a bed in the master bedroom, it sounded like a newsflash I wasn't prepared for. My alarm abated when I was told it was for practical reasons and that other arrangements would be made the next day. That evening, I climbed onto my side of the mattress, bushed from a long day. When a velvety voice asked for my affections, I realised my roommate was propositioning me for sex. I felt my cortisol levels rising, prepared to fight the girl off should she pounce on me. Thankfully, she kept her body away from mine, despite more requests for intimacy. Finally, my refusal was accepted, and we relented to sleep on opposite shores of our king-sized island.

My eyes hurt as they opened to sudden light flooding the room. Realising it was morning, I sat up, swathed in extravagant quilting. As I regulated myself to wakefulness, a figure blurred to and fro. My roommate was in a tizzy. I was a nuisance pet she no longer wanted, so she commanded me. "Get up. Get up! Get your things, and go. You can't stay here. Go now!"

I obeyed without question.

Overloaded with bags, I wheeled my bike to the bus stop, then travelled back to Wodonga. I didn't know where else to go. Aimlessly, I wandered the city's streets until the sun proclaimed it was departing for bed. I also rested from the day. Feeling like a vagabond, I half lay on a park bench amongst my worldly goods. "Maybe I'll stay the night," I said aloud. I prodded a bag to use as a pillow, but it was still lumpy under my head. "Am I homeless?" Again, I spoke to the air, or was I speaking to myself … or God? These questions troubled me, as I didn't have any answers. *Am I going crazy?* I seriously wondered. My forearms formed tiny bumps in the refrigerated air, its chill causing my body to tremor. I was rapidly feeling less drowsy and more sober-minded. *I'm not crazy.* The words came as a sure thought that time. If I slept in the street, I'd be exposed to the elements, among other threats. I had to find somewhere to stay before the night sky cast its shadow over me. Mum wasn't a viable option, as I'd overstayed my welcome last time. Dad was also out of the question, as he lived in another part of the state. Besides, he'd frown at my situation.

The only other person who came to mind was Esther. She was a single thirty-year-old woman, a youth pastor employed at the church I attended. Knowing Esther practised what she preached offered a glimmer of hope. It prompted me to drag my stuff across the road to the public telephone booth. Once Esther received my call, I cut to the chase. "I have nowhere to stay. Can you help me?"

Without hesitancy the pastor threw me a lifeline.

I refused the offer of a lift, reaching her flat by nightfall. With a sheepish smile, I stood on Esther's doorstep, where she eyed me with care and concern. My appearance was bedraggled. I was drained from the day's wind and sun, my shoulders weighted from hoisting too many bags. My feet ached. Esther later described me as "a little lost bunny" when I arrived. I crashed on her couch for some weeks, then shared a skimpy space in her bedroom for many more. It was a great credit to two generous spirits: Esther and her flat mate, Evelyn, who provided a tall glass of cool water when I needed it most.

While I wasn't left to endure life on the streets, I *was* disenchanted. My independent move to Wodonga proved to be futile, as I couldn't find paid work. Unrest simmered away, coming to a head when I attended an interview at Albury's Department of Social Security. I detested that place, as it had contributed to my miserable locust year and a half in Wodonga. I arrived at the government building, dismounted my bike, and positioned it out the front for a quick departure. In the waiting area, I became antsy, shifting in my seat while watching the drawn faces of people who shared a similar predicament to me. The sound of my name brought heat to my face and forced me to stand and greet the public servant who'd called me. I followed the back of his striding slacks to a makeshift booth. The man posed all the usual questions. With officiousness, he reviewed my vocational skills and job-seeking efforts. He then put down his pen and eyeballed me with concern, pausing for longer than felt comfortable. The interviewer then addressed me with a lecture and a disparaging conclusion. I'd made dissatisfactory efforts at getting into the job market, and on that account, I was unemployable. Once I'd been sufficiently discouraged, he indicated that the interview was over. I hastened out of the building and grabbed my bike, soon pumping the pedals hard all the way to the Albury bypass and onto the Wodonga bike path.

I spotted a shrubby area with a small clearing beside the path, so I slowed down, then used the brake. Gracelessly, I dismounted my bike and threw the contraption into the dirt as an unloved piece of junk. With hands on my hips, I leant forward to catch my breath, but the quickening continued, as I was distressed over my dead-end life. Straightening up, I observed a native shrub jutting out, spindly and unappealing. A bird's nearby song came abrasively. Nothing around me, nor within, could bolster my mood. As I paced, stones, leaves, and dirt shifted beneath my shoes. My life was fruitless, and so was my future. And yet, I was not fully defeated. I raised my head and shouted an edgy petition. "Where are you, God? Where are you? You say you have a plan. Do you? I don't see it. God, speak to me!"

The answer came as quickly as I'd demanded it, and God's message was decisive. "You will live with Barbara and work for your father."

At these words, my distress dissolved, and normal breathing returned. The hot, breezeless air didn't bother me as it usually would, and bush sounds came alive as pleasant ambiences. God had renewed my outlook. The Master's spoken plan had sprung up new enthusiasm, pushing me into action.

The context of this plan had arisen more than twelve months earlier. At the time, I was living in Wodonga and looking for work. In an attempt to arm myself for the working world, I asked Dad if he would take me on for work experience. Surprisingly, he did. Benevolence floated up as he warmly welcomed me into his Morwell home and workplace. It was the same town where I'd attended Maryvale High School and a ten-minute drive from where we'd lived in Churchill. Dad accommodated me in his home for a week and a half. I spent the nights on his shabby grey-brown couch in the lounge room as a cosy place for slumbering. Dad's face brightened when he paid my way, treating me to dinner both locally and in the city, where we rendezvoused with Owen. Grandad stopped over for a few days as a rarity, retiring to the spare room. His son willingly played host to the family occupying his home. I watched this unaccustomed scene with enthral.

With pleasure, Dad explained the workings of his practice, clueing me up on administration specifics and errand runner responsibilities. I attended to these tasks with eagerness to ease his burdensome schedule. While traipsing the streets, I greeted old acquaintances, reunited with friends, and a new connection was formed with Barbara, also known as Barb. The endearing grandmother ran a Christian bookshop adjacent to Dad's work building. I frequented Barb's shop during my breaks, browsing the merchandise and connecting with a stream of people, young and old, brash and unassuming, and everything in between, all adding characterful verve to the space.

Gaining work experience meant improving my work skills and building what little confidence I had. Although brief, it was a much-needed change from my jobless life. But it was soon time I returned home. Before leaving, Dad made an unexpected offer of employment.

I could have asked for a starting date, but I declined the offer. "Thanks, Dad," I gushed. "I expect to find work in Wodonga. The work experience should help."

Smiling, Dad nodded and said, "If you change your mind, all you have to do is ask."

After returning to Wodonga, I'd been determined to find my own way. A work opportunity had presented but fizzled out. So I'd picked myself up and continued along the gloomy unemployment path. Over the succeeding weeks and months, I hadn't considered Dad's work offer, at least not as a real solution. I didn't want to inconvenience him, but God thought differently. Undoubtedly, God knew what he was doing. But that didn't mean I wouldn't face trials as his plan unfolded, especially conflicts with Dad, whose sporadic acts of kindness were never a guarantee of the next time. I had trouble finding pluck to contact him, for it had been many months since we'd spoken.

Despite my reluctance, I trundled off to the telephone booth with a bulging purse. *Creaaaaak! Creaaaaak! Clunk!* For a few silent moments, I stood tautly inside the enclosed conspicuous box. I was stalling for time. But the furious pounding in my chest and jutting payphone both urged me to get on with the job. "Okay. Okay." I sighed. My purse reduced in size as silver coins disappeared one by one down the slot. *Clang. Clang. Purr.* My cue to dial away. "Hi, Dad. I've been thinking. Something you said when you took me in for work experience. If I ever needed work, I should ask you."

Irate and unequivocal, he replied, "No! I did not say that. There's no work for you!" Then? *Click!* Dad cut me off. He did so without the slightest concern for my welfare. The man who begot me couldn't care less.

Feeling very much dispirited, I decided to ring Mum for support. Again, I delved into my purse and dialled away. But almost instantly, I knew she was the wrong person to open my heart to. While Mum could be kind and understanding, she could also be uncompassionate, though I don't know why. On this occasion, she had no faith in me. None whatsoever. She claimed I was unqualified for anything remotely vocational, lacking the aptitude for work, except perhaps as a cleaner. "No," she self-corrected. I couldn't even manage a cleaning position. Was she saying I couldn't drag a cloth over a dusty surface or wield a cobwebbing brush to support myself? *Ouch!*

Although these opinions were deeply painful, my closing response consented to them. "Oh. Do you think so? Okay. Goodbye, Mum."

Essentially, we both believed that I had no future work prospects.

My second setback compounded the first. It made me marvel that my parents forgot I was still in my teens, a mere babe all alone in a formidable world. My upsetting reality was an ideal moment for the violinists to appear. If I could, I would have summoned them to play their sad timbres amidst a teary-eyed audience. I desperately needed some fellow feeling, but there was none. I stood forlornly in the booth, confused about what to do next.

Then something divine happened; I heard the psalmist's words from long ago. "When my father and my mother forsake me, then the Lord will take care of me." Psalm 27:10, NKJV.

This verse instantly changed my attitude, as it came with certain clarity and truth, sparking fresh faith and courage. It impelled me to make a third phone call to Barb with my last few coins. Once we connected, I shared my account of what God said and my parents' surprising discouragements. Barb's affirming words came comfortingly. They travelled almost 500 kilometres from her heart to mine, resembling a wonderful, much-needed hug. Barb ended our conversation with an offer to move into her Churchill home, shared with a few other women. I accepted the offer, recognised as God's indispensable care.

I gladly said good riddance to my Wodonga phase, for I was beyond its sweep of grit. The trials I'd endured were many, some being undesirable openings: a cannabis using way of life, a risky connection with a pastor heading off track, and a romantic relationship I'd had misgivings about from the start. The hale and hearty biker expected that we'd ride off into the sunset, dual saddled in his and hers leathers with club colours on our backs. Once I was aware of his pornography addiction and adopted sister obsession, my doubts were verified. I wanted out! Irritatingly, my bearded boyfriend refused to let me go, stating God wanted us to be together. I disagreed, then fended off his negative control. We eventually parted on reasonable terms. By then, I was more than ready to set out on a new path.

PART THREE

*"Imagine yourself as a living house.
God comes in to rebuild that house ..."*
— C.S. Lewis, *Mere Christianity*

EIGHTEEN

Working for Dad: Traversing the Benefits and Drawbacks

With optimism, I sussed out my new living situation. I moved from Wodonga back to my former Churchill town. Barbara resembled the family head. She was well regarded by the women already living in her home. A mature woman, in a prudent sense, Barb's tallness came with an upright carriage. She was proudly English, as expressed in her mannerisms and enunciation. The other residents each held a Christian faith, were about my age, and all looked to Barb for support in some capacity. One of them, I discovered, had been a friend from my Warragul High School days. We were overjoyed, greeting one another with a crushing hug. Barb gave me a tour of the substantial red-brick house and garden, ending with my small bedroom, painted in a calming, neutral colour. There, I plonked my bags by the freshly made bed. I was home.

Contentment floated up from me like a helium balloon ... and then slowly deflated over the thought of my impending call to Dad. I spoke to Barb again about God's direction and Dad's opposition. Her response was that my placement in her home was secure and that things would work out in the end. Even so, I steeled myself while dialling Dad's number. I responded to his greeting, then revisited our last conversation about the work offer, adding my move to Churchill. My anticipation of employment went down like a lead balloon.

"I never agreed. I will not provide you with work. Don't bother asking again, as it's a definite no!" Dad abruptly ended our connection.

Still pressing the handset against my chin and ear, his riled voice remained in my head. His decision was just as loud and clear. And yet, I was not entirely deterred. It was living faith that had prompted me to move into Barb's house and stake my claim for paid work. I expected that my erratic father *would* enable it. God just needed to soften his heart.

While I was armed with unwavering faith, my feelings were all over the place. Dad had bruised me. He said that I was lying about his work offer when it was the other way around. Or else he had a short memory.

I shared my hurt with Barb, who advised me, "Ring your dad later, when he has settled down. He may change his mind."

I shot up a silent prayer. For the remaining afternoon until dark, I wondered when to call and what to say.

Bring! Brring! The landline's sudden shrill ringing caused me to shift in my chair.

I quickly settled, assuming the call wasn't for me, until Barb called out, "Fleur! Fleur, it's for you."

"Dad?" I asked with reticence, taken aback by the buoyant voice.

Dad had thrown aside the weightiness of displeasure at me, uplifted by a shining, bright idea, proposing a business traineeship.

"Yes. Yes." I agreed it was a good idea and that I would meet him at his office at nine in the morning. My feet almost left the ground as I marvelled at God's intervention.

I woke up to a noisy bird fluttering at my window. Its lively tune urged me to get up and organise myself with a bright outlook. So I did, soon ready to meet Dad at his psychology practice in Morwell. Barb and I drove to a car park near our work locations, and we said goodbye with knowing smiles as I embarked on God's plan. A short walk took me to an office building, where I skittered up the stairs, two at a time, and into Dad's rented rooms. He greeted me with optimistic drive in activating our work plans.

The year-long traineeship involved three days of office work with my employer and two days of schooling, through Yallourn TAFE. Depending on the day, I travelled with Barb to work or took a bus to college, so all the logistics were sorted. Daily life became full of activity and purpose. My fraying mental health, caused by long-term unemployment, was mending. As for Dad's earlier harshness and broken word, neither of us brought it up. Instead, I privately absolved him of the hurt he had caused me, nullifying its effect.

While I relished working to the rhythm of Dad's daily practice, my working life was becoming complicated. Our father-daughter relationship wasn't all rainbows and unicorns, and as the months wore on, the sparkle wore off. Dad gave the impression of thriving under pressure, but veritably, his workload weighed heavily on him. He delivered quality consultant and clinical services, kept pace with managerial responsibilities, and stayed abreast of the latest clinical research, among countless other duties. Dad floated with the highs and cursed the lows. It was all a part of running a private practice within his chosen profession.

Our working alliance was a curious arrangement. I often questioned my emotional equilibrium and seriously wondered about Dad's. His intellectual pursuits were something I could rarely escape, not just workwise but on a personal level.

"Fleur, have you completed a Myers and Briggs personality test before?"

This established questionnaire wasn't available online, as there was no internet in our lives. It involved paperwork, which Dad emphatically shoved in front of me after I'd declined. My apprehensions came from being manualised, which distressed me. Dad pressured me to complete an IQ test, among others, and to participate in video self-introductions. I was inclined to shy away from the camera, but Dad reasoned that my self-confidence needed improving. He was keen to video me with the use of his family therapy tool, conveniently fixed on a tripod. He played it back, then re-recorded an improved version, and so it went. Dad's therapeutic assistance, though well-intentioned, was provided against my will. It was unhelpful and humiliating!

I pressed Dad to have casual lunches away from the daily grind. His passing response was always the same. "I'm too busy. Make an appointment in the diary for next week between clients, if there's space."

My manager's attention to business dealings trumped our personal relationship. Also, the psychologist's take on me as a client left me feeling exposed. Our role-switching skirmish was a major hitch in our relationship. I wondered if Dad was even aware.

At an operational level, my manager's expectations left no room for error. His approach was confrontational, should the monthly accounts fail to balance. Dad also disliked administration, and when stress got the better of him, his raised expression came with a condemning rant. Typically, the hot-headed man then disappeared out of my office and into his own. I remained where I was, justifying every condemnation. Evidently, I was a dull-witted twit who couldn't put two and two together. While I was still in my self-loathing state, Dad would re-enter my workspace. His face would be calmer, and knitted brows drew attention to doleful eyes, angrily narrowed just twenty minutes earlier.

"I didn't mean anything I said," Dad professed.

His speech flowed from his mouth and away from my heart. Beyond these words, I took nothing else in. I'd consigned myself to the first identity given. *Bloody idiot. Stupid bitch. Bloody useless!*

Each time this crushing experience occurred, I sombrely wondered why I was there or if Dad even loved me. Away from the work environment, I sought reassurance from my other, more loving father above. Tears wet my face and soaked my pillow as I grappled with my real identity. According to the Good Book, I'd been fashioned by the Creator's own hand, just because he wanted to. His delight in me as his precious daughter was affirmed by our close relationship. Taking this verity into my heart meant surrendering my brokenness. In turn, God lovingly and gradually put me back together. The highly emotional process involved the act of forgiveness towards my father, many times over.

Beneath it all, Dad was at war with himself. Unfortunately, his inner struggle was projected onto whoever was available through negative emotions. Dad did, however, have some self-awareness and quoted Davin Turney's well-known saying every so often. "It is always the one closest to you that hurts you the most." While this truth may have driven him to remedy things between us, his overcompensations did nothing for me. But then again, it may have ebbed away his guilt. At least someone should've benefited.

My unburdening before God was always heartening. The healing effect enabled me to rise in brightness with the sun, ready to return to work for another day with Dad, my employer, the psychologist.

The months slipped away as I continued my business traineeship. I'd come to a point where I wanted to be independent, no longer needing to rely on a bus or Barb to drive me around. I needed a licence and a car of my own. Getting a probationary licence was possible, but purchasing a car wasn't, as I had insufficient funds in the bank. I called on God, who, in my experience, gives good gifts. "I need a car. Please provide one."

It was a simple solution. My prayer was activated the next day, a working Monday. On my way to lunch, I took a shortcut through Morwell's dim and damp-smelling railway underpass. Midway, I came across Arely, a single mother I knew briefly from my church. She revealed that she couldn't afford baby formula to replace a last, depleting tin.

Misty-eyed, I reached into my purse, straining to see two currency notes that only just covered the week. *I'll skip a few lunches*, I thought, shoving the larger one into the fourteen-year-old's hand. Her responding smile showed relief. After a parting embrace, I wondered what it would be like to be a teenage mum. I sent up a voiceless prayer for Arely and her little one.

In my daily bustle, I forgot all about the encounter. That is, until a woman I knew reminded me at church that Sunday. With sureness, she said, "God will bless you." It was strongly implied that these were prophetic words that would be fulfilled before long. I discovered that it was in response to Arely telling her about my charity. *Who wouldn't have helped?* was my immediate thought. But I still took the words to heart. "God will bless you."

The following Sunday, the predicted blessing came into fruition. That morning, I was helping run a kids' church program when a figure caught my vision through the building's front window. I paused to watch the striding man, which I soon recognised as Dad's rectangular frame. His swift, rolling walk told me he was on a mission. As Dad neared the front of the building, I felt confused by his presence. *Why would he want to meet me at church?* I wondered.

At the door, Dad waved away my greeting. With the same hand, he indicated that I should follow him. Neither of us spoke while crunching our way over mottled grey stones in the car park. Stratus clouds above threatened to spit on us, while gusty winds pushed me to keep up with Dad's energetic stride. We passed vehicles of various makes and coloured veneers, then marched beyond the fenced-off area. As we reached the roadside, I realised what was happening. My request for a car and the words "God will bless you" were materialising.

Dad stood beside a second-hand car, exclaiming, "This is for you!" He identified the make and model as a Datsun 120Y, then placed a key in my hand.

I fingered the cool, grooved metal as a satisfying symbol of independence. "Thank you, Dad!" I cooed, looking for an opening to embrace him. But no opening came, as his mind was in another place. My gift giver was busily inspecting the car from every angle.

Dad eventually straightened up and came over to me, his parting lips indicating he had something to say. "The car is in your name. I paid the registration and insurance. The tank is full. The tyre pressure, oil, and water are all done. Oh, and I need a lift home."

I thanked Dad again for everything but didn't allow my effervescence to escape. It was an effort to match his pleased yet moderated mood. Inside, I was elated. It didn't matter that my car wasn't shiny new or had no stand-out features, its duco pale and interior basic. My newly acquired car was in good working order, fitting for a first-time car owner. The only cost from me was passing a small test to aid someone in need.

I slid into the driver's seat, slowly turned the key, and gripped the wheel to transport my passenger home. On the way, Dad pointed out a service station, where he told me I could refuel on his account if I was ever short of money. Three weeks later I took up Dad's offer. But I regretted it when he furiously declared that I wasn't offered access to his account.

"I never said that. Don't *ever* do that again!" Two days later, Dad's memory recall kicked in. "I owe you an apology, Fleur. I did say you could use my account. Just warn me in advance next time."

I accepted his apology but heeded his first "Don't *ever* …" edict from that time on. While Dad's reaction was a blunt reminder of his erratic ways, it didn't diminish my gratitude.

Back at home, I told Barb my car story, and we praised God together. Nearly three decades later, Dad also heard it as he lay upon a hired hospital bed at death's door. I shared his integral part as the gift giver after God whispered thoughts into his head, the precise answer to my prayer. Dad's instinctive gasp and wide-eyed expression told me the events had revealed God's reality.

Early in 1989, I was issued with a Certificate in Vocational Studies in Office/Finance, completed the year before. This proved that I could succeed in a vocation, and my parents acknowledged the achievement. Dad provided ongoing employment, which worked out well, especially as his episodic blow-ups became less frequent. Still, I braced myself for fraught moments in the workplace.

One instance was when Dad offered me an executive director position, overseeing his company. Over a period of time, he had been pressuring me into committing. I eventually signed the contract but later reneged on our agreement. I had foiled Dad's plans. His peeved remarks and accusatory frown certainly conveyed that I'd let him down. But as far as history went, our complex relationship would potentially hurt the business arrangement and, consequently, our personal lives for the long run. With that in mind, I overlooked Dad's romanticised idea of contracting with me as a fruitful father-daughter alliance. My pronouncement came with an unsettled stomach, which continued while I waited for Dad to calm down and accept my decision, and for his sullen expression to clear.

One working day, when Dad was in a better mindset, he suggested that I make an appointment with his dentist friend. The surgery was conveniently located in the same building as Dad's practice. A week or so later, my yawing mouth was inspected for cavities in the usual way. What I hadn't expected was the peppering of questions and strong advice. I responded with subtle head nods and garbled oral sounds while apparatuses prodded and poked my teeth and gums. Apparently, the dentist understood all of my distorted communications. How he and other dentists do that remains a mystery to me. Anyway, I happily left the orthodontic chair with a clean bill of oral health and clarity of mind. During the examination, I was urged to go back to school to obtain a high school certificate. Oh, and to floss daily. It appeared that two close friends had collaborated over my future. I could've kissed their cheeks as an expression of thanks but didn't have the pluck, as I felt way too intimidated by these men. I shouldn't have been, for they were simply kith, while Dad and I were kin.

NINETEEN

A Milestone Birthday

Dad and I were on our way to improving our lives as we developed a healthier family and work association. His light-footed step matched his airy mood. Dad had found a rare gem, a woman considerably younger than himself, perhaps too good for him. Anna swept into our lives as a breath of fresh air. She was able to see beyond Dad's work focus and approved the value of family.

On one occasion, Anna came with Dad and me to visit Nana and Grandad for a brief holiday. Or was it me who joined them? We all relaxed in each other's company the whole time. One glorious sunshiny day, Anna and I took a walk to Terrigal Beach. We soon rested on sun-warmed sand while listening to cheerful seaside sounds. Beach paraphernalia surrounded us and other beachgoers, also soaking up the sun. People frolicked by the glittering sea, plunging in and out of the spray, some with boards to catch a wave, while intrepid swimmers dotted the distant, darker blue waters. The sights and sounds created a lively, brightly coloured display.

In our claimed spot, Anna shared her desire to marry John and raise adopted children together. The words "marriage" and "adoption" stuck in my head for the day and for the rest of our time away. From the moment these topics were broached, my interest in the beachfront disappeared. I'd become far more focused on the woman relaxing beside me, for I was curious to hear what else she had to say. Anna's face enlivened as she discussed her future with the man she loved. All the while, I tried to master a worried expression creeping over my face. I didn't want to crush Anna's dream, but I was sure Dad wouldn't risk marrying a third time. And besides, was he even marriage material? Dad's career was his first love, and he was clearly uncompromisingly devoted! My other concern was that Anna's John was no family man. I was one hundred percent certain that ruling out child adoption was the wisest decision. I gently warned Anna a number of times, but she minimised my apprehensions over her future plans with John. As she spoke, it became increasingly apparent that Anna didn't know my father like I did. For that reason, I believed it was only a matter of time before her glinting eyes dulled with disappointment.

While the couple's relationship was thriving, they generously offered to organise a twenty-first birthday party

"Your dad and I would love to give you a party," Anna told me. She suggested that I get back to them with a theme and other party preferences.

I had time to think about the event, as my birthday date was a couple of months away.

Anna's inclusive wording was a combined offer, but I was certain that it came from her initiative, not Dad's.

Then, without warning, Dad and Anna's relationship entirely collapsed. It happened some weeks before my birthday. I felt a slight loss over my relationship ending with Dad's partner, but not for him. I was more concerned for Anna and her broken dreams. But only a little, knowing the letdown came before they'd made any foolish decisions.

As the days passed, Dad didn't mention my twenty-first event, so I decided to test the waters. The result was my father's crotchetiness and disinterest. With a flinty voice, he expressed an accusation. "You are a *very* presumptuous and selfish person, Fleur."

I sighed out of frustration, then stupidly rang my other parent for empathy. Her comment sounded unfeeling. "I didn't have a twenty-first birthday party. Why should you?"

This only induced more sighing and a protest in my head. I was *not* presumptuous or selfish! Essentially, all I wanted was for Dad to keep his word, signifying that he thought my life was worth celebrating. Was that too much to ask?

I unburdened to Kai and Liana, a pastor couple who ran a youth ministry at my church. They understood my need to feel cherished and offered to host a barbecue at their place on the night after my birthday. As I accepted their offer, my grievance turned into joy. Nothing, at that moment, could tamp down the cheerful mood rising in me.

I was soon sorting and distributing invitations, including a hand-delivered one for Dad. As he received it, I was asked to join him on the evening of my birthday. Dad stated that he wanted to buy me my first cocktail. I dressed up, treating our night out as an esteemed father-daughter date. The tavern, in Traralgon, was more like a restaurant than a bar. There, we enjoyed drinks and dessert at a quiet table. Dad's face lit up as he presented birthday gifts: fluted rim vases and a pair of classic gold hoop earrings. By the tender look in Dad's eyes, he wanted to please me and rid his guilt at the same time. I hid my sadness beneath a wistful smile. What I'd longed for was transparency between us, something Italian vases and fine gold could never make up for.

The next night, I was set apart as the birthday girl amongst friends and my supportive younger brother. Dad came later on in the evening with an obligatory bottle of wine. The coy look on his face was plain as he moved uneasily through a mostly Christian crowd. I felt some relief when Pastor Kai went out of his way to acquaint himself. When it came to the birthday customs, Dad was up for a speech, and it seemed that Dutch courage was helping him along. My slight embarrassment enlarged when Dad told everyone, with a smirk, that I had more than one boyfriend and that I should have as many men as I wanted at one time. I assumed Dad's comments came from a conversation a few weeks earlier, when he had asked after my boyfriend. I had told him I was seeing someone else but may return to my last relationship and said nothing more. Pastor Kai tactfully interjected with a change of direction just as Dad's speech was getting out of hand. He acknowledged my worth and then prayed over me.

Afterwards, Dad decided that Dylan and I were going to his work office to ring distant relatives, telling them I'd come of age. My bid to stall Dad's plans until the next day failed; he'd made up his mind. Was this his excuse to get away from the unfamiliar crowd? Or was he demonstrating a father's pride? Or perhaps possession?

Mum, Barry, and Owen didn't come to my party. I don't recall any interest from them, but I held no expectations, as it was a casual event. All in all, I was grateful to the couple who affirmed me by hosting the evening and to those who attended, including Dad. Later, he gave me a birthday album with black and white photos of me as a small child in the front. In the centre of the same page, Dad placed a photo of a peace rose in pale yellow with a blush of pink, emphasising my name's meaning. It pleased him to tell me the flower came from one of his hybrid tea rose bushes. Knowing Dad, these details undoubtedly came from a mix of guilt and nostalgic sentiment stirring inside of him. But that's not to say that I didn't appreciate Dad's efforts, satisfied that he'd finally created a good feeling between us.

TWENTY

Making a Wide Stride

Going back twelve months to when I'd seen Dad's dentist friend for a check-up, I decided to follow his advice and get my Year 12 certificate. I trundled back to my first high school, the appalling place where I'd received a rude awakening with a culture of underage sex, alcohol binging, and negative peer control, some of which still had an effect on me. The second time around, I was unruffled. I sensed a sociological change, as peer antics were virtually non-existent. The school had a bright new infrastructure, replacing all things drab and outdated. Maryvale High School had been renamed Kurnai College, a far cry from Mary-jail's disreputable connotations. The college had become a senior campus, espousing vision and inclusiveness. I had the impression that those attending wanted to progress, as they were there of their own volition. Endorphins cheered me on as I energetically approached the school office for an interview. A seamless process took place, and I left the grounds enrolled as a student. Rocking up on my first day, some teachers recognised me from my former school days, and this raised hostile emotions in me. Calming myself, I rationalised that they were no longer a threat, and nor was I a threat to their calling. It had the desired effect. I felt freer as teachers affably used my name and oriented me around the campus. I soon settled into class routines as I focused on attaining a certificate.

That year, Dad and I enjoyed a mostly favourable phase in our relationship. He employed me part-time and supplemented my income whenever he felt generous, helping to sustain my independent living situation. By then, I'd moved out of Barb's Churchill home and was flat sharing in Morwell. The two-bedroom place was close to the school I attended, so I walked to and from classes on a regular basis. My TAFE undertakings prepared me for the next step of returning to high school or at least gave me the confidence to tackle three subjects: English, psychology, and human development and society. I worked solidly and turned up for classes throughout the year, and in due course, the postie delivered my Year 12 certificate, issued on December 13, 1989.

Dad was my first port of call to share the news. Mistake number one! I entered his office around nine in the morning, excited to tell him that I'd passed my course. But his response was decidedly mundane. Dismissing my hurt, I figured he was thinking about his hefty workload that day. I also considered Dad to be a good aspirant to discuss future study options. After all, he had been a steady support throughout the year. Mistake number two!

Extending a wad of papers, I explained, "My first preference is an Associate Diploma of Arts in the welfare strain, and a Bachelor of Arts is my second. What do you think?"

"Don't bother applying for either of those courses! You won't get in. They are not for you. Have you thought about primary teaching?" During our conversation, Dad used an insolent and weary mutter, implying I was sapping his energy with the subject I'd brought to him. According to my learned father, I was not cut out for tertiary education. So why was I bothering him? But there was one exception: primary school teaching. It was his former field, which Dad strongly implied would require less intelligence than the other courses. I was appalled over him slighting the teaching profession, and he'd downright insulted me! Dad's unrelated suggestion seemed to be a deflection away from my interest in the social sciences, as though he felt threatened in some way.

Even though Dad's contrariness was troublesome, I persisted, asking him to reconsider my course preferences. It didn't take long for me to realise it was a waste of time.

Far from a weary mutter, Dad retorted, "Do not apply!" He spat more than said it. His rising exasperation was plain to see in his fiery face, frowning eyes, and restive legs. My year with Dad had waxed and then waned!

My pursuit for fatherly guidance turned out to be ill counsel. So I gathered up my paper pile, said goodbye, and hastened out the door, down the stairs, and into the open air. My quickened breath slowed as I leant against the Datsun Dad had given me. It was waiting in the parking area, which was vacant apart from my car, which was located just below his office window. The space, along with the weather, cradled me, though I felt none of their touch. The muggy air was still, and the temperature was neither cool nor warm. I cast my gaze towards the dull sky, hanging heavily like a sodden grey sheet on a line. The thick cloud cover wouldn't rinse the earth, nor fold away for mid-morning sun to shine through. The undetermined weather struck me as inconsequential, even unworthy of small talk amongst acquaintances. In turn, it jeered at me. The message received was that I, too, was inconsequential. I was a mere nobody with nothing to offer, thoroughly unfit for success. While reflecting on Dad's similar view, I smirked at the dreariness above my head, defying its demoralising message. Neither the weather nor the powers undergirding Dad's senseless words could shred my worth or hope for a bright future. I called on God, asking for peace to confirm if my chosen course was the right one. Or if I should not apply, I asked God to withhold peace. My prayer was hardly over when tangible warmth and comfort enwrapped me, like a heavenly embrace. My path was decided.

I woke up feeling energised. Before long, I was breakfasted, preened, and wearing something smart and figure flattering but more casual than business style. I hadn't applied for a corporate job, but I was off to impress an interview panel. I drove my Datsun to Monash University's Gippsland Campus in Churchill. From the car park,

I approached the main building and followed directions to the interview room. By the door, I nervously waited for my name to be called so the interview process could begin. When it was my turn, I shyly extended a hand in response to the lecturers who introduced themselves. The trio fostered a warm glow despite the formal classroom setting. We were seated in a semi-circle, with desks set aside to neutralise positional power, designed for tense interviewees like me. The panel asked measured questions, then intentionally paused for me to think and reply. By the end of the interview, I was congratulated on getting into the welfare course. I hailed the second round of handshakes more than the first, and with a firmer shake.

My university endeavours began in a lecture room with a preamble for new students, who came in dribs and drabs, our backsides plopping into the neatly arranged seating. The lecturers stood out the front, wearing half-smiles for our encouragement. The faculty head, a large and full-voiced woman, made introductions, then oriented us from there. During the session, it slowly dawned on me that I'd entered a higher education labyrinth. Cramming my head full of notes, I organised myself in a bid to avoid getting lost.

Dylan, a Bachelor of Arts student at the same campus, was far less daunted by the establishment and its pressures. His mentorship was invaluable, despite the fact that he was younger than me and was also beginning his first tertiary year.

At one point I asked, "Dylan, why do you get better marks than me?"

His advice was to use impressively long words and waffle on, according to what pleased each lecturer. The approach guaranteed excellent marks. While Dylan could obviously pull it off, it didn't work for me. But his humorous outlook made me laugh. Aside from amusement, my younger brother was a sounding board, levelling me through a haze of study pressure.

Dad no longer employed me, so I lived off a government student allowance. I tended to live minimally anyway, so money was hardly a problem. Regarding Dad's reaction to me gaining my first course preference, I don't remember any.

TWENTY-ONE

Reaching a Crossroads

Church youth happenings were a major part of my life. This involvement began in my teens and followed me through to young adulthood, including my two-year tertiary study period. I attended camps, conventions, music festivals, and many other activities with impassioned preaching and teaching from youth leaders. Connecting with my peers over food was part of the fun.

One classic youth group activity was late night suppers at McDonalds. While hanging out, we removed slimy gherkin slices from our burgers to decorate the ceiling, fallen pieces squelching under our shoes. In fits of laughter, our raucous group left the building, and a gross mess! Other times, our growling stomachs took us to pizzerias filled with heady oregano smells. The boys competed at one pizza shop where the owner joined in on the game, increasing spicy heat with each pizza he made for them. Their bravado provided amusement for us all. The Great Australian Ice Creamery was also a youth group destination. We ordered the kitchen sink off the menu. Our spoons plunged into a specially made sink filled with mounds of ice-cream in a jumble of colours and mouth-watering flavours, syrupy toppings, and fatty whipped cream, sprinkled with sugary confetti and granulated nuts. The frozen dessert became pure decadence on our tongues. As we left the building, my swollen stomach regretted overindulging.

I declared to my friends, "I won't be doing that again." But I inevitably did.

My sphere of youth activity included large-scale events, intimate subgroups, one-on-one bonds, and romantic interludes with the opposite sex. Away from church connections, I revelled in drinking to excess. A combination of boys and boozy escapes gave my world a softer focus, freeing me from inner angst while blithely creating an addiction leeway. I switched from saint to sinner like Stevenson's Dr Jekyll and Mr Hyde, as one boyfriend likened me. Unbeknown to him, that switch came from warring within. What to choose, or rather, who to choose — the living God or the carnal self? I had been looking for a quick fix for my hurting heart. But the lifestyle choice offered no resolution, and it was hurting my relationship with God.

Annoyingly, the God of truth picked me up on my hypocrisy. His challenge was inescapable as the message was always clear-cut. "Stop preaching, and start living it!" These words came forcefully at the college campus one day. My eyes scanned the room, convinced my fellow students had also heard it. But their unfazed faces and behaviour indicated that they hadn't. The disconcerting voice was just for me.

Another time, I sat praying in my parked car when I felt the presence of Jesus beside me. While no vision came, I heard his unswerving message. "If you love me, you will keep my commands."

"Are you saying I don't love you?" The words popped out of my mouth, but I was alone. My unseen friend sought faithfulness. We both knew that I was walking away from the commitment I'd made to him in my early teens.

Such spiritual encounters were boding me to make better life choices. The problem was that my poor choices led to a messed-up love life. I'd been unfaithful to Liam, my boyfriend at the time. He was an unassuming guy who I knew from college, where he studied engineering. I confessed to him that I'd cavorted with someone I hardly knew. Liam's face looked pained, and he called for a cool off period. He needed space to reflect on our future relationship, if we had one.

In tears, I selfishly prayed that Liam would take me back, despite an absence of guilt surrounding the wounding I'd caused him. Evidently, I was in a bad place, as it was out of character for me to be so heartless. Although quite undeserved, around three weeks later, Liam offered to take me back. He suggested that we start over, and soon after, we stayed with his family in their home. During that time, I was surreptitiously confronted by his angry younger brother, whose name is now forgotten. He told me, with teary eyes, that I wasn't worthy of Liam, and if I hurt him again, he would deal with me. Liam's brother was protecting what was his through kinship, but I didn't care. My accoster's words were minimised as I partly tuned out, angering him even more. While my fondness for Liam hadn't been love after all, I still hoped to remain in the relationship.

At that juncture, I came to a crossroad with a hardening heart and a visitation from God. A frightening combination! I had the encounter in my bedroom in the house I shared with three single women in Morwell. They were away the day I threw caution to the wind, openly sharing my love triangle with God. As if he didn't know. The situation involved Liam and a close friend, Peter, who I'd also met on campus. Both had discussed marriage with me. There was also the third entity, and that was the guy I'd used, uncertain if he was even out of the picture. I tried to free myself only to become more entangled, like a fly caught in a sticky web.

God saw my muddle and heard my plea. Our history attested to answered prayer, but he also required fidelity. The solution I sought came as an ultimatum. "Choose this day life or death, blessing or cursing!"

Upon hearing these words, my boldness in approaching the Almighty departed, transforming me into a small and terrified creature in a daunting, hallowed space. My body shook uncontrollably, unable to bear the weighty presence as it forced me to my knees, then prostrate on the floor. I lay without moving as an invisible hand held me there.

Cowering, I uttered my decision in a broken whisper. "I c-choose ... life. I c-choose ... b-blessing." I spoke these words over and over to the one who was listening. I then gave way to sobbing, my chest heavy and heaving. After an unknown period, my watercourse ceased to flow. The dreadful presence had left, along with the tremor I'd felt in my body. I relaxed on the soft carpet pile, my shock replaced with peace and calm. I pulled myself up and stood in the stillness of my room, savouring each lungful of air as I slowly breathed in and out. The formidable experience had restored me with renewed strength and sobriety. Escapism would no longer be my drawcard.

My allegiance was tested the very next day. Lazily, I got out of bed by mid-morning. My housemates were away, so I readied myself for the day in quiet solitude, which was soon interrupted by loud knocking. I dashed to the front door as the repetitive sound demanded. After opening it, my benign smile became slack-jawed as a male form filled my vision. Romeo, as I'll call him, was a blast from the past. Across his brow, a sweep of dark, layered hair drew attention to eyes glittering with desire. A smile played on his lips. Feeling weak and confused, I didn't know what to do. Should I take his hand and lead him in or slam the door in his face? In my quandary, I questioned if God was testing me or if this was the Devil's lure.

Romeo's tight-fitting jeans swaggered in with the rest of him. His firm body brushed against mine, so I stepped aside. My bated breath was alerting me too, lest temptation have its way there and then. Romeo followed me like an adorable puppy, smoothly proposing that we get together. I applied a sisterly smile, acting as if he wasn't leading me on. *He's a friend calling by for a cuppa*, I dishonestly told myself, and I promptly put the kettle on. I asked him to wait for me in the kitchen, as I wouldn't be long. Then I headed towards my bedroom.

Like a disobedient puppy, Romeo's pattering feet trailed mine. In my room, he sidled up to me as I wielded a mascara wand. He told me that I didn't need makeup, as I was pretty enough. I turned away from the mirror and towards my seducer, displeased over his fawning words and close proximity. No longer weak in the knees, I declared there'd be no flirting or sex. Nothing was going to happen between us, not now and not ever.

"You need to leave!" I ended my spiel. At that instant, I drove Romeo out of my bedroom and towards the front door. His large eyes locked on mine as we walked, but I refused his imploring look. He was not my devoted pet. Shooing him out of the house, I closed and locked the door, pressing my weight against the solid wood boundary. I strained to hear footsteps fading into the distance. Then nothing. The only sound was a great sigh escaping my mouth.

Shutting the door meant shutting out an unwanted part of my life, never to be revisited. I then set about making and breaking bonds in an effort to sort out my relationships. I entered through the right door with Peter, the man who became my love interest and who still is.

TWENTY-TWO

Life Lessons for a Sister

One unchanging bond was with my younger brother, Dylan. We shared an affinity and always will. Our relationship contrasted with the emotional dealings I had with Owen. Dylan treated me with dignity. In the early years, I found Dylan to be delightful entertainment, with his blonde, corkscrew curls and bucket loads of innocent charm. He was a constant part of Owen's and my childish quests: roleplays and dress-ups in the shrubby yards of our childhood homes. Aside from our youngster escapades, I kept Dylan in the background to some degree. I venerated Owen as the older and more astute brother. With time, I discerned that Owen was not godlike after all. I also became aware that I'd underestimated my younger brother, noticing his healthy self-determination and heart of faith, steady under Dad's trialling. Dylan had provided valuable lessons for me, specifically relating to our father, though he wouldn't have known it. It's a shame I was impervious to them at the time.

On January 18, 1997, I attended Dylan and Lisa's wedding with Mum and Barry. We travelled part of the way together, arriving the day before at the coastal city of Coffs Harbour, New South Wales. The wedding was held at the Christian Life Centre, a warehouse church, with an ample and comfortable interior. I initially sat with Mum and Barry in the building's extensive seating. While waiting, I became a rubberneck, turning to observe pre-ceremony shifting, settling, and murmuring. All and sundry anticipated the bride's coming. I also scanned the building for Dad and Marion, his latest partner.

I had time to see Dylan. Making my way down the aisle, I veered right towards the groom, where he stood by the sanctified podium. Dylan was appealingly tall and smartly suited, stirring a sense of sisterly pride in me. His familiar sandy curls were tied back, revealing a hale face and enlivened hazel eyes mixed with flecks of blue. I complimented Dylan on his handsomeness, then launched into a question. "Are Dad and Marion coming?" I seemed to forget that Dylan's bride was his main focus, not Dad. Thankfully, Dylan was patient with me. He was also patient with our father. Dylan knew nothing of his attendance, and he hadn't contributed towards the wedding. I seethed at this information but sought to control my emotions, lest I spoil my brother's day.

Back in my seat, I fretted over Dad's lack of love and dedication. The reeling words in my head, that he was a despicable father, stopped when I saw him coming down the aisle with Marion. At least they'd arrived before the bride. With a polite smile, I approached the couple and offered to share the same seating. I was convinced that I ought to sit next to Dad but had no idea why. Behaving like a good daughter, I responded affably while inwardly holding a distinct lack of grace. I was caught up in a jumble of emotions. I felt relief for Dylan, as he'd wanted Dad at his wedding, but I was annoyed that I hadn't suspended judgement before Dad and Marion had arrived. I was also rankling over the father of the groom's poor wedding etiquette. He'd strung Dylan along, never replying to the wedding invitation, and he had denied financial provision. Our father's only commitment was turning up on the day to enjoy all the benefits. How *dare* he treat my brother that way!

During the ceremony, I thought about my amiable brother throughout his teens. He'd favoured Dad's well-meaning efforts over condemning his hurtful actions. While considering Dylan's grace back then, it became obvious that I was witnessing it again at his wedding. He expressed how delighted he was that Dad had actually turned up and graciously ignored any negative aspects. Dylan's cup was overflowing, and so it should on his special day. Unfortunately, his magnanimous attitude did not rub off on me.

I later joined guests at the reception, which took place in another part of the building. The room became an overfilled thermal space as more and more people trickled in. I squirmed on my hard, stackable chair, unable to enjoy the jubilant atmosphere. With no appetite to sample the food, I was worried sick over Mum's discomfort, knowing she shared the same room as her ex-husband. In my head, I asked, *Where is she sitting? Is she okay? Should I be with her?*

Again, I noticed Dylan, who, sensibly, wasn't taking responsibility for Mum's emotions. I should've done the same but wouldn't let go of a weight I carried for her.

Part of the way into the reception, it occurred to me that Dad might embarrass his son with a dubious speech. Sure enough, a hush fell over the crowd when the father-of-the-groom speech was announced. I cringed and began stonewalling at the sound of Dad's nervous high pitch. My intrinsic ability to listen without hearing meant blocking out everything he said. I re-joined the crowd at the sound of applause.

Dylan shared his deep appreciation to our dad's sentiments, which had been expressed through a poem. The whole time, I held contempt, secretly shamefaced, as I was unwilling to give up my negativity. After the event, I felt sorry for my refusal to apply Dylan's life lessons, especially when he'd modelled them so well. I reassured myself that there would be ample opportunity for future application, and there was.

TWENTY-THREE

Graduation Day

Rewinding the clock to November 1991, I had completed my two years of tertiary education. While I put in the effort, I also attributed my achievement to God, who had given me a clear go-ahead the day I prayed for direction in the car park. I also admitted to myself that despite Dad's earlier unsupportive and surly moment when advising me against the course, I felt no negativity coming from him while studying.

Dylan continued as a tertiary student for another year after I graduated from my course. The upcoming celebration date was scheduled for May 16, 1992. I invited Dad as a guest, hopeful that he would readily support me, as he valued further education. Nana was also invited. By then, she was a widow living in an aged care facility in Morwell. My decision to ask Dad over Mum was mostly for proximity reasons. To be sure of my decision, I confirmed with Mum that she was okay with Dad attending in her place.

On the day, I hired an academic gown that shrouded most of me in black, accompanied by a hot-pink satin stole running its path down my front, demonstrating the course I'd undertaken. Dressing for the part brought a sense of joy, especially when I saw my reflection in a full-length mirror. I assured myself it wasn't all vanity. I had earnt the look, and I should relish the occasion. The ceremonial dress's sentiment stayed with me while it covered my body.

I found the ceremony to be a rewarding experience, and time stalled pleasantly during the afterparty. With celebration drinks in our hands, Nana, Dad, and Peter accompanied me in the day's shine, savouring Churchill's sublime autumn weather. We meandered through the university's well-kept grounds, occasionally pausing, as greetings and congratulations were due.

Dad transformed into a proud father for the entire event. His face shone at mine as he planted a kiss on my cheek, then slipped a monetary gift into my hand. "Congratulations, Fleur. You've done well!" Dad's wholehearted response was, and remains, a cherished father-daughter moment.

The event also held an unexpected turn. It involved God's correction, not as a spoiler but as sage, fatherly counsel. During the formalities, the graduation speaker was introduced with a "Very Reverend" title. What followed was a superfluous overview of the religious man. For no justifiable reason, I made a character judgement. *Oh no,* I thought. *Here comes a pompous speech. Such a waste of time. What would he know?*

In that moment, I felt the jolt that comes with a rebuke. God cut through my thoughts with a clear message. "Do not judge!"

I looked around the crowded auditorium, but no one else had heard it. They didn't turn to see my blushing face. Irrespective, I slunk down in the seat as though the entire audience *had* heard God's dealings with me. I repented and modified my attitude accordingly, focusing on the speaker, who sought to inspire us graduates.

It was about six months earlier, just after finishing my course, that I'd had a similar experience. Sitting alone in my lounge room, my thoughts had become misaligned with a clear message that Dad was going to hell. I unreservedly believed the punitive words, echoes of Mum's towards her former husband. She boldly stated that John's behaviour was beyond the pale and that his stiff-necked ways cancelled out God's grace and mercy. He had sealed his own fate: hellfire! I hadn't considered that Mum's staunch belief stemmed from muddled church indoctrination, but I have ever since. Also, at the time I didn't consider that God knew of my judgement.

Then I heard his imposing voice. "Do not judge!"

Deeply sorry, I avowed never to incriminate Dad over his eternal destination again. While I kept my promise, my unfair judgement at graduation against the Very Reverend priest proved I was on a slow learning curve.

PART FOUR

"He has made everything beautiful in its time."
— Ecclesiastes 3:11 (NIV)

TWENTY-FOUR

The Heartbreak of Losing a Brother

From my late teens, I had detected something disturbingly elusive about Owen. He was progressively moving away from my reach, but when we visited, I noticed bouts of extreme introversion and eerily vacant eyes, as if his soul had fled. I mulled over viable reasons why. Dark melancholy moods, drug and alcohol abuse, a lack of healthful living, or even the effect of dabbling in the occult. Whatever it was it persisted and culminated to a point of despair. Owen disappeared without a trace.

By the time my brother had disappeared, when he was in his mid-twenties, I had moved past the offences he had committed by setting me up with Rayleen for sexual relations as a primary school kid and past his sexual interference in my early teens. Or so I thought. While writing about these experiences, more recently, it hit me that I'd endured Owen's offences and then hastily dismissed them at the time. While processing it all, I felt fragments of hurt coming to the surface, and tears flowed from my depths as I forgave him. Once my tears dried up, I was free of the deep distress that had been repressed for so long. The only sadness I felt was that my pardoning can never be shared with Owen, who I have always loved, as he is forever out of reach. It seems that my act of forgiveness was for my wholeness, not his.

Another secret sorrow caused by Owen started from my middle childhood, as from a sister's nearness, I encountered his instabilities. One regular afternoon, I ran upstairs to wash my hands at the bathroom sink. My peripheral vision glimpsed a naked body. "Oh, sorry, Owen," I said genuinely. "I didn't know you were in the bath."

Since he didn't reply, I turned my head towards him. Owen was fully submerged, so he wouldn't have heard my voice. It then occurred to me that there had been no splashing sounds when I entered the bathroom.

How long has he been under? With that question in mind, I edged closer to the rim of the bathtub. Owen's body listlessly rested beneath the smooth, clear water. His unblinking eyes were fixed in a creepy, detached stare. Was he unconscious, or had he drowned? The fluster I felt motivated action. I called Owen's name repeatedly, struggling to pull him up and out of the water. It was hopeless. Owen's head remained below the water's surface as my immersed hands slid off his smooth skin.

With no time to lose, I raced down the stairs. Huffing and puffing, I yelled, "Mum! Mum, it's Owen. I don't know what's wrong. He … He's in the bath. He's underwater!"

We sprinted upstairs and into the bathroom, where my brother lingered under the water. Neither his body nor his expression had altered. My panic increased, addling my mind and bringing a rush of energy. I abandoned my duty of care once Mum stepped in. Turning away from Owen's comatose body, I began toing and froing the length of the bathroom.

"Owen! Owen! Are you okay?" Mum urgently called, heaving his torso forward. Tepid water splashed into the air and onto the floor, soaking Mum's clothes and splashing onto me. Owen's chest expanded as he took an instinctive gasp of air. The sight and sound was a massive relief for us all.

I left the room for Mum to attend her disoriented son. Surely, I had defied time. The seconds seemed like minutes, and the minutes resembled hours. *What was wrong, why hadn't Owen responded earlier? Would he have drowned if I hadn't been there?* While these questions ran through my mind, I didn't want answers. I was a child and was shaken by the ordeal. My big brother was alive, and that was all that mattered.

On another day, I was alerted to Owen's concerning behaviour. It occurred after he'd returned home from a youth camp. During his absence, our family cat, Marmalade, was struck down by a car. I was the unfortunate witness who passed the news on to my family. Dylan and I shared in our loss for the remaining day. A short while after the accident, I watched our dad dutifully cart Marmalade's body to the backyard, depositing it in a freshly dug hole.

While he wore a long face, Mum was far too matter-of-fact about the casualty. "Good fertiliser for the trees," she said unfeelingly. She upset my childish sensitivities, producing a sense of repulsion and bringing more tears to my eyes.

When Owen returned home, he was told the bad news. By then, Dylan and I had worked through our feelings, having accepted Marmalade's fate. Our brother's reaction proved to be entirely different. When I saw his aggrieved eyes, I oscillated between sisterly consolation and giving him space. Neither approach ministered to him, as he was impassive and refused to be comforted. For many days, I observed Owen's withdrawal. It was beyond what I expected of childhood woes. I had unwittingly witnessed a precursor into my brother's future.

It is my firm belief that Owen had a pre-disposition to depression, which was not clinically assessed or treated. The closest evidence I can find is through an investigative report, authorised by the Coroner's Court of Victoria, November 16, 2015. It proposes that Owen plausibly suffered from depression before he disappeared.

"It would appear that Owen has fallen into a depression in late 1990 and early 1991 …"

Another belief I have, poignant as it is, is that Dad contributed to Owen's depressive moods and his subsequent disappearance.

As an adult, Mum told me of an incident when Owen was two years old. At the family dinner table, Dad lost his temper and threw a cup at his toddler's face, causing him to suffer from a swollen black eye. This shocked me, as I have no recollections of Dad physically lashing out at Owen, Dylan, or me, only against our mother. Even so, we were all significantly impacted by family dysfunction. This was discovered when we confided in each other at various times as young adults.

In a rare conversation with Owen in 1990, he exposed deep distress over his fractured father-son relationship. At the time, he was living in Brunswick, an inner-city suburb, while I lived in Morwell during my second year of tertiary study. He shared his struggle about eight months before ebbing away from loved ones. Lamentably, I missed the forewarning over his runaway intentions. Our conversation occurred late one night when we boarded a metro train. We were heading back to his shared house, where I stayed overnight. Although I don't recall where we'd been, I remember our mouths puffing out fog while walking briskly in Melbourne's midwinter air. During the train ride, we warmed up and found our sea legs as the carriage jerked and swayed. We chose to stand for the entire trip. Through the windows, I stared at rushing rainbow-like flashes against nocturnal blackness.

After a while, the relentless bright and dark bothered my eyes, so I turned my attention to Owen. The well-lit carriage offered us a private space, as it was virtually empty. Owen's worn satchel hung from his side, grabbing my interest. I felt privileged as he reached into the secreted space, retrieving three or four sketches to show me. The pages were intricately inked in blue or perhaps black. For the artist, they resembled meaning. For me, each abstract piece was indecipherable, so he interpreted them.

Owen's last sketch revealed his bereft state. "That's the father," he explained as his finger pointed out a disquieting figure on the page, the cause of his inexorable pain. "And that's the son's foot walking out the door because his father rejected him."

Owen's words were lucid, but his hurting heart was on display. His darkly obscure eyes gave it away. My heaviness of heart held a greater intensity than our earlier days, when he was beset by depression. Everything in me wanted to grab Owen's jacket, pull him close, and never let him go. Instead, I kept my hands and body to myself, my eyes blinking back tears of resignation. I'd discerned that Owen's path was bleak, as he was heading towards greater depths of isolation. Owen was lost. I couldn't redeem him because I didn't know how. That night revealed my brother was going astray, but I didn't twig that he would literally leave. If it was our last meeting, then it would have been a doleful parting. Thankfully, it wasn't. We had another night together, with two others who Owen loved. I shared a pleasing and untethered goodbye, not that I knew it would be my last time in Owen's presence. Nor did I know that I'd hear his voice once and for all in February, 1991.

One afternoon, later in the year 1990, I stood in Dad's Morwell office. With gush, he complimented me in front of his client. "You look nice. Doesn't Fleur look pretty?"

The slightest blush tinged my cheeks as Dad's approving client nodded and reflected his open smile. I pocketed

Dad's compliment as a feel-good memento. Why I made a quick pit stop to see him, I can't recall, but the good vibe between us stayed in my mind. It was before I headed towards Melbourne's cityscape. I'd arranged to meet up with my brothers and Julia, Owen's wife, who I'd met only a few times. Their marriage, which I wasn't initially aware of, was an unconventional one, as they resided in separate homes in Melbourne.

The street-lit metropolis took us to St Kilda's foreshore. Owen suggested that we make Luna Park our destination, and we all agreed. Youthful liveliness attended our footfalls and chatter, reverberating through the streets. As we approached Mr Moon's haunting face, his piercing eyes and toothy gape, he forebade our entry through his mouth and into the looming fairground. No razzle-dazzle could be seen or heard. The place resembled an eerie ghost town. We treated the theme park closure as a minor setback, for the night was still young, and we were free to do as we pleased. For me, it was being together that mattered more than doing things. The streets were remarkably unfilled, so we raised our voices and spread ourselves out, advancing across the paved space as though we owned it. The coolish coastline breeze added to our sense of freedom. Coincidentally, we siblings all wore something red. Julia captured the vibrant hue with our images on film. The photo shows us standing against a glass shopfront, my girly appearance happily sandwiched between my brothers. Dylan's height contrasted with my shortness, while his features showed a family resemblance between us. On my other side, Owen leaned his head of long, wavy hair towards mine. With a hand in his pocket, his demeanour appeared to be cool and confident. The photo is a firm favourite for Dylan and me as a precious memory of our sibling trio. I'm stirred with equal joy and sorrow each time I see it. Owen's image was later extracted from the photograph. The Victoria Police used it for an ageing approximation profile for media release and for subsequent investigations carried out through a nation-wide media campaign.

An official report compiled by the Coroner's Court of Victoria, dated November 16, 2015, states that Owen was last seen on February 21, 1991, at 10am. He was likely seen at his shared Brunswick house by his housemate, Ryden. The same document asserts that police were notified of Owen's disappearance two months later when Julia made a statement at the Brunswick Police Station. The coroner also supports this, declaring that April 26, 1991, was when the report was made and that Owen probably died around that time.

Julia, who I recently reconnected with for the first time in thirty years, shared her memories and diary entries from around the time Owen disappeared. Julia's recollection and diary notes disagree with the timing of when she notified the Brunswick police, as stated in their reports. Julia claims February 21, 1991, was more than likely the date when she and Ryden went to the Brunswick Police Station, not the date when Owen was last seen. Julia recounted that Ryden made a point of contacting her, as he was worried that Owen had been absent from the house for about a week prior to that day.

After reporting Owen's disappearance, many weeks passed, and Julia heard nothing from Owen or the police, so out of concern, she contacted her father-in-law. It was not the first time that Julia had contacted him about Owen's mysterious absence, having asked much earlier on if he had seen or heard from his son. Dad had not and regarded his absence as unsurprising, Owen being a free-spirited young man. The next time Julia contacted Dad, he and Dylan immediately went to the Victorian Police missing persons unit in St Kilda, where they reported Owen as a missing person. This kickstarted an official police investigation.

Likewise, I believe the coroner's timeline is incorrect. I am convinced that Julia, who cared for her husband despite their tumultuous relationship, would not have allowed the time lapse between his disappearance and notifying the police. According to Julia, the police officers attending to her at the Brunswick station treated her rudely and did not take Owen's missing person scenario seriously. Julia was doubtful that inquiries were carried out at that point in time. I find it vexing to think that the police attending Julia disregarded the urgency of her missing husband's case. Well after enquiries took place, the coroner recognised the effect of negligible police investigations from the start.

"It is unfortunate that the completeness and accuracy of evidence before me was impacted by the deficiencies in the early investigation of Mr Redman's disappearance."

The coroner went on to mention inadequate "policing standards and technology at the time …"

In 2005, ten years before the coroner's finding and fourteen years after Owen's disappearance, his missing person's case was reopened. It was then that Victoria Police detectives interviewed family members, our statements providing no new information about his set of circumstances. If only these interviews had been conducted in early 1991, they may well have aided opportune police investigations. As for my parents, Julia said they showed little concern when their son first disappeared and later refused to provide DNA samples, viably contributing to police inaction.

There *was* a need for immediate action. When Owen vanished, he did not front for work or collect wages owing to him. Owen had also left personal items in his bedroom, including all his clothing except for those on his back and a contact lens cleaner, which he always took with him for a night away. These particulars are documented in the coroner's report. The same report presumes Owen's depressive state led to suicide as a probable ending, though his body was never recovered, supported by police checks verifying no proof of life indicators.

On November 16, 2015, a detective rang me with a final verdict from the Coroner's Court of Victoria. "The coroner has declared that Owen is dead." It wasn't until the time of my writing, in December 2021, that I gained a copy of the written coronial findings. I slowly read that

Owen was deceased. The meaning of the words I heard and later read was hard to grasp.

Dylan and Dad took measures to find Owen through the media. I commend them, especially Dylan for his tireless efforts over the years. But while I acclaim Dad, I have wondered about his drive to find his oldest child. If Owen was found, would he know how to reach out? My scepticism has some basis, as Dad was ignorant to Owen's distress over their relationship. Dad's words indicate this in the coroner's report, which reads, "Owen is a very quiet person who never really shared his feelings or spoke about them."

Despondently, I realise again that Dad was ill-equipped in supporting his own family. Owen desperately needed to share his struggles and find real solutions, but he was unsupported. He slunk away to who knows where, carrying the weight of a father's rejection.

TWENTY-FIVE

Significant Celebrations and Dad's Indifference

My police statement, made on July 15, 2005, touches on a late insight into Owen's decision to leave.

"Looking back now, it seems obvious that one day, he would disappear. I think I got that indication when he wouldn't give me an answer about coming to my wedding. I just knew he wasn't going to attend."

If I remember correctly, Owen and I spoke on Tuesday, February 12, 1991. It was eleven days before my engagement celebration on Saturday, February 23, 1991. I kept an engagement invitation, proving this date. The party was organised for the last weekend in February so I could focus on study, soon to commence for that year. I'd rung because Owen hadn't RSVP'd to my invitation, sent two weeks earlier. My follow-up call began. "Hello, Owen. Did you get my invitation in the mail? Are you coming?"

I heard a few imprecise words in reply, giving me the gist that he'd received the invite, but he said nothing about attending. I waited impatiently, Owen's long pause causing me to press him for an answer. He said nothing, giving me no indication as to whether he would attend.

At that point, I moved onto the more significant nuptials. "At least come to my wedding. It's important to me. You're my brother."

As I waited for a response, forced, breathy laughter filled my ear. I ignored it, returning to the wedding topic, only to hear more of Owen's strange, joyless laughter. I didn't try to make sense of what was happening. I continued to pretend that everything was fine, mentioning my wedding for a third time. My nonchalance did nothing. Fake laughter again filtered through the line, low and throaty and for a longer period.

Feeling quite shaken, I fidgeted with the telephone's spiral cable, then decided to conclude the call. My final words were, "I hope you come. I love you, Owen. Goodbye." I lingered by the phone, thinking about Owen's off-kilter responses. I was baffled over his loss for words, disturbing laughter, and inability to commit. Little did I know, from that moment onwards, our brother-sister connection was lost.

Soon, I received the startling news from Dylan. "Owen is missing." No one had seen him for a week. Julia had reported it, and the police were involved. These were the only words I took in, along with the panic in Dylan's voice, putting me in a kind of limbo, suspense over Owen's whereabouts.

The rest of my year was both wistful and heart-warming. Owen's disappearance troubled me, while I was delighted as a bride to be.

Back before I telephoned Owen, my fiancé, Peter, and I had been planning a trip around Victoria. It was late January when we met with two sets of parents in their homes to announce our news, which was well received. And then there was Dad.

Peter and I fronted up to his Morwell home by nightfall. Pulling the old wooden fly screen towards me, I listened to it click open, my rapping on the main door, then the fly screen thump shut. I stepped back to join Peter and waited. No answer came, so I knocked again, and we waited. I pressed my ear to the door, straining to hear creaking floorboards, but I heard nothing. We walked around the front yard, searching for signs of life. The home's timber walls screamed that nobody was home, while darkened windows glared in agreement. We left with misgivings about the owner, who I'd previously written to and rung to confirm our visit.

Peter and I had discussed the likelihood of my dad deserting his place to avoid us and our news. Our suspicions were confirmed soon enough. Dylan relayed that our father had made a beeline out of town because he knew we were coming, adding that he looked very pleased with himself over the successful escape.

"That sounds like Dad!" I remarked, feeling annoyed and embarrassed on his behalf. Why couldn't he behave like a loving father or at least a mature adult? Coward! I'd seen Dad sidestepping confrontation since my adolescence. Wait. Did my engagement confront him, and if so, why?

Over a week later, my fiancé and I were back at Dad's front door, not caring that he didn't want to see us or hear what he already knew. Peter and I turned up when he least expected us.

As far as I could see through obscuring flywire, we were met with a distrustful look. Dad flatly asked what we wanted, as though we were a pair of hawkers canvassing unwanted wares.

Peter steadied his bearing to announce our engagement.

Through the gauzy screen, I made out Dad's indifferent expression, which came with a posture change, keeping us at bay.

On the front verandah, I leant on Peter's chest to shelter from the growing chill and Dad's iciness. All the while, I marvelled at the peculiar, self-protecting man standing in the entryway behind the timber screen. Were we a threat to his home-based threshold, an archetypal entry to his diffident heart?

As Dad's unsociability turned into an irate address, he included colourful words for effect. My mind was in a twizzle, questioning if Peter's neglect to request my father's permission to marry me had broken a cardinal rule. If so, since when had the tradition come into our family? Had it been introduced there and then? As far as I understood, Dad expressed his love for me through limited endeavours. But I didn't possess a daddy's little princess epitome, unless I was dearer to my father than I'd realised. Perhaps he feared losing the only daughter he possessed, uniquely bonded through bloodline. Did depth exist between us after all? If any of this was true, was it so vexing to concede his difficulty in letting me go? But it wasn't too late for my fiancé and me to receive a father's blessing. I wanted to talk amicably.

Dad didn't. He hardly stopped to draw breath, ranting and raving like an unreasonable drunk, guarding his house and heart.

Still turned in a partial hug, Peter and I stood slightly back from the doorway. We were silently bemused, for we had simply come to share our good news.

I worked through a to-do list for the upcoming celebration, counting in Dad's invitation despite his disapproval of my engagement. As time passed, I edgily waited for Dad's reply. His decline came on the verge of the party date. Apparently, he had another commitment. I saw straight through the smokescreen, though it came stingingly to my eyes. Hmmm. what could be more pressing than his daughter's betrothal? Perhaps his commitment came with a royal invitation from Her Majesty, Queen Elizabeth. Given Mr John Redman's outstanding community service, his name might have been placed on an exclusive list, invited to attend one of Her Majesty's illustrious garden parties at Buckingham Palace! Ludicrous as this may sound, it was not beyond my father to invent a contingency plan just to avoid me. *Aargh!* Why wouldn't Dad support me and my fiancé at this significant event? It was only reasonable that I should demand an answer. But I couldn't bring up the matter, as I was fearful of another harsh comeback.

Quite unpredictably, Dad offered me a minor consolation at his office one day. His slight smile came with an engagement present and a card in a sealed envelope.

Feeling somewhat encouraged, I also a managed a smile. "Thank you, Dad. I'll open it with Peter later on," I said.

My fiancé and I met at my place, where he urged me to open the gift, as it was from my dad. With shaky hands, I tore away the paper, revealing a box holding a pair of highly polished pewter goblets, marked with Selmark's quality brand. I relaxed as the charming, timeless keepsake filled me with content. These were a token of Dad's love. I was cradling a false notion, as I unhappily discovered soon after. The congratulatory card depicted red wine glasses and a single red rose, along with printed well wishes in the same romantic colour. Everything was so perfect until I realised the connotation behind Dad's rushed penmanship. In black ballpoint, he wrote:

To Fleur and Peter,

From Marion and Dad. Nobless Obige.

Dad's cryptic message was, in fact, a misspelling of the French expression, "*noblesse oblige.*" The words signified a generous obligation from someone of nobility. While it appeared that Dad was flattering himself, "nobless" more likely referred to his paternal position. The other part of his message was what stung me. His gift giving came not from love but from self-expectation as a dutiful responsibility. "Obige."

"Dad gifted us out of obligation!" I exclaimed. The card, I noted, excluded the words "dear" and "love," and Dad had placed his partner's name before his own. These impersonal details devalued any good intentions. Thankfully, Dad omitted Xs and Os, as his kisses and hugs would have been unbearable! If Dad's curt communication was expounded on, it may have been written this way:

> *To Fleur and Peter,*
>
> *As your magnanimous father, I am dutifully providing you with this gift and card. I have no intention of offering love or support, as actioned by my non-attendance at your engagement party.*
>
> *From Marion and Dad*
>
> *P.S. I trust this takes away your joy, as intended.*

Of course, being this transparent wasn't Dad's typical communication style. Perhaps he was trying to soften the blow. Even so, his words and their meaning did strip away my joy but only for a short while. In spite of Dad, and Owen's mysterious disappearance, I was determined to hold onto what I knew should be mine: happiness. After all, I was celebrating my betrothal to the man I loved.

My engagement spanned most of the year. I was overstretched with study while arranging the fine points of all things wedding. My mother pretty much paid for the whole affair, and out of respect, I chose modest wedding merriment. The family I was marrying into offered ample support, from the engagement through to the big event. During the planning phase, Dad's disinterest came to our attention, and my future parents-in-law, understandably, queried his position. I talked with Dad about a dinner date, as Peter's parents were keen to meet him and Marion. His openness to the idea surprised me, especially when he followed through with a table booking at Gastronomy, his favourite restaurant. Dad generously paid for all our meals. It was his way of feeling in control.

Quite reasonable, I thought, though I was not. I failed to check in on my unhealthy need for control, putting the evening's plan to the test. From our moment of greeting, I didn't settle, bringing tensions to the table. Marion and Dad picked up on my argumentative tone. Thankfully, my fiancé's parents were amiable. They steered the conversation towards wedding details, like seating. Dad showed interest, while I stubbornly remained pithy and guarded. Afterwards, I seriously hoped that others had redeemed the situation. At first, it was hard to forecast Dad's final decision.

Over the months, I made intermittent phone calls to Dad, mentioning my upcoming wedding, which was planned for December 21, 1991. I tried to broach matters a bride to be should not have to stress over. They were specifically around his willingness to contribute financially and if he would like to give me away on the day.

My attempts were interjected every time. It was Dad's ploy to avoid answering what he didn't hear, as he'd anticipated what I'd say. My wily father was a master of deflection, and he used it frequently. "You are very selfish, Fleur. All you talk about is your wedding. Don't you care that Owen has gone missing. How can you be so self-centred?"

I persevered with the aim of winning him over, but Dad continued to show no interest in the marriage ceremony or the reception.

I finally relented when Peter advised me to drop the matter. "You've done all you can, and now John can make up his own mind." My fiancé's counsel came from watching me deal with Dad's disobliging ways. He was looking out for my best interests.

While making up a wedding guest list, I somehow found the grace to include my apathetic parent. Over a few weeks, I repeatedly asked Mum if she'd received his reply. Dad's response came as the very last one.

"I'm sorry, Fleur," Mum said. As she handed over his decline, her hazel eyes softened with sympathy.

While the urge to cry was overwhelming, I took a deep breath to force away the feeling. I was mindful that Mum, Barry, and Peter watched me from nearby.

Inside the card, Dad's writing was evenly spaced and courteously written.

> *Thank you for your kind invitation, but Mr John Redman and friend are unable to attend the marriage of Fleur to Peter.*

It ended with Dad's signed initials. I returned to the front image, as I had initially overlooked it. The picture was a reprint of the nineteenth century oil painting *Portrait of My Cousin*. It featured a rosy-cheeked woman in a pink, flowing gown, radiating youthfulness and romanticism. It was typical of Dad's card preferences, and I found them appealing. I looked at the young woman imaginably dressed for perhaps a wedding occasion. My father was a man tinged by romanticism. So why did he refrain from his girl's special day?

As though Dad knew my thoughts, his decline was explained a day later, discovered through a hand-delivered post-card in my letterbox. It featured a Victorian-style image of a winged cherub clasping the letter "F," adorned with a gilded edge and winding stems of delicate blue forget-me-nots. Dad's postcard image suggested nostalgia, as he'd chosen the initial of the name he'd given me. On the reverse side, his scrawl was more hurried than on the wedding decline:

Dec. 1991

Fleur, I would have loved to have come to your wedding, but in the interests of the integrity and unity of the event, I prefer not. My and mine philosophies differ so much that it is better to stand back and let be. If you love someone, then you have to let them be free. Love, Dad.

It appears that Dad used an abridged version of Douglas Horton's quote, "If you love something, let it go free.

If it doesn't come back, you never had it. If it comes back, love it forever." I write this because I would have always come back to my father, then and in the future, not just to create a sense of nostalgia and romanticism but genuinely for us as kin.

While my father no longer supported legal matrimony, or "unity," as he put it, I still felt cheated. Confusingly, Dad attended Dylan's wedding in 1997, six years after mine. Was this decision just another discrepancy, or had his philosophy changed by then? Or perhaps he discriminated against me for some other reason? To my mind, the man who begot me refused to take up his calling as a father. He disregarded his daughter's wedding, treating our affiliation with contempt!

Since Dad attested he wasn't up for the father-of-the-bride role, I sought an alternative. It had to be someone dependable and someone who truly loved me. My stepfather, Barry, was that someone. His broad smile and chuffed manner showed delight and honour in being asked to escort me down the aisle. My emotional inclination was to ask Barry early in the piece. But I chose to follow my conviction that a biological father should be preferred out of respect. It was a chance for Dad to fill his rightful role, regardless of our fitful relationship. I had also hoped that Dad's resistance would melt away and that he would embrace the occasion with tenderness. Dismally, it wasn't in him.

On the upside, Dad's absence at my wedding meant I was unconcerned for Mum's well-being, knowing his character repelled her. When it came to the speeches, my uncle and father-in-law each put something together. Their thoughtful words were very much appreciated. Yet the rousing inside of me didn't come from their speeches, rather a yearning for adoring father-of-the-bride reflections that would never be.

Dad's jilting responses to my engagement and wedding occasions still resonate with sadness today. But that does not mean he's unforgiven. My feelings of resentment faded away once I forgave him, which came before the marriage date. It released me to take pleasure in bridal niceties, shining throughout the day. I'll never renege on my decision, as I believe in the power of forgiveness. One positive side effect was my desire to show decency towards Dad by way of inclusion. He was on my mind when the professional wedding photos arrived. I settled on a couple shot, framed it, and wrapped it in tissue paper. Next, I brandished a knife, slicing away a generous chunk of wedding cake. I sealed its aromatic scent of sugar, spice, and rich fruit in plastic wrap. The goods were delivered to Dad's work location in Morwell, the same town where I lived with my new husband.

I climbed the stairs up to Dad's rented workspace, hugging the fruit-laden slab and fragile package. Choosing the element of surprise, I burst into the reception room, where Dad happened to be standing. "This is for you. A wedding photo and a portion of cake."

He took the offering without words.

I farewelled him and promptly walked back out the door. An indelible image went with me: Dad's retiring face and static pose as he held the gifts I'd handed over.

It should be mentioned that Dad met Peter before our engagement. I was housesitting for a couple in Morwell when Dad arrived early one evening. He'd come to take me out on my twenty-first birthday. Peter was a friend who happened to be visiting me, and so I introduced them. Dad and I were soon buckled up in the car and ready to go, but he sat quietly for a moment as concern crept across his face.

"Don't get involved with that man," he advised. "He has mental health problems."

I felt heat in my face with rising indignation, but I resisted it, as I wanted to enjoy our evening. Exactly how Dad came to that conclusion, I'll never know. If he was sceptical of our long-term relationship, he needn't have been. Our marriage has proven to be a momentous effort, with over thirty years of devotion.

Something I never told Dad was that I prayed for a husband at his hobby farm one summer. If Dad knew, I'm sure he'd have rolled his eyes with weary cynicism. I was between seventeen and eighteen at the time. It had been a hot day, and by evening, I finally found relief between cool, cotton sheets on the mattress in the spare room. There, I rattled off a husband list, then an unrelated request that the possum-sized rats scurrying in the walls and ceiling would stay away, which they did. Incredibly, my husband particulars also came as requested, from his faithfulness to his dark head of hair.

Some months after the wedding, Dad must've reconsidered his new son-in-law. He planned to see Peter and I on his way to a psychology conference. The night Dad visited us, it went effortlessly well. Then, in true Aussie style, Peter took a friendly shoulder slap from his father-in-law.

It came with a compliment before leaving. "You're not a bad bloke," said Dad.

As I walked Dad out, his smiling eyes looked into mine, and he reaffirmed, "Peter's not such a bad bloke after all!"

He must've been speaking to himself. I was curious as to whether his words held any substance. Would he commit to a relationship with my husband and me, and with our future children? Only time would tell.

TWENTY-SIX

Ephemeral Grandparent

When Peter and I dived into parenthood, we lived in Oakey, a rural town located in south-east Queensland. Toowoomba's attractive in-land city was a thirty-minute drive away. Our firstborn was delivered at the Toowoomba Hospital. Peter marked off a significant others list as he passed on our news. The last birth announcement was left to me because it involved ringing Dad. My husband refused, uncertain if his father-in-law even cared. Dad had been on the fringe over the years when it came to family. When I made the call, Dad's congratulations were well received, and I believed he was genuine.

Around fifteen months later, I rang to let Dad know that I was expecting another baby.

His reaction sounded like rudeness to my ear. "Oops! Haha. Oops!" An uncomfortable pause followed. Dad then introduced a topic he was sure of: cricket. As far as I remember, he talked about the England verses West Indies test cricket scores from the month before. Dad prattled on as I tuned out.

Then I cut back in, revisiting my pregnancy with needless justification, using a firm tone. "I'm thirty-one, a grown woman …"

Dad ended the call soon after.

My second son also arrived at the Toowoomba Hospital. I picked up the phone to notify Dad and heard his "Congratulations!" With added pep, he asked, "Did you hear the cricket scores?"

Again, I ignored his after-the-contest commentary. It likely covered the West Indies versus South Africa test cricket match, but I can't be entirely sure. Dad knew that tests ran throughout the year, every year, and while he was an avid fan, his grandson's birth should have been incomparable.

I squirmed in my hospital bed as much as my recovering body allowed, troubled over Dad's indifference. What was blocking him from rejoicing over his new grandson and continued heritage?

Dad may have shown little interest in my pregnancies and was absent after my deliveries, but he did embrace the honoured title of Grandad, at least for a short period. When my sons arrived, Dad and I lived two states apart, so distance justified our lack of face-to-face contact. Consequently, I was thrilled when Dad travelled with Marion to work-related conferences in our northern state. They visited us in our home, giving gifts to my boys and chatting over cups of tea. We also met in Brisbane, where we traipsed around the city centre in the pleasant sunshine with children's paraphernalia in tow.

While my family were still three, we took a trip to Victoria, where Nana met her first great-grandchild. We joined Dad and Marion to see Nana in her aged care home. Her grouchiness slipped away once we walked through the automatic doors, happily escaping hospice care with its relentless fuss and bother. Nana settled into her wheelchair, all cosied up with a vibrant blanket she'd crocheted years before. We all preferred the fresh outdoors, welcoming in the sun's warm rays while breathing the crisp autumn air.

Dad's outing choice was the Morwell Centenary Rose Garden, where he tested his knowledge of rose varieties. Hybrid tea roses were familiar, favoured for their big, beautiful blooms. As we wandered through the garden, a pleasing meadow scent wafted across our path. I strolled with the pram as Peter wheeled Nana around. During our outing, I took some happy snaps, capturing my father delighting in his grandson on the outdoor seating. We were a regular family that day, like all our get-togethers with Dad and Marion.

Another time, my family of four were welcomed into Dad and Marion's two-story place at the beachside town of Inverloch. On arrival, I admired Dad's real estate, its beach position and the native garden he'd established. Later, we wandered through touristy streets at leisurely speed, licking flavoured ice-cream as feathery clouds moved across the blue expanse with the sea breeze. Dad's easy-going manner and newfound cheekiness with his grandsons resembled the characteristics of his own father, my grandad.

What kind of grandparent will Dad become as my family grows? I wondered. I needn't have, as our get-togethers ended after six or so exchanges.

By the time my second child was four months old, we packed up and moved to Kerang, a town in the northwestern region of Victoria. Catching up with Dad would be an easier feat, as the miles between us were significantly less. Also, I would rely on his benign grandparent pattern so far. But as the months passed, Dad's responsiveness was next to none. My decided reality became what felt like a disappointing unreality. Despite Dad's lack of interest and my resultant low moods, I gave him the benefit of the doubt. I wanted to believe that he would make contact at some point.

By November of 2002, I was pregnant with baby number three. I rang Dad to tell him I was expecting and then with the news of the delivery the following year. I took his congratulations as officium, according to the Latin meaning. *A sense of duty.* Dad's *noblesse oblige* gift giving didn't apply, as there was no well-wishing card, flower bunch, or a gift for our precious little one, with lots of love from Dad or Grandad. My daughter's birth was a non-event to the man enshrouded in apathy. He missed the privilege of being called Grandad and all that this implied. And yet, Dad had named himself Grandad, just like his own dad had done for my brothers and me. I was miffed by that stubborn father of mine when I recognised his decision to distance himself.

Dad may have resisted the wonders of new life and the joy of family, but his bowing out didn't mean I had to. Corresponding from my end came with a mention that my door was always open. My address and phone number were often included as a prompt. In my recent writing, I rediscovered the initial impact of Dad's withdrawal, as indicated in my police statement made in 2005. The detective who interviewed me asked pertinent questions, about negative family dynamics, for clues in regards to Owen's disappearance. My children were aged two, four, and six when the detective documented my words.

"He would never contact me," I said. "In the end, I stopped contacting him and left the ball in his court. He contacted me once. That was about a year ago."

At the time, I was disheartened and decided to step back from the relationship. I waited to see if my inattentive father would bother to make contact. Since he didn't, I chose to reach out a few months later. I sent updated photos and cards with descriptions of family progress, and I initiated telephone calls. These calls were kept to a minimum to avoid the appearance of pushiness. Even then, our exchanges were stilted. I longed for the two of us to share openly, but our volatile relationship wouldn't allow for in-depth sharing. In fairness, Dad's responses were good-natured when I rang him early on in the piece. Although he did upset me during one conversation.

"I drove past your town the other week," he told me. "I was heading off to a psychology conference in a neighbouring town. I know where you live." Dad's sprightly voice implied good vibes filled our conversation. He had no clue that he'd hurt me, making no attempt to stop by, despite his close proximity.

I entertained the thought of Dad attending a conference called 'Improving professionals' communication styles: Start with family through time and affirmation.'

Would something like this change his way of thinking? Or was Dad too academic for first principles? The sad truth is that my father never visited me and mine at our country home. He had almost two decades of opportunity to do so while he lived in Gippsland. We lived in the same state, not on different planets!

Once my daughter turned three, I felt sure that Dad should meet her. I would confront her uncaring grandparent with her presence, even if it was just once. It would be an opportunity for Dad to consider what he was missing out on. Perhaps he'd change his mind. Even so, I held low expectations.

An opportunity presented itself during the Christmas holiday season. My family were returning home from a Queensland holiday when we took a detour off the Princes Freeway. Peter parked our car and caravan opposite Dad's Morwell home and worksite, where his private practice had relocated to in the early 1990s.

Without delay, I exited the car, marching across the road and into Dad's pad. My impromptu entry startled the secretary. She was taken aback by my presence, knowing my dad, who she had worked for over a long period of time, had deliberately kept me out of his life. The look of shock on her face was comical, so I smiled broadly at her, trying to hold back a laugh. My unexpected reaction brought me some emotional relief from the tension around seeing my estranged father. After waiting a short while, I entered the consulting room. I braced myself for Dad's negative reaction, caused by my random entrance and pending request.

But there was no negativity. Dad behaved good-naturedly, even though my appearance confused him for a moment. I leaned forward, and we shared a cheek kiss.

Then Dad stood back. He looked at my face questioningly and confessed, "Oh, Fleur. I didn't recognise you!"

Had my father forgotten what I looked like? It had been five years since we'd been in each other's company.

Dad became conversational, as though nothing was amiss in our relationship.

Half-smiling, I nodded away, impatient to state my reason for being there. "I'd like you to meet your granddaughter. She's in the car," I said, signalling that we should leave through the front door.

I could not believe my eyes as Dad complied without protest, following me like an obedient child. We stopped by the open car window. Dad peered in at the small girl with honey blonde hair, her doe eyes gazing back at the conspicuous stranger.

I made a general introduction. "This is Grandad. Say hello. Everyone, say hello."

Dad gave a greeting and attempted small talk with my children. Standing beside him, I heard his higher than usual pitch and noticed his skittish body. These were signs that he was emotionally confronted. Despite Dad's nerves, he provided the connection I'd hoped for, even though it only lasted around twelve minutes. My mission may have been accomplished, but sadly, it had no reformative effect. It was just as well I'd kept my expectations low.

The years rolled by, and my family of five became six. But Dad never met his youngest grandchild, as he'd shown no interest. I'd made the call to announce her birth. I continued with my unrequited stream of mail, including updates on our newest family member. Dad's grandparent deficiency was prevalent. He had no clue about his grandkids' identities. This was very apparent when I telephoned him over the years.

Dad often asked, "How many children do you have again? Is it three, or is it four? What are their names?" These were simple facts he should have known.

During one conversation, when I was in my mid-forties, Dad revisited these questions, making it obvious that he was documenting what had been missed. "How do you spell his name? How old is he?"

Why Dad bothered was a mystery, as these details were always written in my cards and letters. Besides, he had no intention of connecting with his grandkids. This included birthday parties and Christmas celebrations. These should have been joyful grandparent times, but Dad remained uninvolved as he progressed well into his sunset years.

Dad was gifted with twenty years to create meaningful bonds with his grandchildren. Alas, no relationships were forged to make this possible. Instead, he settled on half a dozen interactions with my sons, which they don't remember. One of them vaguely recalls seeing his grandad when he stopped by our car the time he met my oldest daughter. At their grandad's passing, my children didn't pause in contemplation to honour his life, nor did they shed a single tear. How could they grieve the loss of someone they'd never known? To them, he was their mother's psychologist father who persistently ignored her, their dad, and them. He left them an empty legacy.

TWENTY-SEVEN

Emotional Cutoff

For a time, I entirely ran out of steam. Worriedly, I tussled in prayer over my lack of concern for Dad. I'd hit a brick wall. Devoid of feelings, I offered up our relationship to God, believing he'd file it away with care.

Around seven years later, renewed warmth spurred me to intercede in prayer for Dad once again. I don't know how I found the inspiration. What I do know, however, is the cause of my stalemate beforehand: the effects of emotional cutoff. From my return to Victoria in winter 2001 through to winter 2003, I believed Dad's unavailability was related to work. Then his lack of interest in my family, after my third child arrived, told me otherwise. The intractable man had kept away as an enduring choice. Recently, while writing, I tallied up the timeframe during which Dad shut me and my household out, which came to a total of seventeen years! This finished when, at eighty, he passed on from this life.

While Dad alienated himself, I can recall a few exceptions when he initiated contact. One was the 2004 telephone call I specified in my police statement, most likely when he mentioned driving past my town. Another time, Dad rang in an effort to provide solace after Mum's death. And his third phone call surprised me one year on my birthday.

It was in early May 2011 when Dad genuinely reached out, ringing me the day after Mum's funeral. My seven-year-old daughter interrupted my cheerless mood, handing me the landline receiver, saying she didn't know who it was.

Dad's voice came familiarly, though not consolingly, as I pushed down my grief. "I'm sorry to hear about your mother's death. It must be hard for you."

I politely listened to Dad, but his caring words had a stinging effect after many years of his rejection. While he appeared to support me in my time of need, privately, I was not receptive. If I'd let down my guard and sobbed inconsolably, Dad's cutoff behaviour wouldn't have changed. The conscience he had grown would drop off as soon as it had come. My distrust included immense bewilderment. Owen's grim status hadn't driven a penchant in Dad to save our relationship. I couldn't conceive how he resisted his willing daughter while separated from his long-lost son.

An extract from Dad's police statement, as mentioned in the coroner's report, has since reinforced my misgivings.

"John Redman stated that he had moved on with his life but still held a fatherly love for Owen and thinks about him now and then."

As I write, I wonder if Mum's death was a "now and then" moment that motivated Dad to make the call. Did he hold "a fatherly love" towards me? Had he "moved on," accepting my absence like Owen's?

I yearned to shout through the receiver, to heatedly challenge the man speaking so tenderly, the same man who'd caused me tremendous heartache. But I just couldn't, for my strength had gone. Besides, it would've come to nought. Dad would prematurely end the call and resume ghosting me. In the end, all I could manage was a weak "Yes. Uh-huh. Thank you for your call, Dad."

I had no doubts that my father rang with benevolent intent. But his brief attending could never meet my need nor compensate for our fragmented relationship, which he showed no desire to restore. I moped about, thinking of Dad readily assisting his clients, specifically building up family relationships. Did his paradoxical actions stem from deplorable life choices? Or were they purely unconscious? Dad would certainly have used the Johari Window method as a therapeutic tool in improving client self-awareness. The model requires others' input to reveal conscious and unconscious bias, taking away barriers that hinder healthy interactions. If only John, the proficient psychologist, was open to using the Johari model to address such issues in his personal life. Despite my distrust, or perhaps because of it, I would have willingly joined the therapy group.

A few years later, Dad made another phone call at a time when I wasn't steeped in grief. It was my birthday, and I was caught up in a mix of emotions. Birthday blessings were sunnily accepted as my day unfolded.

Then Dad's surprise call came with a chirpy "Hello, Fleur!"

Merely hearing his voice made me twitchy.

Dad described a March calendar page that he was holding. It was an image of a child set amongst a field of wildflowers. "The girl in the picture reminded me of you, and so I decided to ring to wish you a happy birthday!"

As he spoke, I calmed myself, imagining summer's lasting blooms beneath a gentle autumn sun; the unending bright and cheerful spray swayed upon an emerald sea. They were calling me, the carefree girl amongst them, to "pick us before winter's ravage." I'd fallen for Dad's romanticism, as the imagery fitted who I was, but not for long. I withdrew from my fanciful frame of mind and into a reproving one, careful he wasn't looking to rekindle our relationship.

The same day, other birthday wishes came in, and I shared Dad's spontaneity with a relative. Her take was encouraging. She said my father had taken a positive step forward in the relationship. Dad's history of snubbing me over the past decade meant I couldn't agree, but I kept this to myself. I felt, emphatically, that Dad's favour was little more than fleeting kindness. I refused to accept it.

Providentially, I came across another view. It was simple yet profound. Kind acts from the unloving are deliveries of kindness from above, though unawares. It is God's intention to bless those who are hurting, using those who are unwilling. The explanation made sense to me, having experienced God's character as full of love and grace. I accepted Dad's kind-heartedness as a validation of my worth, via God.

As much as I was encouraged that day, Dad's continual ghosting was hard to process. As we lived and breathed, we had ample opportunity for reconciliation and new beginnings. Manifestly, that was not our reality, and so my coldness remained towards Dad. Although deeply hurt, I maintained a firm belief that I was okay. Setting aside my concern for Dad allowed me to work on my self-view, discovering that I was not unlovable and that I had much to give in a relationship. This message was affirmed by those I held dear and most of all by my Heavenly Father.

Despite my feelings towards Dad, I continued to reach out. One effort I made was making an annual phone call around Christmas time. In 2014, I rang Dad on Boxing Day, coincidently the same year I received his birthday wishes. I was surprised by his upbeat mood and genuine interest in our conversation.

Since Dad seemed so relaxed, I asked, "Do you have any plans?"

"No. I'm having next week off work."

His professed availability led me to test the waters further. "I'll be staying near Inverloch next week. Would you like to meet for coffee?"

"Yes." His response came pleasantly to my ear.

The eternal optimist in me believed it. Then over the next few days, I was slightly more realistic, fluctuating between expectancy and self-caution. The neighbouring town, where my family and I stayed, was a ten-minute drive from Dad's Inverloch house. He and Marion preferred their comfortable, coastal-style home to his modest Morwell place, primarily used for work purposes. Once settled, I telephoned Dad but couldn't get through, and he didn't respond to my voice messages. Still hopeful, I considered turning up on his doorstep. The very thought gave me a thrill. Maybe I wanted to see my disaffected father balk at my surprise appearing, reinforcing a sense of entitlement. After all, I *was* his daughter.

The following morning was so lovely, bright, and unclouded that I chose to stay on Dad's nature strip. In solitary bliss, I absorbed the sun's warmth while admiring his native garden. It had grown profusely since I'd visited with Peter and our infant sons. Plants in various forms and shades clumped and sprawled over the sloping corner block, some reaching skyward. Twinging in my stomach spoilt the moment, urging me to forget the garden and knock on the front door. When it opened, I took in Dad's familiar form.

Clearly, mine came as a shock. His jaw dropped, and he blanched at the sight of me. "Fleur!" he gasped.

"Hello, Dad," I said with intentional friendliness. We kissed each other's cheeks, as was our custom, softening Dad's shock. For once, my parent wasn't remiss as he invited me in.

I declined, explaining that Peter and our kids were waiting in the car nearby. As I write this, I wonder why on earth I didn't walk right in. My family could've waited a bit longer. I asked Dad when he'd like to catch up, placing emphasis on my words. "As we agreed."

"I'm … umm … not sure where my diary is. Hold on a minute. Hold on."

Dad took off in a fluster. I guessed he'd dashed up the stairs to consult with Marion on how to handle his ostracised daughter. Dad returned soon after with sureness in his stride and a hint of cunning in his eyes. Apparently, his diary had been misplaced, so he couldn't commit. More like Dad was up to his old tricks! He'd used a diversion to quash our original plan. *Groan!*

I wanted to confront my non-committal father, whose face hardened with a tightly closed mouth, implying we were done and dusted.

Since I wasn't done with the conversation, I bravely reiterated Dad's words about his availability that week. But his jaw remained tight, and his lacklustre eyes carried a look of apathy. "How about I ring you?" I put forward. "We can make a time to meet."

"Okay," Dad muttered unconvincingly, then shut the door.

The next day, I held my mobile to my ear, trying to ignore an unsettled feeling in my gut.

But it only worsened when Dad spoke. "I'm not able to see you, as I have other engagements."

I recognised these words from the past as a rehashed lie to get him off the hook. In view of that, I didn't back down. "Can we meet at the coffee shop?"

Dad fobbed me off, deciding it was time to finish up.

"Wait. Please. Don't go, Dad," I pleaded. "The last time we saw each other was eight years ago, and even then, it was brief. Do you want to see me or not?"

Dad's harsh "No!" ended our call. It was yet another offending moment of rejection.

The optimist in me gave in, accepting defeat. My family rallied round me, but no comfort came. I was numb.

Thankfully, I was better able to process Dad's rejection the day after. I remembered the importance of keeping low expectations, as I had learned to do with Dad over the years. While I knew it was true, I still had the blues that day. My husband was there for me, as always. He caringly gave me a compensatory gift, an elegant ring I'd admired in a jewellery store earlier that week. I called it my acceptance ring, worn as a glittering symbol of love beyond my father's care. It remains a favourite piece in my jewellery collection.

As crazy as it sounds, I rang Dad on Christmas Day the following year. But it would be the last time, as he intercepted these phone calls once and for all.

At the beginning, Marion and I exchanged polite greetings, just as we always did. She then raised her voice, urging her partner to pick up the phone. "John, Fleur's on the phone!"

From what sounded like the back of the room, Dad yelled, "I'm not here!" Then he repeated himself at the same volume.

"Did you hear that?" Marion asked.

"Yes," I replied, irritated over Dad's blatant shiftiness and immaturity.

Marion was ashamed of her partner. She apologised for his unwillingness to cooperate.

It was time to grant Dad's Christmas wish by cancelling my annual greetings.

Nevertheless, I continued to send mail, forcing myself to include Marion's name with Dad's and close with "Love, Fleur." My steadfastness was exhausting, but I just couldn't give up on my fitful father. Some people in my life found this quite confounding. A relative on my husband's side drew attention to my tireless dedication. He likened me to the persistent widow in Jesus's parable about the unjust judge. I found one main difference between Jesus's story and mine; the judge relented to the widow because of her single-mindedness, while my single-mindedness was refused by my unrelenting father. Dad had made the solemn choice to cut me off. I had no idea why. Then out of the blue, he decided I should know.

TWENTY-EIGHT

Dad's Big Reveal

Being estranged from Dad over a considerable period of time meant our individual circumstances inevitably changed. Dylan hadn't been cut off, so by default, he became our unofficial go-between. Some months after Mum's death, Dylan told me Dad had been hospitalised. He'd also spoken to him about my chaplaincy work in aged care. If it weren't for my attentive brother, Dad and I would've had very little knowledge of each other's lives. That is, apart from my mail, which he may or may not have read. Through Dylan, I discovered that Dad occasionally asked after me, and I half-received it as fatherly care. The other half of me took it pessimistically, as I was still regarded from a distance. I found it baffling that it was so hard for a parent to pick up the phone and speak to his daughter.

Dylan said our dad paid particular attention to my work, mostly the implications for him. He expected me to use my chaplain title as a licence to preach. Dylan realised this when he asked Dad for permission to tell me about his hospital admission.

Dad agreed with one condition. "Tell Fleur not to preach."

Huh, I thought. *Dad feels threatened.* But I had no intention of giving a sermon. I simply wanted to ask after his health. I made the call, hoping Dad wouldn't complicate things, as he was inclined to do.

Straight off the cuff, he asserted, "Don't you dare preach!" And again. "Don't preach! I have my own philosophy, and I'll tell you what my philosophy is …"

My dear father was in a vulnerable place, so I calmly acknowledged everything he shared. Dad settled, having aired his opinions. This allowed me to ask after his health. The patient minimised his condition as a minor hitch, rectified through a routine operation. A full recovery was expected.

Dad swiftly moved our conversation in another direction. It was an astounding confession. "I've stayed away from you all these years because you remind me of your mother."

Literally struck dumb, I sat down, trying to comprehend what I'd heard. After all these years, Dad had finally admitted to abdicating from his father role and explained his reason for doing so. I silently grappled with Dad's revelation while he chattered on about nothing memorable. Our conversation ended with polite goodbyes, my only words since his big reveal. Why did nerve and speech abandon me when I needed them most? If I was able, I would've badgered him for answers. I wanted to ask: "Dad, in what ways do I remind you of Mum? And how did they force you to reject me?" I reasoned that if I knew these answers I could change my appearance, mannerisms, or whatever it was that he couldn't bear. Then my dual-self stepped in with a more convincing thought. *No. I must authentically be myself.*

After hearing Dad's lowdown, I could've kissed our affiliation goodbye. Like him, I could've moved on in my life. I could've held the view that my lousy disappointment of a father was no longer worth considering, period! So why didn't I?

A probable answer dates back to my early twenties. At the time, I was employed as a juvenile justice worker in the social welfare sector. The demographic I worked with were predominantly fifteen-to-seventeen-year-old males. All of them had committed criminal offences, some held a criminal record, and virtually all of them came from dysfunctional homes. I compiled reports for the criminal division of the Children's Court of Victoria. These reports concluded with a penalty recommendation for the magistrate. Consequently, I supervised those sentenced to serve court orders. I collaboratively worked with these young people to improve their quality of life, with the goal of decreasing re-offence.

I noticed a negligent father theme in almost all of these vulnerable lives, with issues ranging from alcoholism to violence and a lack of positive and physical presence, among other deficiencies. Many of these young men had also endured a mother's changing partners, bringing further fragmentation and instability into their lives. From infancy, negative dynamics had taken their toll. Testosterone-fuelled youths became angry and out of control. Anarchy was their way of dealing with the losses. For some of my clients, their natural fathers were distant figures, either permanently missing or haphazardly present. These broken youths confided in me as they recounted their stories. Attempts were made to salvage their father-son relationships, only to re-experience rebuff. It shattered their self-confidence and messed with their ability to maintain healthy relationships. With loads of empathy, I reached out to them in their struggle. Like these young men, I yearned for a father's connection, even in the face of rejection. I could not fob mine off.

One day in November 2017, I was doing nothing in particular when Dylan contacted me as the bearer of bad news. Dad had been admitted to the Wonthaggi Hospital, and it wasn't for a routine operation. He'd likely suffered from a minor stroke, although it was not definite at that stage. The news impelled me to travel across the Victorian state for a visit. I wore low-heeled leather boots, a dark sage wrinkle-resistant dress, and a favourite denim jacket. It was a comfortable choice for the long journey and for between-season weather. By rail, countryside with various grazing herds of animals rushed past my window. After reaching Melbourne's transport hub, I made my way to a crowded coach. The driver was soon traversing the ebb and flow of suburban traffic, while the trip was tedious for me. Again, I watched rural scenery flash past, only at a faster pace behind glass as Dylan drove his wife, Lisa, and I to our Wonthaggi destination. My fatiguing trip covered more than 400 kilometres, one way.

Knowing that time spent with Dad could be testing, we united in prayer before leaving the vehicle's innocuous bubble. Upon entering the hospital, the staff provided a warm reception and directed us to Dad's room. The three of us had agreed that I should head in last, hoping that Dylan and Lisa's presence would soften Dad's shock at seeing his distant daughter. From the corridor, I listened to greetings and general natter, waiting nervously for the right time to enter. As I lingered, no right time came, so I entered anyway.

I startled Dad, and he startled me, his wide eyes burning into mine. As I struggled to recognise the contorted face attached to an agitated being, his head lurched sideways as a snakelike hiss escaped his simpering mouth. I stared at the horrid appearance threatening me. Or was it threatened by me? I refused to be distraught or distracted, though I felt slightly unnerved. At that moment, I knew I hadn't been delusional. Even so, it was reassuring to hear Dylan's later confirmation of what occurred, having also witnessed Dad's bizarre alteration. My brother compared what he saw to Gollum's viciousness and uncanny leer. I'm guessing that I wasn't Dad's "precious," although I was the cause of his creepy change. Irrespective of what had ensued, I shifted past the distorted face and kissed the aging forehead.

In a twinkling, Dad returned. His features normalised, and my uncanny feeling dissipated.

The medic's diagnosis was unverified, as test results were pending, though a mini-stroke was still likely. Dad disagreed. I took this response as typical stubbornness. Then, on second thought, I decided to be more understanding towards the disoriented patient as he recuperated. Dad was slow to speech, but for a moment, he became lucid, boldly correcting Dylan for misusing some psychological term during their conversation, showing his true character. The remainder of our time with Dad was pretty much benign. At the end of the visit, I bypassed Dad's handshake to courteously kiss him goodbye. Our company of three moved out of the hospital and into the car for the next challenge. At least, it was challenging for me. We were to spend time with Marion, pre-arranged by Dylan, as I'd been cut out of the picture. She was not keen on me and avidly supported Dad's stance against our relationship. It made for an awkward afternoon in spite of our mutual concern for the same convalescent man.

The Wonthaggi Golf Club offered its patrons ample charm. That being said, it wasn't the picturesque grounds, quaint country décor, or pleasurable foodie experience that I was looking for. My only aim was to have a peaceful connection with Dad's beloved Marion. Achieving my purpose was hard work from the outset. From the time of our arrival, I felt Marion's cold shoulder. Her distrustful eyes darted away from mine. She turned her head in the opposite direction whenever I spoke to her and the rest of our gathering around the table. I was ignored for at least forty minutes. Whenever Dad behaved childishly, I acted as though it wasn't happening, resorting to common curtesy as I would in any other scenario. I used the same tactic with Marion that afternoon, albeit speaking to the back of her head. Marion had invited friends, an affable couple who'd arrived before Dylan, Lisa and me. Their presence eventually caused her to straighten up and acknowledge me, lest they cotton on to her snubbing.

Marion led the conversation, sharing the trials of living with John. She touched on his overachieving work ethic and the burden of his health situation. I couldn't argue with that. But as the minutes became a couple of hours of complaint, I stiffened in my chair, finally escaping to find the bathroom. It felt good to stretch and even better to get away from Marion, who wearied me. I was over her need for undivided devotion and inability to consider others around her. Marion hadn't asked after my life, lengthy trip, or my family in general. Contrastingly, I'd shown polite interest, asking what her family was doing that Christmas. Marion drew attention to her birthday, and I responded aptly with well wishes. It was not enough. I gathered through her mutterings that I'd neglected to make a concerted effort. Her snide remarks came absurdly.

I'd had no idea it was her birthday before arriving because we had no relationship. I was a replica of John's ex-wife and the marginalised daughter.

After returning home, all I thought about was Marion's need to play the victim card, her self-view as the quintessential woman in John's life and the way she considered me to be irrelevant. It all grated on me to the extreme. I had to deal with my negative thoughts and feelings, and so I resorted to goodwill. I'd bless the antagonising woman with a surprise package. It had the desired effect. All my irritation left once it disappeared into the post box. My actions also brought positivity for Marion. This was made apparent when I read her text message, forwarded from my brother.

"Dylan, when you speak to your sister would you thank her for the card and photos and birthday present, please."

Her communication was indirect, and my name was omitted, but hey, it's the thought that counts. That was my attitude at the time.

TWENTY-NINE

Mum's Death Impacts Dad

Back on the night of April 27, 2011, while I was in the second trimester of my last pregnancy, two policemen came to my door. With staid expressions, they brought the news of Mum's fatal car accident. They told me that the first responders at the scene performed cardiopulmonary resuscitation for over an hour, but she had gone.

My world reduced to slow motion through mourning, while heightened hormones upset my stomach. Yet, in the middle of it all, God's strengthening and my chaplain know-how enabled me to step up and officiate Mum's funeral. As I organised myself, I did something completely out of character. I told Dylan, "Promise me one thing, don't tell Dad about Mum's death until after the funeral. You can tell him the minute it's all over."

Dylan gave me his word and followed through as a faithful brother.

On the day, I conducted the service in Corowa, a New South Wales town where Mum had lived with Barry.

The funeral ceremony was officiated with certain ease, knowing Dad wouldn't turn up in an unknown state to unsettle me. While Dad's absence was reassuring, a few close friends and family members, including Dylan and Lisa, who attended the service, also brought a sense of reassurance.

With the officiator job behind me, I reclined in the front passenger seat of our family car. Peter drove as our kids sat quietly in the back. I was pleased to be heading home. My mobile's jingle alerted me to sit up and look at the screen, which told me it was Dylan. His message was that Dad now knew of Mum's untimely death. Dylan had called him moments ago. I assured him that because the funeral was over, the pressure was off and that there would be no negative outcome. Dad's commiserations through his well-meaning phone call the next day made me certain of this. I was mistaken.

Over a week later, my lanyard swung from side to side, legs sauntering as my pregnant body refused to pick up speed. I was moving through the corridors of my work facility when I heard my mobile's familiar tune. It was Dylan, and his tone implied that he was not happy. He conveyed the message that Dad hadn't dealt with Mum's death well. His tempestuous reaction targeted Marion, who targeted Dylan, and then it finally reached me. Apparently, I was the cause of all the turmoil, as I had asked Dylan to keep Mum's death from Dad. I ended the call with my brother, as I was working and needed time to reflect.

While reflecting, it became apparent that I had made a sound decision. Neither Dylan nor I had committed a wrongdoing, despite Dad's offence. Above all else, my decision was hinged on honouring our mother. Grand relief was evident the day her first marriage was severed, and she happily remarried to a man who esteemed her. For Mum, John's name was regarded with contempt, his brutishness lingering as a bad memory. I was certain that Mum would not have wanted him at her funeral.

My inclination to protect Mum from Dad had been strong since I was a child. So there I was, making one final effort to protect her from Dad, even after her death. With all of my assiduousness in trying to include that aloof father of mine in my life, it was the one time I was adamant that he should be excluded.

Dad's unpredictability was also why I wanted Mum's funeral details kept from him. In order to protect myself, I wouldn't take the risk of Dad turning up. Especially when considering my officiate responsibility in taking the service, my pregnancy and raw grief adding to my load. No more justification needed!

Around two months later, I was confronted again about my decision to conceal Mum's death. This time, it was through Marion when I made an unrelated phone call to Dad. I planned to invite him and Marion to an amateur theatre production involving my children. It was another avenue to connect with Dad. Since he wasn't available, I extended the invitation via Marion. She seemed to be interested, so I committed to sending an advertisement through the post.

Our chat was all very pleasant until Marion launched into something pressing on her. "Why did you prevent your father from hearing the news of your mother's death?" Her pointed question came with a spiteful tone.

When I didn't answer the question, Marion shared her concern over John's immense suffering because I had denied him his right to be told. After all, the mother of his children had passed away. She added that divorce wasn't a reason to disadvantage him. I wasn't swayed by Marion's rationale. Instead, I speculated on Dad's state of mind. Now that his former wife was dead, did past regrets come back to haunt him? Did they create a great burden of guilt? I had seen him waning under the weight of guilt before. Dylan had similarly noticed Dad's battle with negative feelings over the years.

Recently, Dylan sent a text touching on Dad's problem. "Unfortunately, he was overcome with guilt from the past."

How we detected Dad's guilt, I'm not exactly sure, but it was undoubtedly there.

Again, Marion demanded an answer to her question, as though she was my source of accountability. I refused to give a direct reply, unwilling to accept the guilt trip. "That's a conversation between Dad and me. He's welcome to talk to me any time." I candidly offered these words as a solution to Dad's apparent problem.

Marion reacted with tetchiness, stating twice, "He would never do that!" Her reaction only served to highlight

Dad's spinelessness, choosing to close his eyes to glaring, unresolved family matters.

I had observed his unwillingness to work through relationship problems over the years, starting in my adolescence. In my head, I had called him the Tin Man, from *The Wizard of Oz*, believing he had no heart. But I've since realised that he was more like the Cowardly Lion, too afraid to play his part in our family. Contrastingly, Dad would never have allowed family members the comfortable position of avoidance in the therapy room.

I became wary when Marion's irritability subsided. Her softer voice connoted sadness as she admitted John had been a negligent father and grandfather. She even apologised for his absence in our lives over the years, conceding that she didn't know why he had made that choice. Marion's sudden change of heart didn't last, as she was intent on returning to her question. I was beginning to wonder how long she'd keep the circular conversation going amid my unchanging response. It was over at last when Marion spoke out of exasperation. "You're as stubborn as your nana!" She ended the call shortly thereafter.

It seemed that my grandmother's stubborn streak had been passed down as healthy determination. If only Dad's acquired obstinacy had been directed in the same way.

My thoughts returned to my original reason for phoning. This drove me to locate the production advertisement, destined for Dad and Marion's letterbox. I didn't expect a reply or their attendance at the performance, and sure enough, they didn't come.

THIRTY

Dad's Terminal Diagnosis

In early September 2019, Dylan let me know of another health predicament regarding Dad. Cancer had been detected in his bowel area, requiring emergency surgery. This news prompted a car journey to West Gippsland, where my family and I stayed with Peter's relatives.

The next day, I travelled with Dylan to Latrobe Regional Hospital in Traralgon. During the car trip, we exchanged concerned looks, as Dad's future was uncertain. Both of us were aware that the same aggressive cancer had killed Grandad. Across the carpark's blackened tarmac, I listened to soft pounding of our rubber-soled shoes. The distance to the building's front seemed absurdly long as I strained to keep up with Dylan's long-legged stride. After entering the hospital, we faced a maze of corridors and closed doors leading into the wrong areas. Eventually, we found the correct door. There, we encountered a change of momentum as medical staff chaotically ran to and fro. I took a moment of their precious time, asking where we could find John Redman. Dylan and I followed a bustling post-operative nurse, pausing every so often to peek through cubical curtains.

Then, with a smile, she affirmed, "Here he is."

Dad was groggy, as he'd just come from the surgery table. While I was uncertain if he recognised us or if he was even up for a visit, I reassured myself that the hospital staff had approved our coming. Dylan and I let Dad know we cared, mostly with our presence because we spoke minimally. The patient sat on a raised chair in a virtual upright position. I observed his laboured breathing and pale face, which had taken a different shape. Dylan and I squeezed into the tight space, avoiding tubing and cabling in a crisscrossing jumble between apparatuses and Dad. A few minutes in, he recognised us, indicated with a subtle blink and nod of the head. I slipped my hand into Dad's, and his slight pressing put warmth between us. His affection was a rarity, but then again, *any* contact was rare. Dylan and I stayed no longer than fifteen minutes, as anything more would've been too much for the post-op patient.

Dad's road to recovery and rehabilitation meant a further stint away from his home. Follow-up care meant specialised services for cancer patients. Meanwhile, I was at home in Kerang, thinking of him. He was also in my prayers, as my lacking feelings were replaced with care and concern. I reached out to Dad, ringing the hospital over a number of days. But all my calls were put through to Dad's room, then disconnected. Two reasons came to mind. I was either accidently cut off, as the hospital lines were inundated with callers, or more realistically, Dad was avoiding me. I rang one last time, explaining to a staff member that I couldn't get through.

The woman assisting me provided a commentary of her walk to Dad's bedside, where I overheard her say, "It's your daughter, John. Would you like to speak to her?"

Although Dad wasn't speaking to me, I caught his distinct answer. "No."

The female voice needlessly apologised.

At least I'd tried.

THIRTY-ONE

A Strategic Mistake

During my recent writing, I came across a forgotten message I'd sent to Dylan in early 2019. It was the same year Dad's bowel cancer was detected, but as far as I know, he was undiagnosed at the time. The text was in reference to my upcoming fiftieth birthday in March.

"Someone asked me what I would really like, and I thought to myself, a catch-up with Dylan and Dad."

What I would've really liked never eventuated, at least not as a birthday wish. Still, my desire to connect with them both remained, despite Dad being out of my reach.

Later, when Dylan told me about Dad's diagnosis, it was apparent that we would connect that year, for as the months progressed, so did the disease. Dylan, Lisa, and I planned a visit to see our father in Morwell five days before Christmas. The day before setting off, I met with a friend in prayer. Jen and I sat in her lounge room, where our petitions centred on my time with Dad and his eternal resting place. As Jen prayed, a vision passed through my mind's eye. I saw an angel suspended in an expanse, an atmosphere within or beyond the earth's layers. The splendid being had strength of form and great stature. Birdlike wings splayed from each side with pure white feathers, singularly defined. Like the hosts I'd seen before, the angel wore a seamless tunic and was brightened by an aura. A golden sash hugged the angel's waist as a distinct feature. The image disappeared the second my friend stopped praying. Filled with faith and verve, I was convinced that the angel was appointed to carry Dad home and into the everlasting arms of the Father. Feeling ready for timely sharing, I couldn't possibly muck up God's scheduling or my delivery, could I?

Boarding the train from Kerang's railway platform, my husband and our eight-year-old daughter waved devotedly. I returned the gesture through an unembellished window frame as my transport juddered forward. The train gained momentum as I watched my loved ones rapidly disappear. I took advantage of the spare seating by spreading myself and my things out. The seat's padding was covered with a predominantly blue, irregular pattern. I guessed it was designed to hide unsightly stains, though more than a hint remained. As a traveller, I was uncurious about what had caused them. The journey was hassle-free, and I arrived almost four hours later at Melbourne's Southern Cross Station. Shaking off lethargy, I adjusted my senses to the scurrying mood and pace, moving hastily from the regional carriage to a metro train line for the next mode of travel. My use of public transport had finally come to a mechanical halt, stiff legs moving me towards the exit, where the door released. Bags swung at my torso as I stepped cautiously over the platform gap, my wheeled case clunking onto the ground. Amongst the thinning crowd, my brother's height and his adorable curls and open face stood out. He spotted me at the same time. We beamed greetings at one another.

Dylan and I were guided by Marion's text updates regarding Dad's health decline, also sharing sensitive details about her loved one. "There is nothing more they can do. He couldn't tolerate the chemo …" Clearly, she thought a great deal of her partner and willingly provided carer support, as indicated in another of her messages. "He has done so much for so many people. I can do this for him."

While I kept up my end of texting, Marion's responses dwindled to nothing. The fact that she'd been communicating with me was unusual, so I'd welcomed it. But I also understood that her priority was her partner, not providing a commentary for his daughter. That afternoon, however, I was treated with hostility and distrust from Marion. Was it the effect of relentless care for her John, his resistance over my visit, or had I simply stuffed up?

When my brother met me at the train station, I asked, "Could we meet Dad tomorrow?"

But Dylan had other plans, factoring in our visit for the same day. I was a free agent, so either day was fine. It was just that I was very much aware of God's predictive plan. He had spoken to me over the past few months, foretelling that I would share with Dad on a Saturday, and it was Friday. Also prophetically, Dad and I would meet exclusively. But it would be five of us if we met that day. I didn't understand. It hadn't occurred to me that this may not be my final meeting with Dad.

Again, I tried to persuade my brother. "Are you sure it has to be today?"

His answer was unchanged, so I dropped the matter.

Dylan picked his wife up on the way, driving us in air-conditioned comfort. Like all my travels that day, I'd avoided the disagreeable outdoor heat. Our Victorian summer had had a spate of high temperatures, soaring to around 40 degrees Celsius. The trip lasted for an hour, finishing at Dad's Morwell property. He no longer stayed in his Inverloch home, as the stairs were impractical. Dylan parked around the corner beside a few Australian native trees with twisted trunks and branches, as though cringing in the heat. The tallest one cast dappled shade on the car. As I got out, I felt an uneasiness thicken the air, beyond the oppressive weather. It was a weighty awareness that Dad lay at death's door.

Our three pairs of shoes trudged up the unkempt driveway leading to a derelict garage. Passing Dad's house on the right, we veered in that direction, through a weathered gate surrounded by lattice, then between two structures. The smaller lodge, where Dad and Marion resided, was on the left with the house on the other side, unoccupied. It was set up for Dad's work practice, used solely for that purpose over many years. We trundled up a short wooden ramp, where Dylan knocked on the flat's door, ready to announce our presence. Marion wasn't ready, and she took a while to answer. We spoke minimally and kept our voices low, and then there was a lull.

I turned to face the rear of Dad's post-war house. Rotting wooden window frames, broken guttering and spouting, and other neglect requiring maintenance was evident. Also, unsightly green mould had moved in and spread across the concrete pathway. I ruminated over a time before the granny flat had been built, just beyond my teens. It had been a glorious spring morning when Dad's roses beckoned me to meander through the garden while he was out. Pricks from rose thorns stung my fingers as I placed flower-filled vases around Dad's austere house. Surely, the roses and their delicate sweet musk would stir feelings of delight, raising his morale for the day. Or not. When he returned, we were both disheartened. Dad called me to his side, near a vase I'd embellished with various coloured roses, their pretty little heads mocking me. Dad expelled a sigh through a partly gaping mouth, and his eyes rolled upwards. His expression conjured the same sinking feeling I'd had as a girl in the principal's office, knowing I was unduly in trouble and about to endure a lecture. With a tight voice, Dad emphasised my ignorance. Clearly, I should have known that roses were picked in their late bud stage, not in full bloom! What followed was a lesson on how to cut roses, strip back their leafage, use the right water temperature when placed in a vase, and so it went on. Yes I was ignorant, but

I was also dismayed. My intended moment of happiness for us had been lost.

Now three decades on, I was back at the same property and wondering how the visit would unfold. Would Dad still consider me obtuse, deserving a lecture of sorts? And what about our last precious moments? Would they be carelessly mislaid?

Marion's voice broke through my thoughts. "Come in." Her attention was divided, as she was engrossed in a phone call.

Dylan, Lisa, and I stood uneasily in the kitchen-dining area. I took in the unappealing 1990s pink colour scheme and varnished pine, thinking that the place needed an upgrade. Immediately after, I berated myself. *It's not my place; get rid of that thought!* It was an indication of negative anticipation.

Marion said goodbye to her mobile screen, then offered us a cup of tea, which we all declined. We'd brought a token gift: treats boxed in gourmet-style packaging, for Marion rather than Dad. She casually tossed it aside, muttering, "I don't know why you bothered. He can't even eat them."

I silently told myself it was inconsequential.

Marion ushered us into the lounge room, filled with couches and a stand-alone recliner, which Dad occupied. The chair was beside covered sliding glass doors and faced a television set. It glowed and chattered for Dad's entertainment. After a kerfuffle, the box was turned off, and greetings were made to Dad as he flaccidly lay on the padded chair. His accustomed woolly hair had turned wispy thin and drained of its last bit of colour. Sunken eyes peered out from a distorted, pale face, much like the one I'd seen after his operation. Dylan later agreed that the wasting man didn't look like our father.

I bypassed Dad's extended hand, reaching over to kiss his forehead. As I did, a sickly odour invaded my nostrils, shifting to my tongue. I wanted to spit and wash away the taste in my mouth. Instead, I sipped water at the kitchen sink, but the putrid taste clung to my tongue. I wondered if cancer had an odour.

Dylan, Lisa, and I stood around our father, silently waiting for coherent words to come from his mouth. Perhaps Dad had something for us to reminisce over in the future. I was wrong.

He spoke without acumen, dishing out insults to each of us on account of our appearances. "You're getting fat!" he told me.

Dad's sheer insolence brought a flash of heat to my face, and then it dissipated.

I rejected the insult, taking it as an untruth. My clothing had recently gained wriggle room, and besides, I was comfortable in my own skin. I just hoped that Dylan and Lisa were unscathed by Dad's pathetic moment. I had seen this childishness in the Redman family many times before. It was an ugly attribute I refused to take on board. The three of us chose to overlook Dad's fault, behaving as though it never happened.

Before entering the flat, we had agreed to mutually support each other. That included uninterrupted one-on-one conversations with Dad. This was honoured. I respected Dylan's time, as he did with me, while Lisa was gracious as always. Marion, on the other hand, was not so obliging, at least towards me. She was, quite understandably, reactive when I launched into preachy mode. At the time, I didn't think it was understandable at all. It wasn't until later on during the visit that I realised my strategic mistake. I had been bent on bringing Dad into conviction by demanding he reconcile with God and me.

Marion, appalled by my insensitivity, shrieked, "You can't speak that way to a dying man!"

A fiery blaze ratcheted up from my depths, hot emotion I didn't know I'd possessed. The fury I felt was directed towards Dad, not Marion, although it sounded like it was for her. I simply wanted her out of my way. Couldn't she accept that I was there to claim a moment of candidness with my father? I was jealous for what had been lost for *so* long.

"This is my time with Dad. Don't interrupt!" I snapped.

Marion was scolded several times, and it worked for a while, as her insulting from the couch decelerated.

It allowed me to broach a heated question with Dad. "Was there ever a time when you wanted to be a grandparent? Because you weren't there!"

If my audience sensed condemnation, they were right! More sneering comments came from Marion, aghast at my inhumaneness.

I felt wholly justified, for I had not shamed, insulted, or cursed the man whose body was indeed crumbling.

Dad's mind was intact, fully aware of his abdication as a parent and grandparent. My directness was meant to bring accountability and settle our messy relationship as a final effort. Surely, Dad's imminent death justified my confrontation.

I understood Marion's angle of care through protection for her deteriorating man. I spoke for the protection of family sanctity, or at least that was what I was trying to achieve. My position proved to be pointless.

Dad answered my impassioned question with a stony "no." His single word came quietly but woundingly.

Immediately after he spoke, I was of a mind to ask Dad the same question about wanting to be a father. But I didn't. Mercifully, my dual-self strove for silence. If I'd asked and Dad's answer was another unhindered "no," it would've taken both Dylan and I down as a final callous rejection.

Concerning Dad's disinterest in being a grandparent, Marion painted an entirely different picture after he died. Her online funeral tribute depicted John Redman as an endearing grandfather, who would be "loved and missed by all his grandchildren and great-grandchildren."

Marion may have been glibly referring to her own family, but she didn't care that her statement would add insult to injury for her late partner's daughter. She knew that my children were John's only third-generation bloodline. She heard his hard-hearted reply when I asked if he wanted to be a grandparent that afternoon, and she witnessed his absence in my family's life over the long-haul.

She'd even admitted it with an apology and a token of sadness during our telephone conversation in 2011. I found it incomprehensible that Marion conveyed a strong family ethic towards her own loved ones while whitewashing who John Redman really was.

Dad's indifferent attitude towards his grandparent role, along with Marion's fabrications and willingness to support him, could've easily sprung up a root of bitterness in me. To the contrary, I fought against it with the belief that everyone has their own will and emotions to contend with before God. Besides, why let bitterness ruin my life, especially over something I cannot change?

Back in the flat, Dad's poker face released. His eyes softened and glistened with tears. "I miss my work." Dad's wavering voice expressed the loss of the nearest and dearest thing in his life.

I was overcome with an anesthetised nothingness with no comfort to offer him.

Dad treasured his profession above and beyond family. It was a choice he'd made that I'd continually found hard to fathom.

While nothing I had hotly declared moved the shell of a man facing me, I continued to rave on for some unknown reason. That is, until Marion's cackle burst into the room. In that moment, my blundering indiscretion stood out. I winced inside with embarrassment. Had I just sabotaged everything, the precious moment I'd intended?

I ended my pathetic moment. "Well, that's about all I have to say." Then I fled out the door, clearing the air for everybody. I could almost hear a chorus of hallelujahs coming from the granny flat.

Dad would've joined in with a whispery voice.

I'd forgotten about the outdoor furnace until hot acrid air rushed up my nose, flushed my cheeks, and made its way all over my body. My fury had been just as disagreeable towards Dad and Marion. I didn't mean to bring conflict into their home. I wanted to have a real conversation for the first and last time with Dad, though he was hardly able. My guilt mingled uncomfortably with the scorching weather, but it was too soon to go back inside. Standing under the building's eaves, I regarded Dad's dishevelled backyard. It was the same yard I'd cavorted around, looking for roses to freshen up the house all those years ago. Many months before that day, Dad and I had circumnavigated the place. He related his plans to fashion a habitation of natural beauty and repose, a "romantic rose garden" as it was named in his how-to reference. I recalled how chuffed I'd been that he wanted to share it with his daughter. With this memory, I forced myself to step away from the shady roof space and into the sweltering sun. I morphed into a sweaty creature, searching for evidence of Dad's garden, but there was none. The patch was nothing more than overgrown plants, spindly undergrowth, and dying vegetation. I treaded mounds of decomposing debris, reeking of pungent, earthy smells. Struggling, I tried to gather words in prayer. They fell to the ground as I spoke, scattered amongst mouldering leaves at my sandalled feet, which prickled from organic matter and heat.

Once I rounded the building, I was back at the main door. I applied a plucky face while re-entering the flat, though I was done in. Even the air-conditioning couldn't revive me.

Nearing the end of our visit, Dad congratulated his son, acknowledging his accomplishments with a proud grin and a sure handshake. Dylan was every bit deserving, but regrettably, my insecurities took over. I foolishly competed, listing my study attainments over the years. While speaking, I hinted at and looked for validation from my father, then waited until my heart sank.

Dad's soul was miles away from mine as he emptily stared at my expectant eyes. His blinked without expression as a stiffly closed mouth formed a straight line. Dad's uncommunicativeness recapped my immense impediment. I was the out-of-favour child!

That night, I grabbed the leather-bound Bible packed away in my luggage, the cover's vibrant butterfly design mismatching my low mood. With a grand effort, I climbed onto the bed in Dylan's spare room, expended in every way. The bed's embrace enabled a short prayer. "Give me something, Lord. Speak to me!" I went straight to the book of Psalms. My fingers randomly separated thin, rustling pages and then stopped in chapter 103, verses 8 to 14. The words practically leapt off the page, as they were already highlighted.

> "The Lord is compassionate and gracious; slow to anger, abounding in love. He will not always

accuse, nor will he harbor his anger forever; he does not treat us as our sins deserve or repay us according to our iniquities. For as high as the heavens are above the earth, so great is his love for those who fear him; as far as the east is from the west, so far has he removed our transgressions from us. As a father has compassion on his children, so the Lord has compassion on those who fear him; for he knows how we are formed, he remembers that we are dust." (NIV)

With solemness, I reflected on these words, which reminded me of the Lord's enduring grace and clemency. His regard towards all people was lavish. God saw me through the eyes of a loving father, and he treated me accordingly. Undoubtedly, my father was regarded in the same way, no matter how impossible I thought him to be. While taking in God's correcting love, I pulled the cover up and over my head. My body furled as a weary lump between the sheets, sobbing softly into slumber. My hot and overwhelming day had ended.

THIRTY-TWO

A Letter for Dad, With Love

God did consider my father, and one clear example stands out. It was back in 2016, when I was prompted to write him a letter.

My pre-schooler and I walked along the short path towards Kerang's local library, named after Sir John Gorton, one of Australia's former prime ministers. I angled my head to gaze at the historic water tower. It resembled a robust redhead, looming above and behind the newer building. Her antique brickwork, in mottled red clay, flowed as an impermeable skirt, reaching a grassy base. She commanded my attention. Not punitively but as a mother overseeing her young one below. It was the library we were about to enter as mother and daughter. What I didn't know was that the mother-daughter theme would soon become father-daughter focused, at least for me.

Once my daughter settled in the children's area, I found myself a study space nearby. I'd planned to watch a lecture on my laptop while she entertained herself. At the time, I was undertaking an online self-paced Bible course. I discovered while in the library that my next course subject was 'Exploring God as Father.' The presenter was a known theological educator. Since I'd met him at a youth camp and heard him speak publicly at a number of events, I readily listened to his teaching.

Part of the way in, God interjected. "You need to write your father a letter."

I delayed the presentation to think about these words. They were succinct and yet vague, as I had no context, so I decided to wait for a deeper insight. Before returning to the lecture, I unwarily shifted my gaze towards innumerable books surrounding me, quickly shaking off a hemmed-in feeling.

The teacher's personal sharing came through his address, lending itself to the fatherhood theme. An important part of his story included writing a letter to his dad, identifying good and commendable attributes. The premise of the message was to, "honour your father," according to God's commandment, a rule without exception. At that point, I knew to follow up on the divine message by copying the teacher's example.

Once the lecture had ended, I shut down my computer, resting my hands in my lap. Again, I looked at the rows of library books coming at me from every angle. There were simply too many books to choose from. The task of composing a letter for Dad felt just as overwhelming. I wouldn't know where to start. And yet, I singled out library books on a regular basis. So I could easily type Dad a letter, right?

Back at home, I sat staring at a glowing white page. My computer demanded that I type something, but I couldn't. My mind was as blank as the page in front of me. Then I remembered the teacher's reference to a father's ability to create life as a starting point. Naturally, I was thankful for the gift of life. The names Dad had lovingly selected at my birth came next. I was beginning to relish the feel-good moment until my grateful mindset fizzled out, eclipsed by painful memories and Dad's relentless rejection. The word "Dad" glowered at me from the top of the page, along with "things I appreciate about you." I allowed pessimism to seep in as bitter tears splashed onto the keyboard. My remiss father was not, nor would he ever be, worthy of my thanks and praise!

Despite my indignant state of mind, I returned to the task. But nothing came of it. I tried again on another day and then another, still unable to move forward. Eventually, I offered up a tearful prayer. "I want to honour you, Lord. I want to acknowledge Dad's efforts. I give you my pain, my disappointments, the impact of all the rejection." After praying, an inner peace restored me. Also, to my astonishment, recollections of Dad's kindnesses came to mind, along with a genuine desire to applaud him. Little by little, I formed simple father-daughter sketches, all good-hearted and commendable.

After two months, the letter was signed, sealed, and ready to send. I held it high above my head while committing it to God. A short while later, I stood facing a bright red post box, then released my letter with a satisfied smile. My expression was taken as a warm greeting from a passer-by.

Almost four years later, I shared my letter at Dad's funeral.

20/04/2016

"Dad, a list of things I appreciate about you:

- *You gave me life.*
- *You named me Fleur Colette, and I like it!*
- *When I was a child, you made some good decisions in order to protect me.*
- *Concern for my well-being was shown by exposing me to the Quit Smoking campaign.*
- *You tried to help expand my horizons through art shows, theatre, concerts, and taking me places to meet a variety of people.*
- *Music was something you included in our family life when I was a child.*
- *Enjoying nature through botanical gardens, bush walks, and visiting the beach are positive memories I have, which you were a part of.*
- *You helped by providing employment through a business studies traineeship and included me as the executive of your company.*

- *The employment you provided enabled me to return to high school and on to uni.*
- *It meant a great deal to me that you and Nana attended my graduation. You also gave me a congratulations gift, which I bought a graduation photo and frame with.*
- *You provided me with a car when I needed it, along with extras such as insurance, rego, and a tank of fuel.*
- *I noticed you made efforts to try and save your marriage to Mum.*
- *Your words of sympathy to me regarding Mum's death were appreciated.*
- *You made efforts to minimise damage to Owen, Dylan, and I at the time of your divorce.*
- *You helped Owen out during his Year 12 studies by accommodating him.*
- *Because of Owen's disappearance, you were willing to go to the media for help.*
- *The interest you have shown in Dylan and Lisa matters a great deal.*
- *I am pleased that you and Marion have stayed together all these years.*
- *You made efforts to reconcile and encourage me after we had arguments.*

- *I am pleased you made sure Owen, Dylan, and I had contact with Nana and Grandad during our childhood.*
- *You encouraged me to maintain contact with relatives on your side of the family.*
- *You attended my twenty-first birthday party, took me out to dinner on my birthday, and gave me lovely gifts.*
- *Your phone call to me a couple of years ago, wishing me happy birthday, was much appreciated.*
- *I appreciated the two times you and Marion visited Peter and I in Queensland, when my boys were in their infancy.*
- *You have good taste in gifts, including the pewter goblets you gave Peter and I for our engagement.*
- *Your love of roses and appreciation of nature is something I like about you.*
- *I admire your hard work and success in your chosen career.*

For all these things, and anything I may have missed, thank you! And thank you also for raising me and doing the best you could have done at the time. I have typed this list for you because I choose to honour you because you are my father!

With love, Fleur."

During the service, I added concluding words to my funeral tribute. This included a lost opportunity to talk with Dad about what I wrote, but I made no mention of his behaviour as the reason why. Instead, I said it pleased me to have shared my appreciation through the letter I sent him and with those who knew him at his funeral that morning.

My homage was delivered to a mostly unknown crowd as a commemorative effort, leaving many specifics unexplained. Once the service was over, I heard a whisper that my funeral tribute "wasn't very helpful to others." It pained me to hear this. God knows I approached the task with good grace and how hard it was to fight off the urge to ditch my speech and tell the congregation some home truths about Dad.

Also, after the service, a woman I didn't know called my name. It was one of Dad's former colleagues, perhaps in her thirties, who promptly introduced herself. I could see she was an amiable person, not just a professional who worked with Dad. Her comely eyes took my attention, along with her perceptive comment. "There's a lot between the lines of your letter."

"Yes. Yes, there is," I replied.

I was pleased when she demanded no further information. Her consideration caused me to entertain an idea, an opportunity to meet while Dad lived. He and I, with his impartial associate, would unpack my letter. We would highlight meaningful father-daughter times, irrespective that they were marked with imperfection. It would reinforce the value of our relationship, allowing Dad and me to start afresh. But it was impossible to turn my thoughts into reality, as time and circumstance prohibited it. More's the pity.

THIRTY-THREE

Slippery Slope of Self-Contempt

The letter didn't miraculously transform our dad-and-daughter association into a flourishing relationship or provide any suggestion of reconciliation from Dad's end, but my decision to honour him was one of integrity. That was enough for me, as I had ultimately honoured God. Producing the letter also pushed me to acknowledge that there *had* been positives in our relationship. It also backed up my belief in the age-old saying, "Credit where credit is due." While God was clearly in the mix when it came to this challenge, my self-loathing was, and at times still is, the greatest mountain I've had to navigate. It began in my teenage years, but I concealed my struggle from others to avoid further vulnerability.

John had a good track record. In the entire time he had been practising psychology, there were no client suicides, and those are very good odds! This was an observation passed on to Dylan and me from some who knew our father well, stating it near the end of his life. While I have no reason to contest this claim, a sad fact remains: Dad assisted others while oblivious to the detrimental impacts of family violence on his children.

According to the official 2015 coroner's report, in 1989 Owen "attended St Vincent's Hospital in Melbourne, where he received ninety stitches to lacerations on his arm."

The lacerations were self-inflicted during a heavy drinking episode. The same report mentions Owen's experimental use of drugs, self-harm, and other risk-taking behaviours. Soon after Owen slashed himself, Julia, who became his wife in January that year, informed her father-in-law of the incident. She also expressed her grave concern for Owen's overall well-being. Dad minimised his son's behaviour as childish attention-seeking, offering no support whatsoever. I wept for my brother when I heard this.

My family dysfunction buttressed poorly managed anger, low self-esteem leading to suicide ideation, aggression, and self-directed violence. Some of these impulses I internalised and outwardly exhibited. I effectively hid my shortfall for a long time. On a social level, I smiled while shedding tears on the inside, tearing myself apart when alone. If I took a risk with someone safe, my confiding was quickly dismissed.

Well-intentioned friends used playful mockery or scepticism. "I doubt it. You wouldn't do that, Fleur. You're much too nice."

Without a word, I smiled and nodded, not wanting to burst the bubble. Once I married and started a family, however, it was virtually impossible to hide my struggle from those closest to me. Dad ghosting me over a prolonged period also compounded my problem. I fluctuated between believing the deep-seated lie that I was valueless and fighting against it. Self-loathing came as a harsh voice in my head, urging me to hurt myself, among other destructions. Graciously, the Holy Spirit's stronger and kindlier voice overpowered it. Slowly but surely, I understood my significance, iterated in the book of Psalms, particularly chapter 139's lyrical verses. The first time I heard these verses from a preacher's mouth, I wept in my seat, trying to absorb who God really is. From verse 1, I discovered his intimate nature and surprising attentiveness, even attuned to my secret sobbing and sighing. God, my Father, in all his completeness, came to me with his comforting presence, imparting a depth of love that I couldn't resist, proving to be steadfast over the years.

With confidence, I can now say that the bulk of the work is done. But every so often, a trigger presents itself. If someone close misjudges who I am or undervalues what I have to offer, a threatened feeling crawls in and expands, belying my worth. I have to fight to overcome it. I begin with forgiving whoever needs to be forgiven, though giving myself grace is by far the more difficult feat. A reeling lie tells me I've failed, that my life is redundant and that suffering is required. With God's strength and reassuring grace, I stand my ground and recommence myself.

Just as importantly, I allowed others to see my loss of traction on the slippery slope of self-contempt. These dependable people have come for a season or still remain in my life. In my need, they applied psychological and spiritual first-aid with unconditional acceptance and heaps of love. Without them, I would struggle all the more to embrace the life that God has given me.

THIRTY-FOUR

Our Final Father-Daughter Exchange

On Thursday, January 16, 2020, news came via a stranger. The caller was Kath, Marion's daughter. Veritably, I have a hazy memory of us having been introduced twenty-seven years before, but that's all. I was told John had been transported to hospital by ambulance. It was the likely place of his final demise. Kath stressed that she and her sister, Ella, would be my points of contact regarding John. That way, I could avoid all communication with their mother to minimise her anxiety. I agreed to comply, quite willingly. Dad was my primary focus and always had been between he and Marion.

After taking the call, I felt certain that my meeting with Dad would be the last one. I'd been praying intently about our relationship during his terminal illness and for a long time before then. God knew that I desired to see my estranged parent, even from years back, when I asked, "If Dad rejects me for the remainder of his life, then so be it, but give me the opportunity to talk with him alone, even if he's on his deathbed."

Our dialogue went two ways as I heard that my request would, indeed, be granted. I got the same response closer to Dad's death. Other pertinent details were divinely revealed too, like God's offer of guidance on what to say at the time and that I would leave Dad's bedside in peace. With these vital insights, I packed a bag with eagerness for my final father-daughter chapter.

My accustomed rail and coach journey was uneventful, ending in Traralgon, a place pleasingly leafy, with a grander, more urban feel than other towns strung along Gippsland's Latrobe Valley. I stayed the night with a couple who generously opened their home, along with its creature comforts. I awakened to a sunlit room amongst comfy bed linen, which caressed me through dreamless sleep. Liveliness filled me, punctuated by a cheery knock and greeting through the door. It was early Saturday morning, and I was ready for my long-awaited moment with Dad.

I travelled to the Latrobe Regional Hospital, driven by one of my friends who had accommodated me. Once we arrived, I followed her steady pace around the clinical labyrinth. Whiffs of antiseptic reached my nose, while veneered policy notices claimed my attention. We stopped just short of the nurses' station, where I was told John's room was around the corner. There, my companion and I parted ways, as she considerately gave me space. I was attended to by gregarious hospital staff, who concluded that I was an integral part of John's supportive family. I played along, having no desire to tell them I'd been written off for years. By then, it felt like a hundred!

I was sure that Marion grudgingly allowed me in — because imminent death does that — or was it because no one could interfere with God's plan? That morning, Dad's three womenfolk anticipated my visit, but what they didn't know was that I'd arrive earlier than most visitors. The tactic was used to avoid tricky liaisons and interrupted time with Dad. It worked perfectly.

Despite being early, the staff allowed me to enter Dad's hospital room. I stopped at the door labelled "John Redman." It confirmed that I wasn't walking in on a stranger, although the inpatient and I were indeed estranged. Gingerly, I stepped into the dusky room, where I heard soft gurgling sounds. Earlier, a nurse had told me to open the curtains. As I did, she had walked into the room, energetically joined me in the task, and then left straight after. We brought the day's clarity into the room, brightening my view of the dozing man. I took in what I saw. Dad's bony arms rested on tightly tucked bedding, revealing reddened marks over loose, transparent skin. He'd shrunken down to the size of a prepubescent boy waiting for muscle and bulk to come in. I stood beside the husk of a man in quiet muse. We were side by side in unobtrusive surrounds. How unusual!

Dad stirred, then blinked me into focus. I offered a slight smile before leaning over to kiss his brow. Despite Dad's parlous state, his faculties were in order, and he recognised me by stating my name.

My moment beside Dad was interrupted by a flurry of nursing and domestic staff. They efficiently and cheerily attended to routine observations and domestic tasks. I wasn't jealous of our time. Dad needed care, and I soon acquired a role, obliging him with little helps that felt strangely satisfying. For Dad, it was an imposition, not by me, but he was exasperated with himself. He apologised for the maintenance he required and swore into the air over his non-compliant body, which was quite evidently shutting down.

Dad settled once breakfast was done, and the staff presence subsided. I repositioned his pillows and pulled up the bedding according to his liking. Dad finally rested, as much as his abating body allowed. For me, our time was more sweet than bitter. I felt bursts of joy each time we addressed each other as "Fleur" and "Dad." It was our habit from days gone by, underused for seventeen years.

There was effectively no strain between us, even when Dad asked, "What was that about?" He was referring to my forced approach at the granny flat while visiting with Dylan and Lisa.

I meekly apologised and confessed that my good intentions had gone awry.

Dad's guard was down, as he accepted my admission of guilt and then graciously left it alone. We sat together like old friends, relaxing in each other's company. I found Dad's features, speech, and mannerisms pleasantly familiar. Nuances I'd missed when angrily confronting him less than a month earlier. At the time, I had seen an ailing man with a distorted face and an absent heart. As Dad spoke, I listened to his nasal Aussie twang, which had turned strained and rasping. I also watched his features move in the same expressive way as they always had, his pursing and parting pinkish-brown lips among them. Smile marks around his blue-grey eyes and the furrows etched between subtle brows also looked familiar. Dad's lines were just more pronounced and on a thinner, paler face. To me, these alterations were inconsequential. Dad was the same old dad I knew. I could only hope that my presence also benefited him.

I believed God attended the hospital room, just as he'd joined me over the previous months when he spoke about my final time with Dad. I anticipated the fulfilment of those words but was mindful that certain aspects hadn't been fulfilled, like his guidance on what to say. So I created an opening for sharing. "If there is anything you would like to say, I'm here to listen."

We had carried our heartaches, and limpid expressions of regret were due, but I wouldn't manipulate the conversation or coerce my ailing father. I felt the minutes pass by, acutely aware that Dad's life hung in the balance. I wanted him to name our blessings or anything else light or heavy upon his heart. Anything relating to us. To hear his sincere apology, "I'm sorry for causing you pain, so sorry I cut you off." If he said this, in tears, I would tell him that all was forgiven. In turn, Dad would soften, replenishing his well of fondness for his girl, which had dried up.

But he remained silent on the matter, so it wasn't to be. Did vulnerability prevent Dad from opening up, from unearthing too many layers, for he was beyond it all? Or was he simply unrepentant? Whatever his reasoning, I accepted there would be no heart-rending moment between us. With that realisation, I put aside my inexorable ache and moved on. I reached out to the man suffering from cancer's atrophy, running its final course.

In that moment, I felt the Spirit's unction as words came effortlessly. Dad's face livened up, as if a spiritual light bulb flicked on as I shared, factoring in my sighting of the angel who would carry his soul away. Very gently, I asked if he had considered his eternal state.

Dad's low, rasping voice drew my face closer to his. "Go away, and I'll think about it."

I immediately left the room, walked through elongated corridors, and then settled by a bay window. Through the glass, I gazed at a patch of clipped lawn, cast in shade between the hospital's walls. I attempted to release Dad to the eternal God, only to offer him prayer afterwards. His quiet but firm refusal was freely accepted, for anything more would have disrespected his feelings. My spiritual onus ended there, for Dad's answer untethered me. Marion's daughter, Kath, arrived shortly after. We exchanged polite greetings before I kissed Dad goodbye, promising to return the next day. Kath remarked that I was leaving so soon.

"I've had a good amount of time with Dad," I replied, unthinking.

My Sunday visit began half an hour earlier than the previous day. The hospital room had the appearance of nightfall as unopened drapes and heavy shade behind them hid the morning sun. I could just make out a trundle bed, which jutted below Dad's bedframe, and a person filling it, but that was all. I backed out of the doorway and into the well-lit corridor. At the nurses' station, I asked, "How did John sleep last night?" I wanted to know if his condition had worsened as a reason for additional support.

The nurse's smiling reply came without hesitation. "Peaceful. Very, very peaceful. He didn't need any assistance at all."

This reassured me, and I returned to Dad's living quarters. Softly, I stepped into the room, where Dad's sleeping shape was unchanged and a woman groggily emerged from the lower bed. She introduced herself as Marion's daughter, Ella. Before long, the tetchy woman explained she'd stayed the night to protect John. Apparently, I represented clear and present danger for the dying man in the room. I resisted blurting out a laugh. Ella, who I'd discovered was a policewoman, had come to intercept me. I knew her mother had put her up to it, since Ella and I weren't acquainted. *What actions would Marion's security force take, should I be found wanting in her eyes? Drag me away from the facility in handcuffs?* If my thoughts came true, such a drama would have caused Dad great distress, or perhaps much-needed entertainment.

Dad's partner and her daughters had, evidently, discussed his menacing daughter, construing that Saturday's early visit involved unsupervised time with John. Consequently, they pre-empted my early Sunday arrival. Yes, they'd got that part right. But I was still unclear about my posing threat towards their John.

I didn't need to speculate for long, as Ella quickly voiced her concern. "I don't know what you said to him, but I've never seen him like it!"

"Like what?" I asked, ready to hear the facts.

Ella was vague and unable to name any outward signs or symptoms troubling Dad. She only suggested that he was upset on account of me, and so he needed a guardian. While I hadn't committed a single felony, I endured Ella's unclear indictments surrounding John's heightened anxiety.

Once Ella's irritated voice let up, I told her I was off to buy Dad flowers. I added that she'd have ample opportunity to get dressed and breakfasted, allowing me time with Dad when I returned. Ella faced me without words, the room's dimness concealing her expression. I turned and walked away, leaving her with the sleeping patient.

At the shop's frontage, I stopped to give myself a moment, deeply breathing in and out. I shot up a prayer for myself and the intrusion at the hospital. Surely, my opposition was more than personal; it was spiritual. Dad's distress, I believed, came from a spiritual awakening, a battle not uncommon for Christians. Much like the disturbing God encounter I'd had as a young woman regarding my life choices. I'd also put Dad's restful night down to making his peace with God. This had been an experience of mine, once surrendered.

Resting from prayer, I rounded the corner, where I found rows of cellophane-wrapped flowers. I snatched up the perkiest bunch with a few essential roses. I added a card to my purchase as a token of thanks to Marion, acknowledging her devotion to my father over the years.

Back with Dad, I presented the flower bunch. "I chose roses for you!"

Dad didn't respond as I'd hoped. His eyes narrowed distrustfully at mine.

I was unsure why until I realised Ella was whispering something in his ear, undoubtedly something unkind about me. Like a cattish schoolgirl, her eyes peered in my direction as her mouth moved. I swept aside her spite, turning my attention to the envelope in my hand. I asked Ella to pass the card on to her mother, placing it beside Dad's flowers. She left soon after. This allowed me to move to the spot she'd occupied by the bedhead. I filled Saturday's same grey, high-back chair by the window. It felt good to have another opportunity to be close to Dad. Kath shortly joined Ella as backup. They sat by the door, assuming a supervisory role, ready to intervene if a threat was detected. I didn't resist or resent the security presence, taking it in my stride while smiling to myself over the ridiculousness of it all.

Speech had evaded my deteriorating parent. I took it as a chance to bask together while classical music drifted from my phone. The music had a palliative effect as the patient's fingers metrically came to life.

When it was time to go, I gently pecked Dad's temple. "Love you, Dad," I said before edging along the bedframe. It didn't feel like it was enough, so I instinctively stopped by the footboard with something more to say. "I won't be seeing you again."

Cancer's gaze looked at me through Dad's weary eyes. He managed an incomplete smile, but a smile nonetheless.

"I won't be seeing you again, Dad," I repeated. My eyes intently fixed on his, wistfully waiting. I was unwilling to leave without a sign of Dad's favour, pending his life's end. Then there it was, a moment of tenderness; his goodbye kiss gently blew in my direction. I took it without words, only raising the corners of my closed mouth in recognition. Dad's little gesture contributed to what God had foretold about leaving his bedside in peace.

That afternoon, my body bumped and swayed with a coach's uneven pulse, then to the rhythm of a rumbling train, taking me home. Their soothing effect matched my holistic state. God's peace and calm defied the impact of long-running fragmentation in my relationship with Dad, causing me to ache beside his deathbed. I just knew he and I would be alright. My father died three days later.

THIRTY-FIVE

A Heartfelt and Healing Funeral ... Yeah, Right!

From the backseat, I felt the car swerve off the Princes Highway. Our destination was the Latrobe Valley Funeral Services in Traralgon East. We slowed to a tortoise-like pace, much like my reduced reflex ability from apprehension over the funeral. In air-conditioned comfort, I remarked on the manicured garden to the couple up front. They were friends who'd accommodated me the night before. I was taken by its bright, pert foliage, in spite of January's high temperatures. The weather was a continuation of December's heatwave, made more unbearable, as arid heat had turned muggy. Opening the car door, sultry air leapt onto my clothes and clung to my skin. I wished for a summer skirt instead of heat trapping denim jeans as I moved towards the next chilled space, the chapel's foyer.

We arrived early, which allowed time to find my ex-boyfriend, Daniel. He was somewhere in the funeral building, where he worked. We had connected some days prior, when I rang for the celebrant's contact details. The unfamiliar male voice provided her mobile number and then took me completely by surprise when he told me, "We were going out. You were seventeen." It sounded like a line from a romantic movie. Mercifully, he couldn't see my glowing face as he described seventeen-year-old me with surprising detail. Daniel seemed decent enough, but I had no idea who he was. On the morning of the funeral, I sought to satisfy my curiosity. Plus, my focus was a wanted distraction before the service.

I waited a short while before the guy from my past showed up, tall and smartly dressed. He imparted a warm smile like we were old friends. I asked if we could briefly chat. Daniel agreed and ushered me into an office, where he offered a swivel chair. I'd hardly sat down when two male colleagues came in. After Daniel introduced me as his former girlfriend, they behaved like awkward schoolboys as they softly chortled into their palms. I didn't pander to them and was pleased when they left shortly after. All I wanted to know was who this Daniel character was and how he fit into my past.

At least ten minutes into our conversation, Daniel grinned as he probed me for a response. "You still don't know who I am, do you, Fleur?"

"Ah, no. Can you help me remember?" My bashfulness was plain to us both as warmth tinged my cheeks.

Still grinning, Daniel obliged me by expounding on our history. We'd met at a youth event at the Belgrave

Heights Convention Centre, south-east of Melbourne. From there, I began to connect the dots. We shared a little of our lives since our late teens, ending with an affirming hug. Our time had effectively side-tracked me from worry over the impending funeral service, my next reality.

It came as no surprise that I was excluded from all the funeral preparations, since I was an outsider. Marion took charge as she directed the celebrant and her family to contribute as she saw fit. That being said, I was pleased that she'd also permitted me, and a few others, six minutes each to pay homage to the departed.

Feeling conspicuous, I timidly made my way down the chapel aisle, then veered to the left, where I parked myself in the second pew from the front. *I'm allowed,* I reassured myself. While taking solace in Dylan and Lisa's company on the seating, a feeling of aloneness also clouded me. Nat King Cole's *Unforgettable* came in tenderly as the sound of sweet sorrow, setting the tone as the late John Redman was on everyone's mind.

Marion, with her daughters and the rest of her clan, arrived right on starting time. I stood with the congregation to honour them, as if they were VIPs. I didn't know why I followed the crowd. Maybe I didn't want to be an unconventional pain. The congregational response also mystified me, as did the family. They sauntered down the aisle as if the service was all about them, with the civil celebrant and a funeral attendant leading the way. The cluster inelegantly plonked themselves onto the front pews, relishing the attention. Perhaps my view was skewed, but I sensed Marion's ownership stamped on foreheads around the room. It was certainly stamped on Dad's lifeless body, sealed inside the obtrusive, darkly veneered, ligneous box.

Marion drew sympathy from those nearby. It was to be expected, as her brokenness was raw beneath a polished appearance. It would be safe to say our grieving worlds could never collide, only repel. She suffered loss over John's departing, their wanted relationship permanently severed. My loss was over a relationship that had died over the years. The grief I suffered came from knowing the relationship I wanted with Dad would never be wanted by him in my lifetime. Our father-daughter relationship would always be marked by detachment. While Dad's death didn't grieve me, I felt the end of his life and what that meant for us acutely. Since I wasn't in a safe place, I postponed my intense grief, steeling myself for the funeral service while taking in a deep breath.

The celebrant, Heather, began the service as I'd expected, with a caring tone and deliberate words. Her warm welcomes segued into generous waves of commiserations, and then grief support was encouraged amongst the congregation. Tedious housekeeping was also covered, including where to find the toilets, all spoken with the same sentimental tone. I could've laughed out loud at the irony but chose not to express it.

Heather's opening words regarding the deceased said that he was a "generous, intelligent, and some say an eccentric man known to you all, of course, as John."

It raised some annoyance in me, as she would have known Dylan and I called him Dad. Was I being unreasonably pedantic? Perhaps so, as Dylan, Lisa, Peter, and I were soon named, along with Marion's children and their partners. Even Owen received a mention. Grandchildren and great-grandchildren were lumped together as one. It was just as well, as my children had no chance to "treasure the memories of their loved John," as Heather concluded. My body trembled, as I could hardly take the homily, flowerily gushing on and on.

I heard one truth about Dad. "Not every memory [of John was] etched in gold." This, I believe, is fitting to us all. I dubbed Heather's remaining speech as nothing more than froth and bubble. Some lines said that "he gave you wonderful gifts of strength, kindness, acceptance, and love," and a standard compliment no one can ever achieve, she told us, "he never had a bad word to say about anyone." Heather continued, "The final analysis was John gave every inch to you of what he had to offer. His door was always open to anyone, and he just loved helping others. He was non-judgemental and gave his all…"

As I heard the final analysis of John, I let out a restrained, sarcastic "wowww" sound. I couldn't help it.

While these words churned in my head, another truth sprang from the officiator's mouth. It was an offer to those most moved within the congregation, and I guessed that included me.

"You are now the representatives and caretakers of John's legacy …"

I realise the rousing counsel is currently being fulfilled through my candid, written deliberation: memoirs of Dad and me. I make no apologies about my contributions as John Redman's daughter, a warranted representative and legacy caretaker!

Magnanimous tributes, including mine, celebrated the departed, ending with Marion's speech. She gave a generous description of John as "my champion, your champion!" Attention was drawn to his positive and endearing influence, apparently modelled to everyone in the room. It was a great shame that Marion's inference didn't resonate with me or my immediate family. Nor did it relate to his first wife or his two sons, as I had testified to throughout the years.

My thoughts shifted with my head towards the funeral slideshow, looping through epochs of Dad's life. I watched a brief cameo featuring our family, excluding Mum. One aging photograph depicted three young siblings with Nana and Dad in the front. I looked closer at the wee girl between her brothers. It was me, and we belonged to each other. In my imagination, I counted Mum in place of Nana. We fit together, though not perfectly, like worn pieces joining comfortably in a favourite puzzle. The puzzle had been pulled apart, pieces separated, tossed, and never brought back together as a whole picture.

With a jolt, I returned to the service as the slideshow moved to Dad, his partner, and her family. They were people I didn't know. I was chronologically fifty, yet emotionally, I'd reverted to the small child on the screen. Her vulnerable eyes were mine, and they wanted to cry. My sadness swiftly turned into an overwhelming urge to tantrum. I could've created a dramatic scene, stood on my seat, and screamed, "Dad never belonged to them. I want my family back!" If only the images were accompanied by the 1980s song *What About Me?* instead of Andrew Lloyd Webber's *Think of Me*, sung by Emmy Rossum. Her angelic voice came displeasingly to my hearing. As did Jim Croce's 1970s *Time in a Bottle*, the second accompanying choice. If I'd had the power, I'd have exchanged their mawkishness for the Moving Picture's single. Their lyrics resonated with my sense of abandon. *What about me? It isn't fair!* I would've screamed it to the rousing music, screaming it over and over to attract attention to my painful family loss. I didn't have the power. Plus, I was very much aware that the rest of the congregation was paying homage to the departed through well-ordered propriety. But I just couldn't relate. I desperately wanted someone, anyone, in that funeral place to acknowledge my family as one enduring collective. That included the man they were mourning and celebrating. And yet, I knew that our family base had died long before Dad had passed away. The puzzle pieces were mostly lost and unredeemed, and *it wasn't fair!*

Somehow, in the thick of my impassioned battle, I sought restraint. My cue came uncomplicatedly as a Christian persuasion. It was *not* all about me. My attitude changed from self-centeredness to reasonableness towards Marion. Dad was entitled to have another partner and her loved ones in his life. It was just too bad that his devotion to them left a yawning chasm in his original family.

Irrespective of how I felt, it was to Marion's credit that she'd considered my family, and rightly so for John's sake. Marion ensured that our names were mentioned and displayed family photographs, acknowledging we'd been a significant part of John's earlier life (and for Dylan, also in recent times). Accordingly, I sought Marion out after the service and planted a polite kiss on her cheek. There were no signs of ill will or resistance, so I stayed to thank her for including Owen, Dylan, and me in the slideshow. She shrugged off my thanks, stating that Kath had put in the work. Still, I didn't withdraw my appreciation, since she'd ultimately approved it.

When I thanked Kath, she responded, "Of course, Fleur."

Her warm candour and kind eyes softened me. I pondered that people can be surprising and easily misjudged.

Platters of funeral repast food were meticulously placed on tables for the gathering. I had no appetite or desire to socialise, so I passed by them, accidently catching my side on a table's corner. The sharp pain I felt was the bruising kind, and while wincing inside, I hoped nobody noticed. Under the porte-cochere outside, I stood in the extreme heat, feeling uncomfortable but pleased to be away from the crowd. Two couples I knew joined me soon after. As we spoke, I busily concocted a plan in my head.

I would centre all my energy on others, behaving benevolently while not having to open up.

With renewed strength, I entered the building to circumnavigate my way around the room, focusing on every living soul I could get a hold of. My words were calm and constant. "Hello. I'm Fleur, John's daughter. What was your connection with John?" I reached out with a listening ear and a gentle smile and gave heartfelt hugs as needed. My actioned idea went flawlessly well.

Feeling quite in control, I went to get a cup of tea, then almost flipped my lid. The emotions I'd capped came close to overflowing when affronted by the tea lady. The flustering woman accused me of queue-jumping. If that was the case, it was entirely accidental. I attempted an apology to keep the peace but was ignored. The woman's face inflamed as her loudened voice continued to reprimand me for rudeness and impatience. Indignation overcame me, convinced that she was unjustifiably uncivil and should be taken to task, not me! *Leave me alone. I'm the daughter of the deceased, you buffoon!* These words were ready on my tongue, but I determined to latch them down. I wouldn't exacerbate the situation. Like a good Christian, I managed to apply a gracious smile and blessed the scowling woman. Heat abated from her face and mine as she handed over the drink. I stepped aside from the counter and its busy people. My nose breathed in aromatic steam before sipping the tea. I found comfort, from my parched mouth all the way down. It must have been Dad's Englishness in me.

I'd almost completed my dutiful stranger connections when a woman demanded my attention. I began my practised line, speaking the last of it into her hair as she rushed at me with a full embrace. I held the mystery woman as she feverishly sobbed. Her wetness soaked through my silk-blend blouse and onto my shoulder. Her outpouring grief was over the loss of the man who'd turned her life around. Between sobs, she explained her story. The late John Redman, in his professional capacity, had carried her through the anguish of living with ghosting from her two adult daughters. They'd been separated over a significant period, though nowhere near the many changing seasons I'd endured as an estranged daughter. Much to the mother's relief, she'd reunited with her family in recent years.

After hearing the woman's story, I burst Dad's bubble, but only in my imagination. In actuality, I made no mention of her champion's shortfall. I wasn't that heartless. But I did wonder what thoughts scudded across Dad's mind while counselling his troubled client, rejected by those she dearly loved. Did he consider the effect of cutting off his own daughter, and did it ever trouble him? I believed Dad wasn't play-acting in his psychologist role. He worked according to a positive mantra; it was just that his lacking personal life made him look like a fraud. Was he a wounded healer, assisting others with the use of his narrative for attentiveness and empathy, meanwhile neglecting his own therapeutic needs? The stranger's poignant story provided greater reason to believe it. I was sure that most of the gathering wouldn't have known of his discrepancy, while some had turned a blind eye, and a few who knew were saddened by it. I was one of the sad ones.

Fortunately, by then, I was no longer heated, having moved on from my *What About Me?* encore. With sincere condolences, I ministered to Dad's grief-stricken client at his funeral, the same vulnerable person he'd ministered to over the repercussions of her emotional cutoff, though I still felt uneasy over the irony of it all.

THIRTY-SIX

Embracing a New Season

Ecclesiastes 3:1 reads, "There is a time for everything and a season for every activity under the heavens" (NIV). I believe the tenor of this poetic verse transcends time, affecting all people. This includes my trifling life along history's continuum. My season of rejection was over, as John William Redman no longer held a place on this earth. It was time for me to break from my industriousness in chasing a dead-end relationship. Terminating my immense efforts over such a lengthy period almost felt surreal, but my grief *was* real. The source of my rejection may have gone, but it had left its mark.

After returning home from Dad's funeral service, I found that my family didn't share in my sorrow. And why would they? Aimlessly, I careened around the house in a bubble of isolation. I needed to grieve, so I looked for support through my abiding friend, Deb. When I rang, her naturalness in meeting my need brought tremendous mental relief. Soon after, I grabbed my car keys to meet her at Kerang's levee bank on the Loddon River. I parked in the shade of a weeping peppercorn tree, where I sat peering through the windscreen. A sandy path rose up to join a walking track. The sky behind it was filled with rustic Australian native trees, home to an array of calling birds, all flying in and out of the branches. It was all familiar to me; like other locals, I'd walked the path many times. But that day, I had no desire to leave the car.

When I saw Deb's approaching figure, I gestured for her to sit in the front passenger seat. There, I faced her pensive brown eyes, brimming with tears of compassion, making it plain that I had chosen the right confidante. Shamelessly and uncontrollably, I released a flood of tears without hiding my fury at Dad, allowing the flow to lather away depths of misery. Healing had begun, but my release could not wipe away what had been. That included Dad's refusal in righting our relationship, even to the end. I was certain that more tides of tears would well up over the months and years to come, easing with time. Once my need to cry ended, I sighed heavily. Thankfulness flowed from my heart to my friend, still beside me. She had been full of empathy and offered no advice. It was exactly what I needed.

While striving to be the good Christian daughter was no longer a part of my life, what remained was the comfort of my Heavenly Father. He had been present throughout my entire journey with Dad.

THIRTY-SEVEN

Joy and Sadness

At the age of twenty-two, I had an unambiguous thought. In the event of Dad's death, he would not bequeath me property or financial inheritance, small or large. It was around the time of my wedding, a point where Dad's rejection stood out. My father would never include my name in his last will and testament, and that was that! Surprise came when I realised my belief had been wrong, as Dad had factored me into his will. At one point, Marion tried to convince her dying partner to remove mine and Dylan's names, but he remained firm in his decision. Dad had always been his own determined person.

I blinked repeatedly at Dad's will on the computer screen. It had been emailed to me that day. Judiciously, I read and reread the testator's wishes. My name was favourably inserted near John Redman's and by his decision. While I could see it was true, it also seemed unbelievable. Factoring me into his will meant more than assets or monetary gain. I was the recipient of a sweet ending to our rollercoaster relationship, though the ups and downs I'd lived through were still impactful.

As I deciphered the legal jargon, my high became a low. Owen was factored out of Dad's will, as cited in the document:

> "I make no provision for my son OWEN STEWART REDMAN under the provision of this Will, as he has chosen not to maintain contact with me for many years."

Dad's avowed words lashed out at his firstborn son as blatant rejection and incongruity, especially as I considered Dad's treatment towards me. I felt a weight of despair. My face fell into my hands, and I wailed inconsolably into them. If Owen had shown up at that time, he'd have been rejected by Dad all over again. I couldn't bear the thought of it. My head wouldn't lift nor cease from whimpering.

In my distraught state, I heard my Lord's tender voice. His affecting words were to the point. "Owen is dead." His invisible hand then reached into me and removed my dreadful burden for Owen, along with a taxing sense of injustice. The words came as an epiphany. Owen was not elusively hiding in this world somewhere but was forever gone. Never again would he endure our father's rejection. Grand relief steadied me as my head slowly lifted. I parted my hands and face, slippery wet from crying.

This revelation of Owen's death occurred later in the year Dad died, in 2020. Previously, the only information

I'd received was in 2015 from the detective handling Owen's missing person's case. He said that due to the lengthy case, it had been brought before the Coroners Court of Victoria to establish a finding into his death but without an inquest, since his body hadn't been found. I was shocked when he told me the outcome. I took my four-year-old to a friend's farm residence to mourn the loss of my brother. Vast paddocks lay beyond the backyard's garden, where we sat under a spreading variegated elm, the family dog joining us. My friend reached out as I wailed into the open air. The dog barked, and my little girl clung to me with wide-eyed concern, both confused over my distress. I grieved nonetheless.

While I accepted that Owen was gone, over the years, I couldn't help but wonder if he was still alive because there was no direct proof of his death. By December 2021, when I finally read the coroner's report, I'd already received the divine message about Owen's passing. Consequently, yet not easily, I accepted the written coronial findings, despite being based on the balance of probabilities, rather than proof of when, where, and how.

As I write, a sense of illusoriness over Owen's shadowy set of circumstances still lingers but not overwhelmingly. As for Dad and Owen, although departed, in my heart I reconciled that their relationship was their own. Whatever went wrong, I released to the omniscient God.

With Dylan, I took up ownership of Dad's Morwell property. It had loads of potential, but that would be someone else's project. We chose to sell. As we decluttered and cleaned, Dylan offered me a sledgehammer. He urged me to smash up furniture as a way of taking out my anger towards Dad. I declined, as my mood was neither happy nor sad, not in an apathetic way; I was just contentedly unconcerned.

While Dylan and I sorted through the house, a rare find was discovered. It was a VHS tape featuring a modest performance from Owen while Dad's voice came from behind the video camcorder. Owen's expansive smiles, lustrous blue eyes, and dimpled chin all captivated me. It also unnerved me, as his final curtain call bow depicted him bowing out of life. Owen's auburn brown hair hung matted from a rustic leather hat, and a crimson scarf embellished his neck, creating an Aussie bush style. It suited him. As the living image came into my office, a wave of longing washed over me. My big brother became real again, and all I had to do was reach through the screen and touch him one last time. Oh, to defy what I knew to be impossible! For the sake of sanity, my thoughts were brought back to life as I knew it. I looked for the footage date. It was August 1989, a time when it was uncommon to view people in our personal lives through video footage. It was also a year and a half before Owen's disappearance. With my emotions in check, I replayed the fifteen-second clip over and over, as it ended all too soon. Although brief, it is a precious keepsake for Dylan and me, capturing our brother in a well-focused close-up with colour, movement, and sound.

Thanks to Dad, the inheritance I received paid off my family home. He would have approved, as I'd heard him say several times that it was good to invest in real estate. I also bought fine jewellery pieces, which I decided were gifts from Dad, making up for many lost birthdays and Christmases. I can imagine myself wearing them in front of Dad, who'd gushingly say, "You look nice. Doesn't Fleur look pretty?"

My feel-good keepsake from 1990 reclaimed.

THIRTY-EIGHT

Restoration is Just Beyond the Veil

I had a dream early in the year Dad died. In faith, I was almost certain of Dad's eternal resting place. But admittedly, I looked for further confirmation. God didn't oppose me by asking where my faith had gone. Rather, he provided a porthole into Dad's new habitation. The dream came as a bird's-eye view, but I was also present in the scene. I'd been newly transported to a heavenly place. Not in the Holy City illuminated with God's glory but in a natural environment on the edge of an immense plantation. Perhaps I was on the outskirts of Heaven. I had no knowledge of how or when I arrived. My lack of direction wasn't troubling, as I somehow felt cared for. Absorbing my new reality, it became clear that my earthly life was over. *Oh, I'm dead!* I thought to myself, and I accepted the fact without sadness.

Standing up, I straightened my back and took in the view. Fields of sun-kissed wheat stretched far and wide, ripe for the harvest. In the distance, I saw a great forest of ancient evergreen trees, which prevented me from viewing the timberland's yonder. Instinctively, I accepted that an Eden-like garden existed beyond the tree line, but it was not yet available to me. Looking to the right, I saw a figure heading in my direction.

A man steadily moved at an angle with the sprightliness of youth. I watched his pace increase while brushing with golden ears of wheat, ardent in reaching me. As he came closer, I recognised Dad's rectangular form, then his face, which was aglow with a reassuring smile. Although I couldn't determine his age, he wasn't frail or elderly, portraying a picture of health and vitality. Dad was altered, depicting lightness and freedom. I couldn't fathom the change, but I knew it was a heavenly effect, his very essence belonging to Christ's eternal kingdom. My father's countenance radiated fondness, and without words or hesitation, his gentle arms enclosed me. I melted into his warm embrace.

My eyes opened abruptly, then stared at the darkness cloaking the bedroom. Smiling into nothingness, my dream vividly remained in my heart and mind. I felt the warmth of my husband beside me, heavy with sleep. Lying in our bed, I pondered that the dream's fulfilment can only occur after death, at God's appointed time. In the meantime, I'm living my mortal life in a fallen world. So ever and anon, my dad-insecurities will rise up.

During my recent writing, I pawed over family photographs in Dad's albums. I rediscovered how affectionate my family had been. Our closeness included smiles and arms around each other in numerous shots. It made me think about my lack of feelings towards Dad over the many changing seasons. Even after my wilderness patch, due to his ongoing rejection, fondness didn't return in spades. Similarly, Dad's waning warmth was patent when I randomly showed up during the cutoff years. It seems that our lacking relationship stunted natural affection in both directions. Interestingly, my dream not only revealed Dad's eternal home but also emphasised his eagerness to lovingly embrace me, affection beyond a dutiful kiss and a distant handshake.

While my father is transformed, I am not even close. My emotions are unchanged from when I stood by the hospital bed, telling Dad that I loved him. I meant those words as an act of the will, not based on effusive emotion. But then again, I consider that my affections will be renewed. I believe this is something only God, in his unfathomable ways, can do.

My God-given dream heartens me with future expectation, for I am fully confident that the Lord will restore all things at the right time. Only then, in our happily ever after beyond the veil, will perfect love flow between Dad and me.

Acknowledgments

To Dylan, many thanks for your loving support and contributions along the way. You have been a tremendous help in my walk down memory lane.

Barry, I am so very grateful for your contribution to my memoir. Your memory is still as sharp as ever!

Aunty Joy, thank you for your recollections relating to my parents' early relationship. This filled a small gap within my larger narrative.

To Lisa Jane, thank you for helping me remember our teenage Revival Centre days.

To Rachel, my dear friend and indispensable beta reader, I am truly thankful for your assistance in the early stages of crafting my memoir. I couldn't have done it without you!

Julia, thanks for sharing your introspective thoughts on Owen's life while you were a part of it, in relation to his disappearance. You've helped me connect the dots in a poignant part of my story.

Thank you to my developmental editor, Virginia. You thoroughly reviewed my manuscript as a professional, with an added touch of personal grace.

A massive thank you to the team at Aurora House, who have provided the expertise required to get my book to publication.

Finally, but not least of all, I am perpetually grateful to my family on the home front. Your love and understanding has been invaluable as I attend to my writing.

About the author

Shaped by hardship, Fleur C. Boal built resilience from childhood through to her adult years, developing a passion for helping others. She has studied and worked in various fields, including social work, chaplaincy, and generalist counselling. Fleur has worked with a broad range of people, including toddlers, teenagers, new parents, and the elderly, providing emotional support, practical help, and pastoral care both professionally and as a volunteer. Her chosen career in the helping profession was motivated by conflict in her upbringing that initiated a desire to facilitate positive change in others.

Fleur and her husband have raised four children in a country town in north-west Victoria, Australia, three of whom are now independent adults. She currently works and resides with her husband and youngest child in a residential hostel for high-school-aged students in the Eastern Highlands province of Papua New Guinea. The school students' parents work with Mission Aviation Fellowship (MAF) in providing assistance to people living in remote parts of Papua New Guinea. This enables the students to get a good standard of education in a country where this is not generally available.

A firm believer that every life holds a story, Fleur shares her own journey of healing and hope to help readers find personal restoration.

www.ingramcontent.com/pod-product-compliance
Lightning Source LLC
Chambersburg PA
CBHW022049160426
43198CB00008B/175